Basic Math Skills

by
August V. Treff
and
Donald H. Jacobs

AGS Publishing
Circle Pines, Minnesota 55014-1796
1-800-328-2560

About the Authors

August V. Treff, M.Ed., was a mathematics teacher and department head, director of research and evaluation, and chief of accountability with the Baltimore City Public Schools. He is now an information analyst with Bank of America. He is also coauthor of AGS *Life Skills Math*.

Donald H. Jacobs, M.Ed., taught mathematics for many years in the Baltimore City Public Schools. He is currently with the Upton Home and Hospital School Program in the technology department. Other AGS textbooks that he has coauthored include *Life Skills Math, Physical Science,* and *General Science.*

Photo credits for this textbook can be found on page 398.

The publisher wishes to thank the following educators for their helpful comments during the review process for *Basic Math Skills.* Their assistance has been invaluable.

Beverly C. Allen, Learning Disabilities Coordinator, L.D. Office, Norman Center, Kansas City, MO; **Delores Anderson,** Director of Exceptional Education, North Forest Administration Building, Houston, TX; **Bryan Backes,** Special Education Instructor, Apollo High School, St. Cloud, MN; **Patricia Baylis,** Coordinator of Special Education, School District of Kansas City, Kansas City, MO; **Maria Buchwald,** Special Needs Teacher, Southeast High School, Springfield, IL; **Roselle D. Clark,** Special Education Teacher, Bailey Bridge Middle School, Midlothian, VA; **Rhonda Dunning,** Curriculum Specialist, Mt. McKinley and Delta Vista High School, Martinez, CA; **Leslie P. Ellis,** Special Education Teacher, Grades 9-12, Woonsocket High School, Woonsocket, RI; **Willietta Merrick Gilbert,** Vocational and Transitional Programming Facilitator, New Orleans Public Schools, Exceptional Children's Services, New Orleans, LA; **Ledru Gowin,** Special Education Local Curriculum Teacher, William H. Taft High School, San Antonio, TX; **Jean Harrington,** Learning/Emotional Support Teacher, Pleasant Hills Middle School, Pittsburgh, PA; **Susan Harrington,** Special Education Teacher, Option III, Salamanca Middle School, Salamanca, NY; **Mike Kozak,** Teacher, West Credit Secondary School, Mississauga, ON, Canada; **Steve Little,** Special Education Teacher, Springfield Southeast High School, Springfield, IL; **Cecilia Lozano,** ESL Teacher, Douglas High School, Oklahoma City, OK; **Margaret-Anne McKibben,** Ph.D., Director of Special Education and Pupil Personnel Services, Penn Hills School District, Pittsburgh, PA; **Niki Pennington,** SLD Teacher, Durant High School, Plant City, FL; **Berlyenn C. Poe,** Resource Teacher, Oak Ridge High School, Oak Ridge, TN; **Marie Ramey,** Department Chairperson, West Side High School, Newark, NJ; **Jim Steinwart,** Special Education Math Teacher, Springfield High School, Springfield, IL; **Theodore S. Wiaterowski,** Special Needs Teacher, Mathematics, John S. Fine High School, Greater Nanticoke Area School District, Nanticoke, PA

Publisher's Project Staff

Director, Product Development: Karen Dahlen; Associate Director, Product Development: Teri Mathews; Senior Editor: Patrick Keithahn; Assistant Editor: Emily Kedrowski; Development Assistant: Bev Johnson; Graphic Designer: Linda Rodriguez Nuñez; Design Manager: Nancy Condon; Desktop Publishing Artist: Jack Ross; Desktop Publishing Manager: Lisa Beller; Purchasing Agent: Mary Kaye Kuzma; Marketing Manager/Curriculum: Brian Holl

Printed in the United States of America

ISBN 0-7854-2952-2

Product Number 93560

A 0 9 8 7 6 5

Contents

How to Use This Book: A Study Guide

Welcome to *Basic Math Skills*. This book includes many of the math skills that you will need now and later in life. Why do you need these skills? Think about the world of mathematics around you. When you buy something, you use math to count money. When you measure something, you use numbers to calculate units of measurement. Most jobs require at least some sort of math. You will use the basic math skills in this book almost every day of your life at home, at school, and on the job.

As you read this book, notice how each lesson is organized. Information will appear at the beginning of each lesson. Read this information carefully. A sample problem with step-by-step instructions will follow. Use the instructions to learn how to solve a certain kind of problem. Once you know how to solve this kind of problem, you will have the chance to solve similar problems on your own. If you have trouble with a lesson, try reading it again.

Before you start to read this book, it is important that you understand how to use it. It is also important to know how to be successful in this course. This first section of the book is here to help you achieve these things.

How to Study

These tips can help you study more effectively:
◆ Plan a regular time to study.
◆ Choose a quiet desk or table where you will not be distracted. Find a spot that has good lighting.
◆ Gather all the books, pencils, paper, and other equipment you will need to complete your assignments.
◆ Decide on a goal. For example: "I will finish reading and taking notes on Chapter 1, Lesson 1, by 8:00."
◆ Take a five- to ten-minute break every hour to keep alert.
◆ If you start to feel sleepy, take a break and get some fresh air.

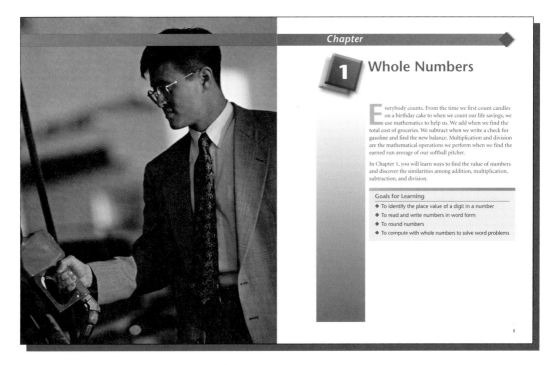

E verybody counts. From the time we first count candles on a birthday cake to when we count our life savings, we use mathematics to help us. We add when we find the total cost of groceries. We subtract when we write a check for gasoline and find the new balance. Multiplication and division are the mathematical operations we perform when we find the earned run average of our softball pitcher.

In Chapter 1, you will learn ways to find the value of numbers and discover the similarities among addition, multiplication, subtraction, and division.

Goals for Learning
◆ To identify the place value of a digit in a number
◆ To read and write numbers in word form
◆ To round numbers
◆ To compute with whole numbers to solve word problems

Before Beginning Each Chapter

◆ Read the chapter title and study the photograph. What does the photo tell you about the chapter title?
◆ Read the opening paragraphs.
◆ Study the Goals for Learning. The Chapter Review and tests will ask questions related to these goals.
◆ Look at the Chapter Review. The questions cover the most important information in the chapter.

Note the Chapter Features

Application
A look at how a topic in the chapter relates to real life

Notes
Hints or reminders that point out important information

Look for this box for helpful tips!

Technology Connection
Use technology to
apply math skills

Try This
New ways to think about
problems and solve them

Writing About Mathematics
Opportunities to write about
problems and alternate solutions

Before Beginning Each Lesson

Read the lesson title and
restate it in the form of
a question.

For example, write:
What is place value?

Look over the entire lesson,
noting the following:
◆ bold words
◆ text organization
◆ exercises
◆ notes in the margins
◆ photos

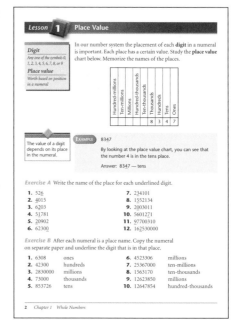

As You Read the Lesson
◆ Read the major headings.
◆ Read the subheads and paragraphs that follow.
◆ Read the content in the example boxes.
◆ Before moving on to the next lesson, see if you understand
   the concepts you read. If you do not, reread the lesson.
   If you are still unsure, ask for help.
◆ Practice what you have learned by doing the exercises in
   each lesson.

Using the Bold Words

Knowing the meaning of all the boxed words in the left column
will help you understand what you read.

These words appear in **bold type** the first time they appear in
the text and are often defined in the paragraph.

Addition is combining numbers to form a total.

All of the words in the left column are also defined in the **glossary**.

Addition (ə dish´ ən) the arithmetic operation of combining
numbers to find their sum or total (p. 7)

What to Do with a Word You Do Not Know

When you come to a word you do not know, ask yourself:

◆ **Is the word a compound word?**
Can you find two words within the word? This could
help you understand the meaning. For example: *rainfall*.

◆ **Does the word have a prefix at the beginning?**
For example: *improper*. The prefix *im-* means "not,"
so this word refers to something that is not proper.

◆ **Does the word have a suffix at the end?**
For example: *variable, -able*. This means "able to vary."

◆ **Can you identify the root word?**
Can you sound it out in parts?
For example: *un known*.

◆ **Are there any clues in the sentence that will help you
understand the word?**

Look for the word in the margin box, glossary, or dictionary.

If you are still having trouble with a word, ask for help.

Using Tables to Solve Problems

Four tables can be found in the back of this book. There is one for each of the four main math operations: addition, subtraction, multiplication, and division. You are encouraged to memorize these tables or refer to them as needed. If you are allowed to use a calculator, you may choose to use one instead of these tables.

Multiplication Table

×	2	3	4	5	6	7	8	9	10	11	12
2	4	6	8	10	12	14	16	18	20	22	24
3	6	9	12	15	18	21	24	27	30	33	36
4	8	12	16	20	24	28	32	36	40	44	48
5	10	15	20	25	30	35	40	45	50	55	60
6	12	18	24	30	36	42	48	54	60	66	72
7	14	21	28	35	42	49	56	63	70	77	84
8	16	24	32	40	48	56	64	72	80	88	96
9	18	27	36	45	54	63	72	81	90	99	108
10	20	30	40	50	60	70	80	90	100	110	120
11	22	33	44	55	66	77	88	99	110	121	132
12	24	36	48	60	72	84	96	108	120	132	144

384   *Multiplication Table*

Using the Chapter Reviews

◆ For each Chapter Review, answer the multiple choice questions first.
◆ Answer the questions under the other parts of the Chapter Review.
◆ To help you take tests, read the Test-Taking Tips at the end of each Chapter Review.

Test-Taking Tip

When learning math vocabulary, make flash cards with words and abbreviations on one side and definitions on the other side. Draw pictures next to the words, if possible. Then use the flash cards in a game to test your vocabulary skills.

Preparing for Tests

◆ Complete the exercises in each lesson. Make up similar problems to practice what you have learned. You may want to do this with a classmate and share your questions.
◆ Review your answers to lesson exercises and Chapter Reviews.
◆ Test yourself on vocabulary words and key ideas.
◆ Practice problem-solving strategies.

Problem-Solving Strategies

Following these steps will help you to solve math problems in this textbook.

1 Read

- Read the problem to discover what information you need.
- Make sure you understand the math concepts.
- Study the problem to decide if you have all the necessary information and if there is information you do not need.
- Begin thinking about the steps needed to solve the problem.

2 Plan

Think about the steps you will need to do to solve the problem. Decide if you will use mental math, paper and pencil, or a calculator. Will you need to draw a picture? Are measurements in the same units? Will you use a formula? Will you need to do more than one step?

These strategies may help you find a solution:

- Reword the problem.
- Draw a picture.
- Estimate your answer.
- Write an equation.
- Divide the problem into smaller parts.
- Make a chart or graph.
- Use a formula.
- Work backward.

3 Solve

- Follow your plan and do the calculations.
- Make sure to label your answer correctly.

4 Reflect

- Reread the problem.
- Does your answer make sense?
- Did you answer the question?
- Check your work to see if your answer is correct.

Whole Numbers

Everybody counts. From the time we first count candles on a birthday cake to when we count our life savings, we use mathematics to help us. We add when we find the total cost of groceries. We subtract when we write a check for gasoline and find the new balance. Multiplication and division are the mathematical operations we perform when we find the earned run average of our softball pitcher.

In Chapter 1, you will learn ways to find the value of numbers and discover the similarities among addition, multiplication, subtraction, and division.

Goals for Learning

◆ To identify the place value of a digit in a number

◆ To read and write numbers in word form

◆ To round numbers

◆ To compute with whole numbers to solve word problems

Digit

Any one of the symbols 0, 1, 2, 3, 4, 5, 6, 7, 8, or 9

Place value

Worth based on position in a numeral

In our number system the placement of each **digit** in a numeral is important. Each place has a certain value. Study the **place value** chart below. Memorize the names of the places.

Hundred-millions	Ten-millions	Millions	Hundred-thousands	Ten-thousands	Thousands	Hundreds	Tens	Ones
						8	3	4	7

The value of a digit depends on its place in the numeral.

EXAMPLE 8347

By looking at the place value chart, you can see that the number 4 is in the tens place.

Answer: 8347 — tens

Exercise A Write the name of the place for each underlined digit.

1. 52<u>6</u>

2. <u>4</u>015

3. 6<u>2</u>03

4. 5<u>1</u>781

5. <u>2</u>0902

6. 6230<u>0</u>

7. 2<u>3</u>4101

8. 1<u>5</u>52134

9. <u>2</u>003011

10. 56012<u>7</u>1

11. 97700<u>3</u>10

12. 16<u>2</u>530000

Exercise B After each numeral is a place name. Copy the numeral on separate paper and underline the digit that is in that place.

1. 6308   ones

2. 42300   hundreds

3. 2830000   millions

4. 73000   thousands

5. 853726   tens

6. 4523306   millions

7. 25367000   ten-millions

8. 1563170   ten-thousands

9. 12623850   millions

10. 12647854   hundred-thousands

Whole numbers

The set of numbers 0, 1, 2, 3, 4, 5, 6, . . .

Reading and writing **whole numbers** can best be explained by using a place value chart. Notice the addition of the group names. Always read the numeral and then the group name. Read from left to right. Commas are inserted every three places to help identify place values.

Writing About Mathematics

Look for large numerals in a newspaper article. Copy each sentence that uses a large numeral. Write the numeral and the words for the numeral.

EXAMPLE

		Millions			Thousands				
	Hundred-millions	Ten-millions	Millions	Hundred-thousands	Ten-thousands	Thousands	Hundreds	Tens	Ones
A				7	4	0	4	7	3
B		4	2	0	0	9	6	0	5

A is read: Seven hundred forty thousand, four hundred seventy-three.

B is read: Forty-two million, nine thousand, six hundred five.

Technology Connection

Demographics is a field of study that uses large numbers. People who work in this field study large groups of people. They try to find out such information as how many people live in a certain place. They also look for things such as age or income for certain groups. Use the Internet to find information about your state, city, and community. Can you find the population and average income? What other demographic measures can you find?

Exercise A Write the following numerals in words.

1. 465,721

2. 7,350,023

3. 26,003

4. 200,463

5. 91,008

6. 21,000,000

7. 14,005,006

8. 3,946

9. 315,621

10. 437

11. 12,400,600

12. 9,203,020

13. 535,000,495

14. 700,463,000

Occasionally, you may wish to round a whole number so that you will have simpler numbers to work with. To round to the nearest tens place, follow these steps:

Step 1 Find the place that you are rounding to.

Step 2 If the digit to its right is five or more, add one to the place that you are rounding to. If it is less than five, do not add anything and round down.

Step 3 Change all of the digits to the right of the place to which you are rounding to zeros.

EXAMPLES	9,346	8,472
Step 1	9,346 Tens place	8,472 Tens place
Step 2	+1 9,346 5 or more, add one	8,472 Less than 5, round down
Step 3	9,350	8,470

Exercise B Round each number to the nearest hundreds place.

1. 365
2. 9,127
3. 98
4. 23,091
5. 971
6. 5,209
7. 36,972
8. 23,068
9. 95,057
10. 27,981

11. 8,163
12. 12,149
13. 44,513
14. 62,891
15. 37,267
16. 21,048
17. 50,910
18. 126,341
19. 367,682
20. 856,750

Try This

For each problem in Exercise B, try rounding to the tens place. Make a chart comparing each number rounded to the tens and to the hundreds place.

Rounding is a useful skill when shopping. You can round prices to estimate total costs before you reach the checkout.

Exercise C The first number in each row is to be rounded to the nearest tens place. Write the number in the row that is correctly rounded.

1. **451:**   450   500   460

2. **3,169:**   3,100   3,160   3,170

3. **708:**   710   700   800

4. **1,509:**   1,510   1,600   1,500

5. **3:**   10   4   0

Write the number in each row that is correctly rounded to the nearest hundreds place.

6. **29,631:**   29,610   29,600   29,700

7. **6,309:**   6,310   6,400   6,300

8. **783:**   800   790   700

9. **49:**   150   100   0

10. **85:**   0   100   80

Round these numbers to the nearest tens place.

11. 375

12. 92

13. 96

14. 281

15. 3,516

16. 6,583

17. 9,217

18. 3,151

19. 22,984

20. 31,659

Round these numbers to the nearest hundreds place.

21. 7,203

22. 861

23. 1,939

24. 2,065

25. 91

26. 49

27. 220

28. 1,658

29. 3,421

30. 82,638

Exercise D Round these whole numbers to the nearest thousands place.

1. 56,266		**9.** 7,230	
2. 9,486		**10.** 27,864	
3. 13,472		**11.** 2,935	
4. 6,700		**12.** 11,906	
5. 98,716		**13.** 13,388	
6. 61,825		**14.** 20,635	
7. 22,464		**15.** 189	
8. 19,130		**16.** 38,612	

Exercise E Complete the chart by rounding to the place named.

Try This

Try tracking the cost of items during your next trip to the grocery store. Mentally round prices to the nearest dollar. Add the rounded prices in your head to get a total. At the checkout, compare your estimate to the actual cost. Was your estimate close?

		Tens	Hundreds	Thousands
1.	463		500	
2.	8,259			
3.	91,612			92,000
4.	83			
5.	915	920		
6.	9,200			
7.	36,155			
8.	3,919			
9.	16			
10.	623			
11.	18,800			
12.	499,792			
13.	30,209			
14.	92,314			
15.	68,197			

Lesson 3 — Adding Whole Numbers

Addition

The arithmetic operation of combining numbers to find their sum

Addend

A number that is added to one or more numbers

Order

Sequence from smallest to largest

Sum

The answer to an addition problem

Zero

The first whole number

Addition is combining numbers to form a total. Each number being added is an **addend.** The **order** in which you add two numbers does not change the answer, or the **sum.** Adding **zero** to a number does not change the number.

EXAMPLES Add 8 and 6.

$$
\begin{array}{r} 8 \\ + 6 \\ \hline 14 \end{array}
\quad \text{OR} \quad
\begin{array}{r} 8 \\ + 6 \\ \hline 14 \end{array}
\begin{array}{l} \text{— addend} \\ \text{— addend} \\ \text{— sum} \end{array}
$$

Add 9 and 0.

$$
\begin{array}{r} 9 \\ + 0 \\ \hline 9 \end{array}
\quad \text{OR} \quad
\begin{array}{r} 9 \\ + 0 \\ \hline 9 \end{array}
\begin{array}{l} \text{— addend} \\ \text{— addend} \\ \text{— sum} \end{array}
$$

Exercise A Add the following addends.

1. $\begin{array}{r} 4 \\ +6 \end{array}$ **2.** $\begin{array}{r} 3 \\ +3 \end{array}$ **3.** $\begin{array}{r} 6 \\ +5 \end{array}$ **4.** $\begin{array}{r} 9 \\ +7 \end{array}$ **5.** $\begin{array}{r} 8 \\ +8 \end{array}$ **6.** $\begin{array}{r} 3 \\ +2 \end{array}$ **7.** $\begin{array}{r} 7 \\ +0 \end{array}$ **8.** $\begin{array}{r} 4 \\ +4 \end{array}$ **9.** $\begin{array}{r} 4 \\ +0 \end{array}$

10. $\begin{array}{r} 5 \\ +5 \end{array}$ **11.** $\begin{array}{r} 5 \\ +0 \end{array}$ **12.** $\begin{array}{r} 4 \\ +3 \end{array}$ **13.** $\begin{array}{r} 7 \\ +9 \end{array}$ **14.** $\begin{array}{r} 8 \\ +6 \end{array}$ **15.** $\begin{array}{r} 9 \\ +1 \end{array}$ **16.** $\begin{array}{r} 0 \\ +8 \end{array}$ **17.** $\begin{array}{r} 3 \\ +0 \end{array}$ **18.** $\begin{array}{r} 6 \\ +1 \end{array}$

19. $\begin{array}{r} 8 \\ +1 \end{array}$ **20.** $\begin{array}{r} 6 \\ +7 \end{array}$ **21.** $\begin{array}{r} 0 \\ +1 \end{array}$ **22.** $\begin{array}{r} 1 \\ +1 \end{array}$ **23.** $\begin{array}{r} 3 \\ +4 \end{array}$ **24.** $\begin{array}{r} 5 \\ +9 \end{array}$ **25.** $\begin{array}{r} 7 \\ +8 \end{array}$ **26.** $\begin{array}{r} 9 \\ +5 \end{array}$ **27.** $\begin{array}{r} 2 \\ +0 \end{array}$

28. $\begin{array}{r} 5 \\ +6 \end{array}$ **29.** $\begin{array}{r} 5 \\ +3 \end{array}$ **30.** $\begin{array}{r} 7 \\ +3 \end{array}$ **31.** $\begin{array}{r} 9 \\ +2 \end{array}$ **32.** $\begin{array}{r} 9 \\ +4 \end{array}$ **33.** $\begin{array}{r} 8 \\ +3 \end{array}$ **34.** $\begin{array}{r} 8 \\ +4 \end{array}$ **35.** $\begin{array}{r} 7 \\ +4 \end{array}$ **36.** $\begin{array}{r} 6 \\ +3 \end{array}$

37. $\begin{array}{r} 4 \\ +5 \end{array}$ **38.** $\begin{array}{r} 5 \\ +7 \end{array}$ **39.** $\begin{array}{r} 2 \\ +5 \end{array}$ **40.** $\begin{array}{r} 2 \\ +9 \end{array}$ **41.** $\begin{array}{r} 6 \\ +8 \end{array}$ **42.** $\begin{array}{r} 2 \\ +7 \end{array}$ **43.** $\begin{array}{r} 2 \\ +6 \end{array}$ **44.** $\begin{array}{r} 9 \\ +0 \end{array}$ **45.** $\begin{array}{r} 8 \\ +5 \end{array}$

Horizontal
Parallel to the horizon
Vertical
Straight up and down

When you are adding two-digit numbers, add the ones first. Then add the tens. Like place values must be added to like place values. If the sum of two numbers is more than 9, then add the ones column first. Then carry over the tens to the tens column.

EXAMPLE

Add 47 + 6

```
   1
  47
 + 6
  53
```

Add the ones first. 7 + 6 = 13
Write the 3 in the ones column.
Write the 1, which stands for 10, in the
tens column. Add the tens. 1 + 4 = 5.

```
  1
 48      8 + 7 = 15
+17
 65
```

```
  1
 39      9 + 2 = 11
+12
 51
```

Exercise B Add the following problems.

1.	23	**2.**	54	**3.**	57	**4.**	68	**5.**	63	**6.**	24	**7.**	35	**8.**	64
	+ 6		+ 8		+ 9		+ 6		+ 5		+ 8		+ 7		+ 9

9.	46	**10.**	39	**11.**	64	**12.**	25	**13.**	54	**14.**	18	**15.**	62	**16.**	15
	+37		+52		+17		+64		+29		+35		+28		+37

Remember that when the whole numbers are added, all places of the same value must be kept in the same column.

EXAMPLE

Read the **horizontal** problem. Write the problem in **vertical** form.

Add 236 + 2,453 + 38.

```
    236
  2,453
 +   38
  2,727
```

Notice that 6, 3, and 8 are all in the ones place. They are all written in the same column.

Exercise C Write these problems in vertical columns as shown in the example at the bottom of page 9. Then add.

Keeping the columns straight will help you get the correct answer.

1. 23 + 467 + 8
2. 98 + 29 + 435
3. 28 + 400 + 81
4. 731 + 42 + 100
5. 300 + 20 + 6
6. 9,213 + 84 + 172
7. 503 + 1,007 + 76
8. 1,551 + 2,003 + 8,711
9. 356 + 4,215 + 768
10. 3,005 + 23 + 36,011
11. 7 + 62 + 853 + 9,134
12. 10 + 235 + 10,062 + 3,412
13. 96 + 9 + 231 + 139 + 2,007
14. 1 + 11 + 1,101 + 2,011

Exercise D Find the sums.

1. 23, 693, 85
2. 353, 9, 72
3. 41, 603, 9143
4. 7, 703, 26, 4111
5. 31, 6211, 923
6. 9, 13, 831, 4111
7. 4, 35, 291, 6234
8. 52, 7, 206, 4110
9. 321, 6351, 8, 91

PROBLEM SOLVING

Exercise E Solve these word problems.

1. Baylor High School has 935 twelfth-grade students, 862 eleventh-grade students, and 1,036 tenth-grade students. What is the school's total enrollment?

2. Vaughn's family drove their economy car on their vacation. They used 15 gallons of gas on Monday, 16 gallons on Tuesday, and 18 gallons on Wednesday. How much gas did they use in all?

3. Konika's test grades during the first quarter are 75, 80, 92, 100, 83, 60, and 85. What is her test grade total for the first quarter?

4. Round each of the following numbers to the nearest hundred and then add: 2633, 493, 160, 55, 49.

5. A bowler bowls nine games. Her scores are 238, 93, 179, 217, 64, 278, 108, 76, and 240. What is her pin total?

Subtraction

The arithmetic operation of taking one number away from another to find the difference

Difference

Answer to a subtraction problem

Subtraction and addition are opposite operations. The answer to a subtraction problem is the **difference.** You can check a subtraction answer by adding.

EXAMPLES

$$8 - 5 = \blacksquare \qquad\qquad 16 - 4 = \blacksquare$$

8	Check: 3	16	Check: 12
−5	+5	−4	+4
3	8	12	16

Exercise A Subtract. Find the differences. Check your answers by adding.

1. 8
−5

2. 7
−6

3. 8
−3

4. 5
−3

5. 9
−2

6. 8
−4

7. 6
−3

8. 5
−2

9. 9
−6

10. 6
−4

11. 8
−6

12. 7
−1

13. 7
−2

14. 8
−7

15. 9
−5

16. 6
−1

17. 13
− 6

18. 15
− 7

19. 14
− 4

20. 12
− 7

21. 16
− 8

22. 14
− 9

23. 19
− 5

24. 15
− 4

25. 17
− 6

26. 15
− 8

27. 13
− 8

28. 16
− 5

29. 17
− 5

30. 17
− 7

31. 12
− 8

32. 12
− 5

33. 13
− 5

34. 14
− 6

35. 19
− 7

36. 12
− 6

37. 13
− 3

38. 15
− 9

39. 15
− 6

40. 12
− 4

41. 14
− 3

42. 16
− 3

43. 13
− 4

44. 14
− 7

45. 16
− 4

46. 15
− 3

47. 19
− 3

48. 18
− 5

Sometimes you must **rename** tens and ones to subtract.

Renaming is like getting change for money. Ten one dollar bills is the same as one ten dollar bill.

EXAMPLE

$$95 - 7 = \blacksquare \qquad \begin{array}{r} 95 \\ -\ 7 \\ \hline \end{array}$$

You cannot subtract 7 from 5. The ones must be renamed to 15.

$$\begin{array}{r} 95 = \quad 9 \text{ tens} + 5 \text{ ones} \\ -\ 7 = -\ \phantom{9 \text{ tens} +} 7 \text{ ones} \\ \hline \end{array} \quad \text{or} \quad \begin{array}{r} 8 \text{ tens} + 15 \text{ ones} \\ -\ \phantom{8 \text{ tens} +} 7 \text{ ones} \\ \hline 8 \text{ tens} + \ 8 \text{ ones} = 88 \end{array}$$

Here is a shorter way to rename:

$$\begin{array}{r} {}^{8}\ {}^{15} \\ \cancel{95} \\ -\ 7 \\ \hline 88 \end{array}$$

Exercise B Subtract.

1. $\begin{array}{r} 23 \\ -\ 5 \\ \hline \end{array}$
2. $\begin{array}{r} 34 \\ -\ 6 \\ \hline \end{array}$
3. $\begin{array}{r} 48 \\ -\ 9 \\ \hline \end{array}$
4. $\begin{array}{r} 32 \\ -\ 8 \\ \hline \end{array}$
5. $\begin{array}{r} 21 \\ -\ 5 \\ \hline \end{array}$
6. $\begin{array}{r} 37 \\ -\ 8 \\ \hline \end{array}$
7. $\begin{array}{r} 36 \\ -\ 7 \\ \hline \end{array}$
8. $\begin{array}{r} 25 \\ -\ 7 \\ \hline \end{array}$

9. $\begin{array}{r} 31 \\ -\ 4 \\ \hline \end{array}$
10. $\begin{array}{r} 46 \\ -\ 8 \\ \hline \end{array}$
11. $\begin{array}{r} 52 \\ -\ 5 \\ \hline \end{array}$
12. $\begin{array}{r} 63 \\ -\ 6 \\ \hline \end{array}$
13. $\begin{array}{r} 26 \\ -\ 9 \\ \hline \end{array}$
14. $\begin{array}{r} 42 \\ -\ 7 \\ \hline \end{array}$
15. $\begin{array}{r} 55 \\ -\ 8 \\ \hline \end{array}$
16. $\begin{array}{r} 72 \\ -\ 6 \\ \hline \end{array}$

17. $\begin{array}{r} 67 \\ -\ 9 \\ \hline \end{array}$
18. $\begin{array}{r} 35 \\ -\ 9 \\ \hline \end{array}$
19. $\begin{array}{r} 36 \\ -18 \\ \hline \end{array}$
20. $\begin{array}{r} 42 \\ -15 \\ \hline \end{array}$
21. $\begin{array}{r} 53 \\ -26 \\ \hline \end{array}$
22. $\begin{array}{r} 31 \\ -15 \\ \hline \end{array}$
23. $\begin{array}{r} 63 \\ -27 \\ \hline \end{array}$
24. $\begin{array}{r} 81 \\ -18 \\ \hline \end{array}$

25. $\begin{array}{r} 37 \\ -28 \\ \hline \end{array}$
26. $\begin{array}{r} 40 \\ -39 \\ \hline \end{array}$
27. $\begin{array}{r} 54 \\ -36 \\ \hline \end{array}$
28. $\begin{array}{r} 46 \\ -27 \\ \hline \end{array}$
29. $\begin{array}{r} 55 \\ -38 \\ \hline \end{array}$
30. $\begin{array}{r} 74 \\ -36 \\ \hline \end{array}$
31. $\begin{array}{r} 90 \\ -63 \\ \hline \end{array}$
32. $\begin{array}{r} 54 \\ -25 \\ \hline \end{array}$

33. $\begin{array}{r} 75 \\ -66 \\ \hline \end{array}$
34. $\begin{array}{r} 82 \\ -54 \\ \hline \end{array}$
35. $\begin{array}{r} 80 \\ -52 \\ \hline \end{array}$
36. $\begin{array}{r} 21 \\ -18 \\ \hline \end{array}$
37. $\begin{array}{r} 48 \\ -39 \\ \hline \end{array}$
38. $\begin{array}{r} 35 \\ -17 \\ \hline \end{array}$
39. $\begin{array}{r} 67 \\ -19 \\ \hline \end{array}$
40. $\begin{array}{r} 72 \\ -36 \\ \hline \end{array}$

When whole numbers are subtracted, all places of the same value must be placed in the same column. It is necessary to rename in this example.

EXAMPLE   3,648 − 459 = ■

```
    5 13 18
 3, 6  4  8
 −    4  5  9
 3, 1  8  9
```

Exercise C Write these problems in vertical columns as shown in the example. Then subtract.

1. 2,803 − 532

2. 5,036 − 987

3. 7,260 − 463

4. 98,217 − 463

5. 40,317 − 8,234

6. 20,103 − 8,234

7. 12,665 − 2,666

8. 4,831 − 965

9. 20,398 − 8,643

10. 91,131 − 222

11. 1,200 − 268

12. 4,000 − 865

13. 29,143 − 9,269

14. 14,209 − 7,610

15. 25,311 − 3,167

16. 9,512 − 9,422

17. 23,716 − 1,875

18. 223,618 − 9,233

19. 112,130 − 16,832

20. 59,176 − 2,341

In subtraction problems, the number following "from" is always placed on top.

EXAMPLE   From 6,435 subtract 856.

```
   5 13 12 15
 6, 4  3  5
 −    8  5  6
 5, 5  7  9
```

Exercise D Write the problems in vertical columns and find the answers to these subtraction problems.

1. From 2,963 subtract 875.

2. From 39,002 subtract 8,723.

3. From 21,093 subtract 463.

4. From 4,238 subtract 829.

5. From 17,163 subtract 8,999.

6. Subtract 683 from 908.

7. Subtract 9,031 from 37,425.

8. Subtract 617 from 100,923.

9. Subtract 9,233 from 9,873.

10. Subtract 4,008 from 7,893.

PROBLEM SOLVING

Exercise E Solve these word problems. Include the name of the units in your answer.

1. Tom weighed 136 pounds. At the end of two months of exercising, Tom weighs 128 pounds. How much weight did Tom lose?

2. Lakeside High School prints 15,000 raffle tickets. The twelfth grade sells 483 tickets. How many tickets are left?

3. Manuel, a plumber, has several pieces of pipe on his truck. He has a piece 6 feet long, a piece 7 feet long, one 9 feet long, and a piece 13 feet long. Find the total length of pipe in feet. If he uses 5 feet of pipe on a job, how many feet of pipe are left?

4. During inventory, the librarian finds that of the 2,482 books on the shelves, 482 are biographies, 726 are art books, and 534 are mysteries. The rest are fiction stories. How many books are fiction stories?

Multiplication

The arithmetic operation of adding a number to itself many times

Factor

Number that is multiplied in a multiplication problem

Product

Answer to a multiplication problem

Addition and **multiplication** are similar. When you multiply a number, you simply add that number many times.

EXAMPLE   Addition:
$$\begin{array}{r} 4 \\ 4 \\ +\ 4 \\ \hline 12 \end{array} \left.\right\} \text{ three 4's}$$

Multiplication: $3 \times 4 = 12$

$$\begin{array}{r} 4 \ — \text{factor} \\ \times\ 3 \ — \text{factor} \\ \hline 12 \ — \text{product} \end{array}$$

Like addition, the order in which you multiply two **factors** does not change the **product.**

EXAMPLE
$$\begin{array}{r} 5 \\ \times\ 4 \\ \hline 20 \end{array} \qquad \begin{array}{r} 4 \\ \times\ 5 \\ \hline 20 \end{array}$$

The product of any factor and zero is zero.

EXAMPLE
$$\begin{array}{r} 0 \\ \times\ 8 \\ \hline 0 \end{array} \qquad \begin{array}{r} 8 \\ \times\ 0 \\ \hline 0 \end{array}$$

Exercise A Multiply the following problems.

1.	**2.**	**3.**	**4.**	**5.**	**6.**	**7.**	**8.**	**9.**
4	6	5	3	2	4	4	2	3
×5	×7	×6	×0	×8	×3	×2	×7	×6

10.	**11.**	**12.**	**13.**	**14.**	**15.**	**16.**	**17.**	**18.**
7	3	6	5	0	2	4	3	7
×7	×5	×9	×9	×6	×5	×5	×4	×7

19.	**20.**	**21.**	**22.**	**23.**	**24.**	**25.**	**26.**	**27.**
5	9	2	5	6	5	2	3	9
×8	×9	×4	×7	×4	×0	×9	×5	×5

Exercise B Multiply the following problems.

1. 23	**2.** 42	**3.** 31	**4.** 73	**5.** 82	**6.** 61	**7.** 54	**8.** 70
× 3	× 4	× 7	× 3	× 4	× 8	× 0	× 7

9. 63	**10.** 52	**11.** 61	**12.** 72	**13.** 81	**14.** 63	**15.** 64	**16.** 64
× 2	× 3	×3	× 4	× 8	× 3	× 2	× 1

17. 46	**18.** 32	**19.** 42	**20.** 51	**21.** 90	**22.** 84	**23.** 72	**24.** 81
× 1	× 4	× 3	× 7	× 9	× 0	× 3	× 7

25. 44	**26.** 53	**27.** 23	**28.** 41	**29.** 50	**30.** 61	**31.** 62	**32.** 85
× 2	× 3	× 1	× 9	× 7	× 6	× 4	× 0

When the product of the ones is greater than 9, you must rename the tens and ones. In the following example, notice that 48 ones were renamed as 4 tens and 8 ones. The 4 tens were added to the tens column.

EXAMPLE $36 \times 8 = \blacksquare$

$$
\begin{array}{r}
36 = \quad \text{3 tens and 6 ones} \\
\times\ 8 = \times \underline{\qquad\qquad \text{8 ones}} \\
\text{24 tens and 48 ones} = \\
\text{28 tens and 8 ones} = 288
\end{array}
$$

$$
\begin{array}{r}
36 \\
\times\ \ 8 \\
\hline
48 \\
+240 \\
\hline
288
\end{array}
\quad
\begin{array}{l}
8 \times 6\ \ =\ \ 48 \\
8 \times 30 = 240
\end{array}
\left.\vphantom{\begin{array}{c}1\\1\end{array}}\right\}
\text{These products are added.}
$$

$$
\begin{array}{c}
48 \\
240 \\
\hline
288
\end{array}
$$

Here is a shorter way to mutiply with renaming.

Step 1

$$
\begin{array}{r}
^4 \\
36 \\
\times\ 8 \\
\hline
8
\end{array}
\quad 8 \times 6 = 48
$$

Step 2

$$
\begin{array}{r}
^4 \\
36 \\
\times\ 8 \\
\hline
288
\end{array}
\quad
\begin{array}{l}
8 \times 3 = 24 \\
\text{and} \\
24 + 4 = 28
\end{array}
$$

Exercise C Practice multiplying with renaming.

1.	34	**2.**	45	**3.**	67	**4.**	58	**5.**	79	**6.**	53	**7.**	62	**8.**	92
	× 6		× 7		× 4		× 3		× 6		× 7		× 3		× 8

9.	64	**10.**	86	**11.**	49	**12.**	63	**13.**	47	**14.**	83	**15.**	24	**16.**	39
	× 7		× 0		× 1		× 5		× 8		× 5		× 9		× 3

17.	64	**18.**	75	**19.**	75	**20.**	95	**21.**	48	**22.**	69	**23.**	57	**24.**	37
	× 6		× 0		× 8		× 9		× 1		× 6		× 4		× 2

Partial products

Answers obtained by multiplying a factor by a digit in the other factor

Sometimes you must multiply by a factor that contains two or more digits. Then you have to write **partial products.** The partial products must be written in the correct columns before they are added.

Multiplication is a quick way to add the same number several times. 34 × 6 is the same as 34 + 34 + 34 + 34 + 34 + 34.

EXAMPLE   52 × 43 = ■

Step 1
```
    52
  × 43
   156
```

Step 2
```
    52
  × 43
   156    partial product
 +208    partial product
```

In Step 1, you multiply by the 3 in 43. 3 × 52 is 156. You write the first digit of the partial product in the ones place. The first digit is 6. 6 is written directly below the 3.

In Step 2, you multiply by the 4 in 43. 4 × 52 is 208. You write the first digit of the partial product in the tens place, or one column to the left.

Step 3
```
      52
    × 43
     156 ⎫
  + 2 08 ⎭  Add these partial products.
   2,236    product
```

Exercise D Multiply the following problems.

1. 45
$\times 57$

2. 56
$\times 45$

3. 47
$\times 90$

4. 87
$\times 54$

5. 35
$\times 34$

6. 97
$\times 63$

7. 75
$\times 21$

8. 90
$\times 51$

9. 66
$\times 51$

10. 83
$\times 38$

11. 99
$\times 51$

12. 75
$\times 50$

13. 67
$\times 45$

14. 34
$\times 34$

15. 23
$\times 75$

16. 75
$\times 37$

Any number times zero equals zero. When zero is part of a factor,
follow these steps.

EXAMPLES $34 \times 0 = 0$ $34 \times 20 = \blacksquare$

Step 1   34   Multiply by 0.
              $\times\ 20$ Write one 0 in the product below the 0
                0   you multiplied by.

Step 2   34   Multiply by the 2. $2 \times 34 = 68$
              $\times\ 20$ Write the first digit of the product under 2.
              680

Study these examples:

35	56	75	787	567
$\times\ 50$	$\times\ 70$	$\times\ 80$	$\times\ 10$	$\times\ 100$
1,750	3,920	6,000	7,870	56,700

Rules   When you multiply a number by 10, write the number. Then write a zero
to the right as shown. $38 \times 10 = 380$

When you multiply a number by 100, write the number. Then write two
zeros at the end. $84 \times 100 = 8,400$

When you multiply a number by 1,000, write the number, and write three
zeros at the end. $23 \times 1,000 = 23,000$

Exercise E Practice multiplying with zeros.

1. 45
$\times 40$

2. 56
$\times 50$

3. 86
$\times 70$

4. 94
$\times 40$

5. 35
$\times 30$

6. 86
$\times 10$

7. 75
$\times 70$

8. 44
$\times 40$

9. 45
$\times 10$

10. 56
$\times 10$

11. 33
$\times 10$

12. 675
$\times 100$

13. 745
$\times 100$

14. 455
$\times 100$

15. 677
$\times 100$

16. 897
$\times 100$

Multiplying with a 3-Digit Factor When you multiply whole numbers, you have to keep the digits in the partial products lined up in the proper columns. The first digit of the first partial product goes in the ones column. The first digit of the second partial product goes in the tens column, one space to the left. The first digit of the third partial product goes in the hundreds column, two spaces to the left.

EXAMPLE $604 \times 126 = \blacksquare$

$$
\begin{array}{r}
604 \\
\times \quad 126 \\
\hline
3\ 624 \\
12\ 08 \\
+60\ 4 \\
\hline
76,104
\end{array}
$$

604 ⎫
× 126 ⎬ factors

3 624 ⎫
12 08 ⎬ partial products
+60 4 ⎭

76,104   product

Exercise F Rewrite the following multiplication problems in vertical form. Then multiply.

1. 741 × 16

2. 358 × 72

3. 539 × 41

4. 222 × 22

5. 465 × 55

6. 902 × 36

7. 1,103 × 112

8. 6,101 × 270

9. 3,817 × 311

10. 4,831 × 717

11. 9,613 × 831

12. 4,018 × 763

13. 8,106 × 4,102

14. 6,313 × 7,011

15. 1,202 × 4,011

16. 2,963 × 6,291

17. 237 × 462

18. 981 × 373

19. 425 × 631

20. 137 × 355

21. 239 × 414

22. 731 × 262

23. 5,821 × 135

24. 6,345 × 217

Exercise G Find the product of each pair of numbers.

1. 23 and 67
2. 854 and 68
3. 403 and 42
4. 679 and 73
5. 703 and 261
6. 785 and 362
7. 1,235 and 69
8. 6,304 and 390

9. 4,107 and 627
10. 8,931 and 3,007
11. 6,707 and 4,823
12. 4,113 and 6,305
13. 5,077 and 4,063
14. 2,011 and 3,579
15. 8,963 and 4,934
16. 5,169 and 4,551

Exercise H Round each factor to the nearest hundreds place. Then multiply.

1.
$$7,382 \times 401$$

2.
$$4,600 \times 2,030$$

3.
$$2,991 \times 233$$

4.
$$20,909 \times 2,016$$

5.
$$9,261 \times 784$$

6.
$$40,101 \times 30,102$$

PROBLEM SOLVING

Exercise I Find the answers to these word problems. Include the units in your answer.

1. Jennifer saves $13.00 a week. There are 52 weeks in a year. How much will she save in one year?

2. Mr. Tanaka's new car gets 52 miles on one gallon of gas. How many miles will he get from 260 gallons?

3. Nadine is figuring out the amount of money collected from ticket sales for the drama club's play. They sold 248 $3.00 tickets and 506 $2.00 tickets. What is the total amount of money they collected?

4. Each package of school printer paper contains 500 sheets of paper. How many sheets of paper are contained in 17 packages of paper?

5. Carlos makes $35.00 a week from his part-time job after school. How much money will he make over a 52-week period?

6. Laura's cat has five kittens. Each kitten eats 3 ounces of kitten food per day. How many ounces of food do the five kittens eat in 7 days?

Division

The arithmetic operation that finds how many times a number is contained in another number

Dividend

A number that is divided

Quotient

Answer in a division problem

Divisor

Number by which you are dividing

Division is the opposite of multiplication. The **dividend** is the number being divided. You may check division by multiplying the **quotient** by the **divisor.**

EXAMPLE $54 \div 9 = \blacksquare$

$$\begin{array}{r} 6 \text{ — quotient} \\ \text{divisor — } 9\,\overline{)\,54} \text{ — dividend} \end{array}$$

Check

$$\begin{array}{r} 6 \text{ — quotient} \\ \times\ 9 \text{ — divisor} \\ \hline 54 \text{ — dividend} \end{array}$$

Exercise A Divide these problems.

1. $4\,\overline{)\,36}$ **10.** $2\,\overline{)\,6}$ **19.** $6\,\overline{)\,18}$ **28.** $7\,\overline{)\,21}$ **37.** $9\,\overline{)\,27}$

2. $2\,\overline{)\,14}$ **11.** $2\,\overline{)\,12}$ **20.** $4\,\overline{)\,20}$ **29.** $6\,\overline{)\,48}$ **38.** $2\,\overline{)\,8}$

3. $5\,\overline{)\,10}$ **12.** $8\,\overline{)\,16}$ **21.** $6\,\overline{)\,30}$ **30.** $3\,\overline{)\,18}$ **39.** $7\,\overline{)\,35}$

4. $4\,\overline{)\,16}$ **13.** $9\,\overline{)\,45}$ **22.** $8\,\overline{)\,48}$ **31.** $3\,\overline{)\,21}$ **40.** $4\,\overline{)\,24}$

5. $9\,\overline{)\,54}$ **14.** $5\,\overline{)\,15}$ **23.** $2\,\overline{)\,16}$ **32.** $5\,\overline{)\,25}$ **41.** $8\,\overline{)\,32}$

6. $4\,\overline{)\,32}$ **15.** $7\,\overline{)\,42}$ **24.** $7\,\overline{)\,49}$ **33.** $4\,\overline{)\,12}$ **42.** $3\,\overline{)\,27}$

7. $4\,\overline{)\,20}$ **16.** $9\,\overline{)\,81}$ **25.** $2\,\overline{)\,10}$ **34.** $3\,\overline{)\,6}$ **43.** $4\,\overline{)\,8}$

8. $7\,\overline{)\,14}$ **17.** $5\,\overline{)\,35}$ **26.** $8\,\overline{)\,64}$ **35.** $9\,\overline{)\,63}$ **44.** $5\,\overline{)\,40}$

9. $6\,\overline{)\,36}$ **18.** $5\,\overline{)\,30}$ **27.** $7\,\overline{)\,56}$ **36.** $8\,\overline{)\,40}$ **45.** $8\,\overline{)\,72}$

When you divide, place the digits correctly in the quotient.

Remainder
Amount left over when dividing

EXAMPLES $168 \div 7 = \blacksquare$

Step 1   The 2 is written above the 6 because the 7 divides into 16.

Step 2 $2 \times 7 = 14$. 14 is subtracted from 16.

Step 3   The 8 in the dividend is brought down and written next to the 2.

Step 4   7 divides into 28 four times. A 4 is placed in the quotient above the 8. $4 \times 7 = 28$. 28 is subtracted from 28. The remainder is 0.

Step 1	Step 2	Step 3	Step 4
$\begin{array}{r} 2 \\ 7\overline{)168} \end{array}$	$\begin{array}{r} 2 \\ 7\overline{)168} \\ -14 \\ \hline 2 \end{array}$	$\begin{array}{r} 2 \\ 7\overline{)168} \\ -14 \\ \hline 28 \end{array}$	$\begin{array}{r} 24 \\ 7\overline{)168} \\ -14 \\ \hline 28 \\ -28 \\ \hline 0 \end{array}$

$$432 \div 12 = \blacksquare$$

Step 1	Step 2	Step 3	Step 4
$\begin{array}{r} 3 \\ 12\overline{)432} \end{array}$	$\begin{array}{r} 3 \\ 12\overline{)432} \\ -36 \\ \hline 7 \end{array}$	$\begin{array}{r} 3 \\ 12\overline{)432} \\ -36 \\ \hline 72 \end{array}$	$\begin{array}{r} 36 \\ 12\overline{)432} \\ -36 \\ \hline 72 \\ -72 \\ \hline 0 \end{array}$

Exercise B Divide these problems.

1. $8\overline{)568}$ **3.** $9\overline{)207}$ **5.** $6\overline{)126}$ **7.** $5\overline{)165}$ **9.** $4\overline{)248}$

2. $4\overline{)52}$ **4.** $9\overline{)108}$ **6.** $5\overline{)85}$ **8.** $8\overline{)248}$ **10.** $6\overline{)258}$

Division with Remainders Often, division problems have a **remainder.** Write the remainder after the quotient. Check the division by multiplying. Then add the remainder to the product.

EXAMPLES $349 \div 8 = \blacksquare$

Check

$$
\begin{array}{r}
43 \text{ r } 5 \\
8 \overline{)\, 349} \\
-32 \\
\hline
29 \\
-24 \\
\hline
5 \text{ remainder}
\end{array}
$$

$$
\begin{array}{rl}
43 & \text{quotient} \\
\times \quad 8 & \text{divisor} \\
\hline
344 & \\
+ \quad 5 & \text{remainder} \\
\hline
349 & \text{dividend}
\end{array}
$$

$243 \div 5 = \blacksquare$

Check

$$
\begin{array}{r}
48 \text{ r } 3 \\
5 \overline{)\, 243} \\
-20 \\
\hline
43 \\
-40 \\
\hline
3 \text{ remainder}
\end{array}
$$

$$
\begin{array}{rl}
48 & \text{quotient} \\
\times \quad 5 & \text{divisor} \\
\hline
240 & \\
+ \quad 3 & \text{remainder} \\
\hline
243 & \text{dividend}
\end{array}
$$

Exercise C Divide and check your answers by multiplying.

1. $8 \overline{)\, 408}$ **6.** $6 \overline{)\, 837}$ **11.** $5 \overline{)\, 306}$ **16.** $8 \overline{)\, 651}$ **21.** $9 \overline{)\, 568}$

2. $5 \overline{)\, 338}$ **7.** $6 \overline{)\, 178}$ **12.** $9 \overline{)\, 888}$ **17.** $9 \overline{)\, 253}$ **22.** $7 \overline{)\, 268}$

3. $6 \overline{)\, 369}$ **8.** $7 \overline{)\, 376}$ **13.** $4 \overline{)\, 461}$ **18.** $7 \overline{)\, 278}$ **23.** $2 \overline{)\, 917}$

4. $6 \overline{)\, 228}$ **9.** $4 \overline{)\, 173}$ **14.** $7 \overline{)\, 298}$ **19.** $7 \overline{)\, 586}$ **24.** $9 \overline{)\, 699}$

5. $4 \overline{)\, 213}$ **10.** $2 \overline{)\, 369}$ **15.** $6 \overline{)\, 148}$ **20.** $8 \overline{)\, 508}$ **25.** $6 \overline{)\, 259}$

Division of Numbers That Have Zeros When you divide numbers that contain zeros, be sure that you keep your columns straight. Otherwise, you may leave a necessary zero out of the quotient.

EXAMPLE $2,380 \div 17 = \blacksquare$

$$
\begin{array}{r}
1 \\
17 \overline{)\, 2,380} \\
-1\,7 \\
\hline
6
\end{array}
\qquad
\begin{array}{r}
14 \\
17 \overline{)\, 2,380} \\
-1\,7 \\
\hline
68
\end{array}
\qquad
\begin{array}{r}
140 \\
17 \overline{)\, 2,380} \\
-1\,7 \\
\hline
68 \\
-68 \\
\hline
0
\end{array}
$$

Exercise D Divide and show your work.

1. 4,550 ÷ 7

2. 1,260 ÷ 3

3. 27,720 ÷ 9

4. 3,080 ÷ 7

5. 1,600 ÷ 8

6. 2,760 ÷ 23

7. 21,730 ÷ 53

8. 12,880 ÷ 46

9. 2,520 ÷ 63

10. 13,020 ÷ 42

11. 27,200 ÷ 85

12. 7,140 ÷ 17

13. 14,300 ÷ 22

14. 28,080 ÷ 72

15. 8,010 ÷ 89

Keep your columns straight when you are dividing. This will help you write zeros in their proper place.

EXAMPLE	$1,484 ÷ 14 = \blacksquare$

Step 1 14 ÷ 14 is 1. Write the 1 above the 4 in the quotient.

$$\begin{array}{r} 1 \\ 14\overline{)1,484} \\ -1\,4 \end{array}$$

Step 2 The 8 is brought down. 8 ÷ 14 is less than 1. Write a zero above the 8.

$$\begin{array}{r} 10 \\ 14\overline{)1,484} \\ -1\,4 \\ \hline 8 \end{array}$$

Step 3 Then the 4 is brought down and written next to 8. Now 84 ÷ 14 = 6. Write the 6 above the 4.

$$\begin{array}{r} 106 \\ 14\overline{)1,484} \\ -1\,4 \\ \hline 84 \\ -84 \\ \hline 0 \end{array}$$

Exercise E Divide and show your work.

1. 1,734 ÷ 17

2. 4,466 ÷ 22

3. 8,016 ÷ 16

4. 13,938 ÷ 23

5. 4,066 ÷ 38

6. 3,366 ÷ 11

7. 15,238 ÷ 19

8. 21,624 ÷ 24

9. 32,246 ÷ 46

10. 25,888 ÷ 32

11. 25,323 ÷ 23

12. 44,142 ÷ 21

13. 66,429 ÷ 33

14. 16,032 ÷ 16

15. 5,720 ÷ 55

Exercise F Divide and show your work.

1. $26 \overline{)5,278}$ **5.** $29 \overline{)14,674}$ **9.** $28 \overline{)10,640}$ **13.** $32 \overline{)29,056}$

2. $35 \overline{)23,100}$ **6.** $41 \overline{)82,451}$ **10.** $31 \overline{)62,341}$ **14.** $57 \overline{)96,957}$

3. $39 \overline{)5,850}$ **7.** $60 \overline{)66,180}$ **11.** $13 \overline{)40,391}$ **15.** $28 \overline{)64,568}$

4. $89 \overline{)10,680}$ **8.** $35 \overline{)70,105}$ **12.** $28 \overline{)12,320}$ **16.** $16 \overline{)36,640}$

 PROBLEM SOLVING

Exercise G Solve these word problems.

1. Yuneng has a job after school. He earned $868.00 over a 14-week period. What is Yuneng's average weekly salary?

2. On Saturday, Jamal works with his father at the flour mill. They load 5,580 pounds of flour. If each bag of flour weighs 45 pounds, how many bags are loaded?

3. Ada's car gets 23 miles on a gallon of gas. How many gallons will she use to take a 4,715-mile trip?

4. Thumbtacks are sold on cards of 48 tacks each. How many cards must be bought if you need 1,104 tacks?

Division is like splitting an amount into equal groups. You can split 629 blocks into 23 groups of 27. There will be 8 left over.

The quotient (answer) of a division problem may not always be a whole number. When this occurs, the remainder may be written as a fraction. The remainder is written over the divisor.

EXAMPLES

$$43 \tfrac{7}{32} \quad \begin{matrix} \text{remainder} \\ \text{divisor} \end{matrix}$$
$$32 \overline{)1,383}$$
$$\underline{-1\ 28}$$
$$103$$
$$\underline{-\ 96}$$
$$7$$

$$150 \tfrac{13}{41} \quad \begin{matrix} \text{remainder} \\ \text{divisor} \end{matrix}$$
$$41 \overline{)6,163}$$
$$\underline{-4\ 1}$$
$$2\ 06$$
$$\underline{-2\ 05}$$
$$13$$

Exercise H Divide and write any remainders as fractions.

1. 35) 742

7. 22) 4,144

13. 18) 19,111

19. 31) 6,263

2. 11) 483

8. 9) 63,631

14. 23) 6,606

20. 8) 3,649

3. 63) 415

9. 38) 7,879

15. 51) 3,110

21. 17) 9,437

4. 39) 563

10. 45) 9,093

16. 18) 6,113

22. 29) 10,006

5. 91) 458

11. 16) 4,801

17. 24) 1,009

23. 26) 13,548

6. 19) 3,839

12. 23) 3,020

18. 47) 6,151

24. 36) 11,056

Exercise I Divide and check by multiplying.

1. 29) 6,951

6. 33) 4,123

11. 8) 2,341

2. 69) 4,123

7. 28) 5,312

12. 6) 413

3. 12) 81,235

8. 36) 7,208

13. 17) 5,136

4. 8) 6,595

9. 42) 42,015

14. 10) 2,031

5. 12) 2,438

10. 125) 300

15. 81) 6,235

PROBLEM SOLVING

Exercise J Solve these word problems.

1. Joe's new car averages 25 miles per gallon. How many gallons will he need to drive 455 miles?

2. Ms. Roland drives 650 miles on her vacation. If she drives for 14 hours, how many miles will she average per hour?

3. Sandra paid $816.00 for heat last year. How much did she pay each month?

4. Chen cuts 168 feet of rope into 5 pieces. How long is each piece?

Average

The number obtained by dividing the sum of two or more quantities by the number of quantities

The **average** of a set of numbers is found by adding all of the numbers and dividing their sum by the total number of numbers added.

EXAMPLE Marvin's test grades in mathematics are 76, 75, 85, 90, 95, and 65. What is Marvin's average grade?

Step 1 Add the test grades.

```
  76
  75
  85
  90
  95
+ 65
 486
```

Step 2 Divide by the number of scores.

```
                    81  — average
number of scores — 6 )486 — sum
                   -48
                    06
                   - 6
                     0
```

You may have a remainder when you divide. Write the remainder over the divisor to express the remainder as a fraction.

EXAMPLE Megan's mathematics test scores are 60, 82, 75, 80, 70, 90, and 70. What is Megan's average grade?

Step 1 Add the scores.

```
  60
  82
  75
  80
  70
  90
+ 70
 527
```

Step 2 Divide by the number of scores.

```
        75 2/7  average
    7 )527
      -49
       37
      -35
        2
```

$75\frac{2}{7}$ average

Exercise A Find the average of each set of numbers.

1. 52, 55, 96, 87, 89, 75, 98, 97, 89
2. 95, 76, 53, 72, 63, 67, 94, 92, 50, 82, 75, 63
3. 37, 89, 71, 56, 92, 96, 83
4. 69, 76, 97, 81, 65, 74, 86

Exercise B Solve these word problems about averages.

1. Gail's first-quarter grades are 85, 68, 90, and 75. Find her average.

2. Mr. Hiroshi receives these test scores in a course that he is taking: 83, 90, 77, 93, 67, and 70. What is Mr. Hiroshi's average in the course?

3. These temperatures are recorded in Seneca County: 75°, 75°, 82°, 63°, 91°, 72°, 60°, 59°. What is the average temperature?

4. In 18 basketball games, Sam scores 92 field goals (2 points each) and 60 foul shots (1 point each). What is the average number of points that Sam scored each game?

5. The five members of the twelfth-grade bowling team each bowl three games. Their scores are given in the chart below. Find the average for each member of the twelfth-grade team.

6. In the first football game of the season, the Fighting Irish gain 112 yards in 28 plays. What is the average number of yards gained on each play?

7. The airplane leaves Burtonville at 2 P.M. and arrives at Meadowfield, 1,095 miles away, at 5 P.M. Find the average speed of the airplane in miles per hour.

8. Anita's grades in her night school course are 93, 72, 85, 81, and 73. What is her average grade?

Team Member	Game 1	Game 2	Game 3
Nick	182	207	166
Eddie	201	106	200
Tony	145	203	102
Frank	225	198	207
Roberto	106	114	132

Use your calculator to find the average of a set of numbers. Remember to check each calculator entry to make sure the correct numbers have been entered. Round these averages to the nearest whole number.

EXAMPLE Find the average of 435, 683, and 315.

Step 1 Add.
Press 435 $+$ 683 $+$ 315 $=$
The display reads 1433.

Step 2 Divide by the total number of numbers.
Press $÷$ 3 $=$
The display reads 477.66666. Round to the nearest whole number. The average is 478.

Averaging is like sharing. If three towers of 9, 4, and 11 blocks shared the blocks evenly, each tower would have 8 blocks. This is the average height of the towers.

Calculator Exercise Use a calculator to find the average for each set of numbers. Round to the nearest whole number.

1. 236, 414, 500, 502, 700, 308

2. 9063, 9060, 8021, 8913, 1006

3. 7000, 8000, 9000, 5000, 5555

4. 36200, 75120, 80602, 77314

5. 72000, 28000, 56100, 43900, 60105

6. 18, 26, 37, 17, 59, 49, 18

7. 412, 438, 319, 389, 372, 420, 422

8. 6, 54, 95, 83, 72, 61, 65, 64, 64

9. 17000, 22630, 29004, 19621, 20000

10. 5816, 5806, 5820, 5812, 5818, 2001

Exponent

Number that tells how many times another number is a factor

Exponents make many math problems easier to write. The exponent tells how many times the same number is to be used as a factor.

Using exponents is a shortcut for multiplying numbers again and again.

EXAMPLE

4^2 means $4 \times 4 = 16$

4^3 means $4 \times 4 \times 4 = 64$

3^2 means $3 \times 3 = 9$

3^3 means $3 \times 3 \times 3 = 27$

3^4 means $3 \times 3 \times 3 \times 3 = 81$

5^3 means $5 \times 5 \times 5 = 125$

2^5 means $2 \times 2 \times 2 \times 2 \times 2 = 32$

12^3 means $12 \times 12 \times 12 = 1,728$

Exercise A Write each as a multiplication problem. Then find the product.

1. 3^2
2. 5^2
3. 6^3
4. 5^4
5. 8^2
6. 7^3
7. 8^3
8. 9^3
9. 6^2
10. 13^2
11. 3^5
12. 2^6
13. 8^4
14. 5^6
15. 4^4
16. 10^3
17. 10^4
18. 3^6
19. 11^2
20. 12^2

21. 15^2
22. 20^3
23. 17^2
24. 15^3
25. 30^2
26. 7^4
27. 16^2
28. 14^2
29. 50^3
30. 100^3
31. 1000^2
32. 60^3
33. 25^3
34. 40^2
35. 60^2
36. 2^7
37. 6^4
38. 5^5
39. 7^2
40. 2^8

When you have several operations in the same number statement, it is important that you perform the operations in the correct order. You should perform the operations in this order:

1. Evaluate any expressions with exponents.
2. Multiply and divide from left to right.
3. Add and subtract from left to right.

$2 + 4 \times 5$ is 22, not 30, because you multiply first before you add.

This phrase can help you remember how to evaluate expressions with exponents:
Elementary, **M**y **D**ear **A**unt **S**ally. (**E**xponents, **M**ultiply and **D**ivide, **A**dd and **S**ubtract.)

EXAMPLES

$$3^2 + 5 \times 6$$
$$= 9 + 30$$
$$= 39$$

$$2^3 + 6 \times 3 \div 2$$
$$= 8 + 18 \div 2$$
$$= 8 + 9$$
$$= 17$$

Exercise A Find the answers.

1. $12 - 18 \div 2$

2. $25 + 16 - 12 \div 2$

3. $5 + 6 \div 2 \times 3$

4. $2 + 8 \times 3 - 6 \times 2$

5. $16 - 9 \times 2 \div 3 + 3$

6. $25 - 4 \times 9 \div 2 + 12 \div 4 \times 2$

7. $12 + 6^2 \div 12 + 5 \times 2$

8. $2^4 + 2^2 \times 9 \div 6$

9. $8^2 - 4^2 \div 2 + 8^2 \div 2^2$

10. $9 - 6 \times 2 \div 2^2 - 6 \times 4 \div 8$

11. $8 + 5 \times 2 - 6 \times 3 \div 3^2 + 2$

$$\Omega\,\sqrt{}\,+\,\$\,\div\,<\,\nearrow\times\,\%\,\$\,\geq\,\nabla\,30°$$

Good Gas Mileage = Savings

Owning a car that gets good gas mileage can save you money. Gas mileage is the average number of miles driven per gallon of gas.

EXAMPLE Suppose you drive an average of 15,000 miles per year, mostly in the city. If the price of a gallon of gas is about $1.50, how much money can you save in one year driving Car A compared to Car B? (Use the table to the right.)

Vehicle Miles Per Gallon Rates		
Car	City	Highway
A	20 mpg	28 mpg
B	8 mpg	12 mpg
C	15 mpg	25 mpg
D	16 mpg	30 mpg
E	20 mpg	35 mpg

Step 1 Find the cost of one year of city driving for Car A.
$15,000 \div 20 = 750$ gallons
$750 \times \$1.50 = \$1,125.00$

Step 2 Find the cost of one year of city driving for Car B.
$15,000 \div 8 = 1,875$ gallons
$1,875 \times \$1.50 = \$2,812.50$

Step 3 Compare Car A and Car B.
Car B: $2,812.50
Car A: $-$ $1,125.00
$\overline{\$1,687.50}$

You would save $1,687.50 in one year driving Car A.

Exercise Use the information in the table above to solve these problems.

1. Ms. Roland is comparing cars A and C. She drives about 28,000 miles per year mostly on the highway. The price of gas is about $1.25 per gallon. Which car should she buy? How much money could she save?

2. Don's mother is looking at cars D and E. She drives about 20,000 miles per year mostly in the city. The price of gas is about $1.80. Which car should she buy? How much money could she save?

Chapter 1   R E V I E W

Write the letter of the best answer to each question.

1. What is the place value of the underlined digit?
64098
   A   Ones
   B   Tens
   C   Hundreds
   D   Thousands

2. What is the correct way to write this number?
215,832
   A   Two hundred thousand, fifteen hundred, eight thirty-two
   B   Two thousand, fifteen hundred, eight hundred thirty-two
   C   Two hundred fifteen million, eight hundred thirty-two thousand
   D   Two hundred fifteen thousand, eight hundred thirty-two

3. The sum of 560, 39, and 26 is—
   A   495
   B   552
   C   625
   D   567,840

4. Subtract 200 from 1,600 and you get—
   A   8
   B   1,400
   C   1,800
   D   320,000

5. The product of 66 and 264 is—
   A   4
   B   198
   C   330
   D   17,424

Write the name of the place for each underlined digit.
  6. 2<u>4</u>6
  7. <u>5</u>103
  8. 2019<u>6</u>
  9. 8<u>4</u>1276

Write these numerals in words:
  10. 25,602
  11. 7,003,417
  12. 32,001
  13. 25,039,041

Round these whole numbers to the nearest . . .
Ten:
  14. 351
  15. 146
  16. 658

Thousand:
  17. 31,056
  18. 19,738
  19. 25,329

Solve these problems.
  20. 26 + 209 + 3,512
  21. 8 + 208 + 16
  22. 1,803 − 736
  23. From 90,123 subtract 8,341.
  24. $3 \times 2^3 - 5 \times 2$
  25. 457 × 203
  26. 21,730 ÷ 53
  27. 3,264 ÷ 16
  28. 931 × 21
  29. 2 + 5 × 4

Solve these word problems.

30. Miss Bonika drives 450 miles on her vacation. If she drives for 9 hours, how many miles does she average per hour?

31. Marshall pays $2.59 for bread and $2.75 for a package of cheese. He also buys some butter for 99¢. If he gives the salesclerk $20.00, how much change will he receive?

32. Marina earns $75.00 a week from her part-time job. How much will she earn in 8 weeks?

33. Ken notices that there are 150 boxes of pens in inventory at the end of the day on Monday. On Tuesday, 28 boxes are sold. An additional 36 are sold on Wednesday. How many boxes are left?

34. Mr. Jenkins pays $550.00 per month for his rent. How much rent does he pay each year?

35. Lincoln High School has 315 seniors. The rest of the students at Lincoln total three times this amount. How many students attend Lincoln?

Test-Taking Tip

Use a calculator to check your answers on tests, if permitted.

2 Number Theory

Many games and tricks that you can play with numbers are not what they seem. Rather, the fun of mathematics is often based upon the patterns that are found there. Art and architecture are pleasing to our eyes because of the patterns that the artist or designer uses. Patterns are only part of what is appealing about mathematics.

In Chapter 2, you will explore and discover some of the patterns in mathematics.

Goals for Learning

◆ To identify prime and composite numbers

◆ To factor numbers

◆ To find the least common multiple for pairs of numbers

◆ To find the greatest common factor for pairs of numbers

Whenever two or more numbers are multiplied together, each number is a factor of the product. The letter F represents factor.

$$1 \times 18 = 18 \qquad 2 \times 9 = 18 \qquad 3 \times 6 = 18$$

The factors of 18 are 1, 2, 3, 6, 9, and 18.

$$F_{18} = \{1, 2, 3, 6, 9, 18\}$$

You can find all of the factors of a number by trying the whole numbers in order. When the factors start to repeat, you have found all of them.

Factors of a number divide evenly into that number.

EXAMPLES

F_{12}
1 × 12
2 × 6
3 × 4
4 × 3 Factors repeat,
      so we stop.

$F_{12} = \{1, 2, 3, 4, 6, 12\}$

F_{42}
1 × 42
2 × 21
3 × 14
4 × No number works.
5 × No number works.
6 × 7
7 × 6 Factors repeat,
      so we stop.

$F_{42} = \{1, 2, 3, 6, 7, 14, 21, 42\}$

Exercise A Find the set of factors of each number.

1. F_{36}

2. F_{20}

3. F_{7}

4. F_{50}

5. F_{30}

6. F_{8}

7. F_{1}

8. F_{11}

9. F_{25}

10. F_{32}

11. F_{4}

12. F_{49}

13. F_{44}

14. F_{15}

15. F_{28}

16. F_{12}

17. F_{10}

18. F_{24}

19. F_{13}

20. F_{48}

> **Multiples**
>
> The product of a given number and a whole number
>
> **Infinite**
>
> Without end or limit

The **multiples** of a number are the answers that you get when you multiply that number by the whole numbers.

> **EXAMPLE** The multiples of 8:
>
> 8×0 8×1 8×2 8×3 $8 \times 4 \ldots$
>
>   0   8   16   24   32 $\ldots$
>
> $M_8 = \{0, 8, 16, 24, 32, \ldots\}$
>
> The three dots show that the set of multiples continues forever. We say that the set is **infinite**.

Exercise A Find the set of multiples of each number. Include 10 numbers in each set.

1. M_4

2. M_9

3. M_3

4. M_{12}

5. M_2

6. M_{10}

7. M_5

8. M_6

 **Calculator Practice**

Use your calculator to find the set of multiples for any whole number.

> **EXAMPLE** Find the multiples of 17.
>
> Write 0 because $17 \times 0 = 0$. Zero is the first multiple in each set.
>
> Press $\boxed{+}$ 17 $\boxed{=}$
>
> The display reads 17. Write 17 because $17 \times 1 = 17$.
>
> Press $\boxed{=}$ $\boxed{=}$ $\boxed{=}$ $\boxed{=}$ $\boxed{=}$ $\boxed{=}$ $\boxed{=}$ and write the multiple after each $\boxed{=}$.
>
> $M_{17} = \{0, 17, 34, 51, 68, 85, 102, 119, 136, 153, \ldots\}$

Calculator Exercise Use a calculator to find the set of multiples of each number. List the first 10 numbers in each set.

1. M_{13}

2. M_{29}

3. M_{15}

4. M_7

5. M_{36}

Lesson 3 Prime and Composite Numbers

Prime number

Any whole number which has only 1 and itself as factors

Composite number

A number with more than two factors

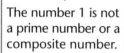

The number 1 is not a prime number or a composite number.

If a number has exactly two factors, we say that it is a **prime number.** If a number has more than two factors, we say that it is a **composite number.**

EXAMPLES   Look at the factors of these three numbers.

1

1×1 Factors repeat, so we stop.

$F_1 = \{1\}$

5

1×5
$2 \times$ No number works.
$3 \times$ No number works.
$4 \times$ No number works.
5×1 Factors repeat, so we stop.

$F_5 = \{1, 5\}$

12

1×12
2×6
3×4
4×3 Factors repeat, so we stop.

$F_{12} = \{1, 2, 3, 4, 6, 12\}$

$F_1 = \{1\}$ $F_5 = \{1, 5\}$ $F_{12} = \{1, 2, 3, 4, 6, 12\}$

5 is a prime number because it has exactly two factors.

12 is a composite number because it has more than two factors.

1 is neither a prime number nor a composite number because it has only one factor.

Exercise A Find the set of factors of each number.

1. F_{12}
2. F_9
3. F_{13}
4. F_8

5. F_{18}
6. F_5
7. F_{20}
8. F_7

9. F_{21}
10. F_2
11. F_{15}
12. F_3

Exercise B Answer the following questions.

1. Which of the numbers in Exercise A are prime numbers?

2. Which of the numbers in Exercise A are composite numbers?

The set of whole numbers is infinite. This set begins with zero and continues forever. You will use this set of whole numbers to find number patterns. This is the set of whole numbers:

$$\{0, 1, 2, 3, 4, 5, \ldots\}$$

Exercise A Follow the directions for each question.

1. The multiples of 2 are called even numbers. List the first six numbers in this set. Use three dots to show that the set is infinite.
Even numbers =

2. The rest of the whole numbers are called odd numbers. List the first six numbers in the set of odd numbers. Use three dots to show that the set is infinite.
Odd numbers =

3. If you begin with 0, and then add 1, and then add 2 to your answer, and then add 3 to your new answer, and continue in this manner, you get the set of triangular numbers. List the set of triangular numbers less than 100.
Triangular numbers = __, __, __, __, __, __, __, __, __, __,

__, __, __, __

4. If you multiply each whole number by itself, you get the set of square numbers. List the set of square numbers up to 100:
Square numbers = __, __, __, __, __, __, __, __, __, __, __

5. What set of numbers does each of these patterns suggest?

a) • ⋰ ⋰ ⋰ etc.   b) • ∷ ∷∷ ∷∷∷ etc.

Technology Connection

Graphic designers make use of patterns and shapes. A designer's job often includes using computers to create pictures and art. Look at how items are packaged for sale in the store. See how things like thumbtacks and candy are presented. Describe any patterns you see. Why do you think the items are displayed the way they are?

In the third century B.C., a Greek mathematician named Eratosthenes (ār ə tos´ thə nēz) invented a way to find prime numbers. It is called the Sieve of Eratosthenes. You may use his method to find the prime numbers less than 100. There are 25 of them. First, list the numbers from 1 to 100. Numbers that are not prime numbers are to be crossed out.

EXAMPLE

Follow these directions to make a Sieve of Eratosthenes and find prime numbers the way Eratosthenes did. Can you find all 25 of them? The numbers that you do not cross out are the prime numbers less than 100. The first two steps are done for you.

Step 1 1 is not a prime number, so it is crossed out.

Step 2 2 is the first prime number, so we circle it and cross out all of the other multiples of 2, like 4, 6, 8, 10, 12, . . .

Step 3 3 is a prime number. Circle it and cross out all of the other multiples of 3, like 6, 9, 12, . . .

Step 4 Circle 5 and cross out the other multiples of 5.

Step 5 Circle 7 and cross out the other multiples of 7.

1̸	②	3	4̸	5	6̸	7	8̸	9	1̸0̸
11	1̸2̸	13	1̸4̸	15	1̸6̸	17	1̸8̸	19	2̸0̸
21	2̸2̸	23	2̸4̸	25	2̸6̸	27	2̸8̸	29	3̸0̸
31	3̸2̸	33	3̸4̸	35	3̸6̸	37	3̸8̸	39	4̸0̸
41	4̸2̸	43	4̸4̸	45	4̸6̸	47	4̸8̸	49	5̸0̸
51	5̸2̸	53	5̸4̸	55	5̸6̸	57	5̸8̸	59	6̸0̸
61	6̸2̸	63	6̸4̸	65	6̸6̸	67	6̸8̸	69	7̸0̸
71	7̸2̸	73	7̸4̸	75	7̸6̸	77	7̸8̸	79	8̸0̸
81	8̸2̸	83	8̸4̸	85	8̸6̸	87	8̸8̸	89	9̸0̸
91	9̸2̸	93	9̸4̸	95	9̸6̸	97	9̸8̸	99	1̸0̸0̸

Exercise A Answer these questions about prime numbers. Use your Sieve of Eratosthenes to help you.

1. List the prime numbers less than 100: 2, 3, . . . 97.

2. 3 and 5 are called twin primes because they are both prime numbers, and they are separated by only one number. What are the other seven twin primes less than 100?

3. What prime number is also an even number?

4. Why is the number 57 not a prime number?

Mathematicians believe that any even number larger than 2 may be written as the sum of two prime numbers.

> **EXAMPLE** 24 = 11 + 13, or 13 + 11
> However, we cannot use 3 + 21, because 21 is not a prime number.

Exercise B Write each of these even numbers as the sum of two prime numbers. The first one has been done for you. Use your Sieve of Eratosthenes to help you.

1. 16 = 3 + 13	**5.** 84	**9.** 66
2. 44	**6.** 30	**10.** 42
3. 8	**7.** 52	**11.** 48
4. 28	**8.** 10	**12.** 80

Mathematicians also believe that any odd number larger than 5 may be written as the sum of three prime numbers.

Exercise C Write each of these odd numbers as the sum of three prime numbers.

1. 17	**6.** 77
2. 25	**7.** 29
3. 59	**8.** 51
4. 41	**9.** 13
5. 21	**10.** 39

Divisible

Able to be divided without a remainder

Divisibility

Able to be divided evenly

If one number divides into a second number and there is no remainder, then the second number is **divisible** by the first number.

EXAMPLE

$$\begin{array}{r} 706 \\ 8\overline{)5,648} \\ -56 \\ \hline 048 \\ -48 \\ \hline 0 \end{array}$$

We can say that 5,648 is divisible by 8 because the remainder is zero.

Sometimes, you can tell if a number is divisible by another number by using a **divisibility** test instead of dividing by the number.

EXAMPLE

Rule A number is divisible by 2 if the digit in the ones place is an even number.

These are the multiples of 2:
0, 2, 4, 6, 8, 10, 12, 14, 16, 18, 20, . . .
They are all divisible by 2. Notice that the digit in the ones place is always 0, 2, 4, 6, or 8.

Exercise A Use the divisibility test to tell which of these numbers are divisible by 2.

1. 16,287

2. 15,298

3. 6,750

4. 387,207

5. 4,393

6. 3,561

7. 21,422

8. 392,556

9. 487,215

10. 31,224

Rule A number is divisible by 5 if the digit in the ones place is 0 or 5.

Here are the multiples of 5:
0, 5, 10, 15, 20, 25, 30, 35, . . .

The digit in the ones place is always 0 or 5.

Exercise B Use the divisibility test to tell which of these numbers are divisible by 5.

1. 48,295

2. 50,553

3. 160,280

4. 17,008

5. 2,007

6. 25,600

The divisibility tests for 2 and 5 used the digit in the ones place to tell if the number was divisible by 2 or 5. The divisibility test for 3 uses all of the digits in the number.

EXAMPLE

Rule A number is divisible by 3 if the sum of its digits is a multiple of 3.

Here are two large numbers: 32,451 and 32,067
These numbers are both divisible by 3.
Find the sum of the digits in each number.

32,451   32,067
3 + 2 + 4 + 5 + 1 = 15   3 + 2 + 0 + 6 + 7 = 18

The sums of the digits are both multiples of 3.
M_3 = {0, 3, 6, 9, 12, 15, 18, 21, . . .}

Exercise C Use the divisibility test to tell which of these numbers are divisible by 3.

1. 48,296

2. 52,872

3. 30,782

4. 16,005

5. 75,913

6. 31,425

Exercise D Use the divisibility tests for 2, 3, and 5. Fill in each space with *Yes* or *No* on a separate piece of paper.

	Number	Divisible by 2?	Divisible by 3?	Divisible by 5?
1.	128,295		Yes	
2.	486,394			
3.	308,460			
4.	268,465			
5.	758,484			
6.	254,751			
7.	396,730			

Any number less than 121 is a prime number if it is not divisible by 2, 3, 5, or 7. You may use the three divisibility tests and then try to divide the number by 7. This will tell you if a number less than 121 is prime or composite.

> If a number has a factor other than 1 or itself, the number is a composite number.

EXAMPLES

314
Divisible by 2.
Composite

75
Divisible by 5.
Composite

423
4 + 2 + 3 = 9
Divisible by 3.
Composite

91
Divisible by 7.
Composite

$$\begin{array}{r} 13 \\ 7\overline{)91} \\ -7 \\ \hline 21 \\ -21 \\ \hline 0 \end{array}$$

83
8 + 3 = 11 Not divisible by 3.
Not divisible by 2.
Not divisible by 5.
Not divisible by 7.
83 is a prime number.

$$\begin{array}{r} 27 \\ 3\overline{)83} \\ -6 \\ \hline 23 \\ -21 \\ \hline 2 \end{array}$$

Exercise E Tell whether each of these numbers is prime or composite. Use the divisibility tests and division by 7.

1. 115	**5.** 120	**9.** 106
2. 117	**6.** 111	**10.** 112
3. 107	**7.** 101	**11.** 103
4. 119	**8.** 105	**12.** 113

There are other divisibility tests that can be useful. These are the divisibility tests for 4, 9, and 10.

EXAMPLES

Rule A number is divisible by 4 if 4 divides evenly into the last two digits.
2,634 is not divisible by 4 because 4 does not divide evenly into 34.

Rule A number is divisible by 9 if the sum of the digits is a multiple of 9.
4,374 is divisible by 9 because 4 + 3 + 7 + 4 = 18, a multiple of 9.

Rule A number is divisible by 10 if the digit in the ones place is a zero.
27,690 is divisible by 10 because the ones digit is a zero.

Exercise F Use the divisibility tests for 4, 9, and 10. Fill in each space with *Yes* or *No* on a separate piece of paper.

	Number	Divisible by 4?	Divisible by 9?	Divisible by 10?
1.	45,666		Yes	
2.	65,320			
3.	73,980			
4.	84,350			
5.	32,436			
6.	88,650			
7.	52,324			

Prime factorization

A number shown as the product of its prime numbers

Every composite number can be written as the product of prime numbers. The expressed product of prime numbers is called the **prime factorization** of the number. One way to find the prime factorization of a number is to make a factor tree.

EXAMPLE

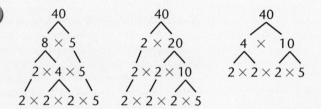

These three factor trees for the number 40 show that you will get the same factors in a different order if you begin with different factors of 40. You still have three 2's and a 5 in the prime factorization of 40. You may think of many factor trees for a number that all end with the same prime numbers.

Writing About Mathematics

A tessellation is the covering of a surface with the same shape. Checkerboards and honeycombs are examples. Find other examples and draw each tessellation. Write about how each suggests factors.

Exercise A Use factor trees to do the prime factorization of the composite numbers below. Do not stop until the last row contains only prime numbers.

1. 40	**7.** 28
2. 24	**8.** 32
3. 15	**9.** 16
4. 63	**10.** 36
5. 54	**11.** 42
6. 30	**12.** 80

Another way to find the prime factorization of a composite number is to use short division and the divisibility tests. The only divisors to be used are 2, 3, 5, and 7. The prime factorization is all of the divisors and the last quotient.

EXAMPLE Find the prime factorization of 420.

	$\dfrac{7}{5\overline{)35}}$	Prime.	Stop.
	$5\overline{)35}$	Ends in 5.	Divide by 5.
	$3\overline{)105}$	$1 + 0 + 5 = 6.$	Divide by 3.
	$2\overline{)210}$	Even.	Divide by 2.
Begin here.	$2\overline{)420}$	Even.	Divide by 2.

$$420 = 2 \times 2 \times 3 \times 5 \times 7$$

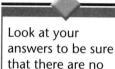

Look at your answers to be sure that there are no composite numbers.

Exercise B Use division to find the prime factorization of these composite numbers.

1. 70

2. 96

3. 72

4. 27

5. 120

6. 84

7. 65

8. 91

9. 48

10. 51

11. 78

12. 110

13. 105

14. 112

15. 150

Try This

You can perform a mind reading act. Neatly write numbers on five cards like this:

| 1 3 5 7 |
| 9 11 13 15 |
| 17 19 21 23 |
| 25 27 29 31 |

| 2 3 6 7 |
| 10 11 14 15 |
| 18 19 22 23 |
| 26 27 30 31 |

| 4 5 6 7 |
| 12 13 14 15 |
| 20 21 22 23 |
| 28 29 30 31 |

| 8 9 10 11 |
| 12 13 14 15 |
| 24 25 26 27 |
| 28 29 30 31 |

| 16 17 18 19 |
| 20 21 22 23 |
| 24 25 26 27 |
| 28 29 30 31 |

Ask a friend to think of a number from 1 to 31. Show your friend the cards one at a time. Ask if the number is on the card. If it is, mentally note the number in the upper left of the card. After you have shown all five cards, say the number your friend was thinking of. It will be the sum of the numbers in the upper left of the cards your friend said the number was on.

Least common multiple (LCM)
Smallest number that two numbers will divide

There is always a *smallest* common multiple of two numbers. This number is called the **least common multiple (LCM)** of two numbers. Zero is a multiple of every number. This is because 0 times any number is always 0. If you look at the nonzero multiples of these numbers, you will see other common multiples.

The LCM is a multiple of both numbers.

EXAMPLES

You have found the multiples of 6 and 9:
$M_6 = \{0, 6, 12, 18, 24, 30, 36, 42, 48, 54, 60, \ldots\}$
$M_9 = \{0, 9, 18, 27, 36, 45, 54, 63, 72, 81, 90, \ldots\}$

These are the common multiples of 6 and 9:
$\{18, 36, 54, \ldots\}$. There is always a least (smallest) common multiple of two numbers.
The LCM (6, 9) = 18.

To find the LCM of two numbers, follow these steps:

Step 1   List the first few multiples of both numbers.

Step 2   Find the smallest nonzero number that is in both sets.

Step 3   If no nonzero number is in both sets, list more multiples of both numbers.

Find LCM (9, 15)
$M_9 = \{0, 9, 18, 27, 36, \underline{45}, \ldots\}$
$M_{15} = \{0, 15, 30, \underline{45}, 60, \ldots\}$
LCM (9, 15) = 45

Exercise A Find the LCM of these pairs of numbers.

1. LCM (12, 18)

2. LCM (6, 8)

3. LCM (3, 9)

4. LCM (3, 7)

5. LCM (12, 15)

6. LCM (8, 20)

7. LCM (6, 15)

8. LCM (10, 8)

9. LCM (6, 12)

10. LCM (8, 9)

11. LCM (4, 6)

12. LCM (15, 18)

Common factors

For any two numbers, all the numbers that divide evenly into both numbers

Greatest common factor (GCF)

Largest factor of two numbers

The GCF is a factor of both numbers.

You have listed all numbers that divide into a number evenly. These are the number's factors. Factors that occur for two numbers are **common factors.** The *largest* of these is the **greatest common factor (GCF)** of the two numbers.

EXAMPLE   List all of the factors of two numbers, 24 and 36.

24	36
1 × 24	1 × 36
2 × 12	2 × 18
3 × 8	3 × 12
4 × 6	4 × 9
5 × No number works.	5 × No number works.
6 × 4 Factors repeat, so we stop.	6 × 6
	7 × No number works.
	8 × No number works.
	9 × 4 Factors repeat, so we stop.

$F_{24} = \{1, 2, 3, 4, 6, 8, 12, 24\}$
$F_{36} = \{1, 2, 3, 4, 6, 9, 12, 18, 36\}$

These two sets have numbers in common:
$\{1, 2, 3, 4, 6, \underline{12}\}$
GCF (24, 36) = 12

Exercise A Find the GCF of these pairs of numbers.

1. GCF (10, 16)

2. GCF (16, 24)

3. GCF (4, 12)

4. GCF (10, 15)

5. GCF (8, 20)

6. GCF (7, 12)

7. GCF (18, 15)

8. GCF (16, 20)

9. GCF (8, 15)

10. GCF (12, 24)

11. GCF (4, 6)

12. GCF (16, 32)

13. GCF (16, 48)

14. GCF (2, 5)

Both the least common multiple and the greatest common factor of two numbers can be found by using the prime factorization of these two numbers.

Learning how to find the LCM will help you add fractions.

 EXAMPLE   Find the LCM of 36 and 40 by using prime factorization.

36
6 × 6
2 × 3 × 2 × 3

40
4 × 10
2 × 2 × 2 × 5

36 = 2 × 2 × 3 × 3
40 = 2 × 2 × 2 × 5

LCM (36, 40) = 2 × 2 × 3 × 3 × 2 × 5
= 360

Exercise A Use prime factorization to find the least common multiple of these pairs of numbers.

1. LCM (8, 10)

2. LCM (6, 15)

3. LCM (10, 12)

4. LCM (6, 18)

5. LCM (15, 20)

6. LCM (8, 12)

7. LCM (12, 16)

8. LCM (8, 15)

9. LCM (8, 14)

10. LCM (6, 9)

11. LCM (15, 24)

12. LCM (10, 14)

13. LCM (6, 12)

14. LCM (9, 20)

The GCF of two numbers may also be found by using prime factorization. Use this method to find the GCF of 36 and 48. If there are no common factors, then the GCF is 1.

The GCF will help you reduce fractions to lowest terms.

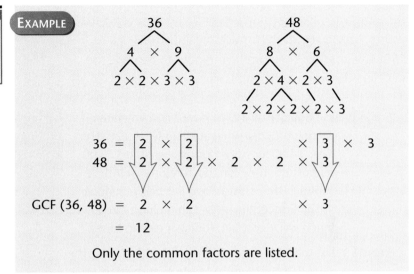

EXAMPLE

$$36 = 2 \times 2 \qquad \times 3 \times 3$$
$$48 = 2 \times 2 \times 2 \times 2 \times 3$$

$$\text{GCF } (36, 48) = 2 \times 2 \qquad \times 3$$
$$= 12$$

Only the common factors are listed.

Exercise B Use prime factorization to find the greatest common factor of these pairs of numbers.

1. GCF (24, 36)

2. GCF (15, 18)

3. GCF (4, 6)

4. GCF (30, 45)

5. GCF (14, 16)

6. GCF (24, 54)

7. GCF (26, 39)

8. GCF (12, 17)

9. GCF (12, 18)

10. GCF (24, 56)

11. GCF (36, 28)

12. GCF (15, 20)

13. GCF (24, 16)

14. GCF (50, 75)

TLC for the Lawn

To maintain a healthy lawn, it must be watered, cut, and fertilized regularly. Sometimes businesses and homeowners hire lawn care companies to provide the TLC (tender loving care) all lawns need.

EXAMPLE Mr. Marshall wants to have his lawn watered every fourth day and cut every tenth day. The fee is $8.00 for watering the lawn and $20.00 for cutting it. According to a one-month contract, the first watering will begin on June 4. The first cutting will begin on June 10. How much will it cost him for lawn care in June?

Step 1 List the days for watering and cutting. (Use the calendars to the right.) Days that overlap are combined for watering and cutting.
Watering at $8.00: June 4, 8, 12, 16, ~~20~~, 24, 28
Cutting at $20.00: June 10, ~~20~~, 30
Watering and Cutting at $28.00: June 20

Step 2 Calculate the fees.
6 payments of $8.00 = $48.00
2 payments of $20.00 = $40.00
1 payment of $28.00 = $28.00
$116.00

The lawn care costs in June will be $116.00.

June						
Sun.	Mon.	Tues.	Wed.	Thurs.	Fri.	Sat.
			1	2	3	4	5
6	7	8	9	10	11	12
13	14	15	16	17	18	19
20	21	22	23	24	25	26
27	28	29	30			

July						
Sun.	Mon.	Tues.	Wed.	Thurs.	Fri.	Sat.
				1	2	3
4	5	6	7	8	9	10
11	12	13	14	15	16	17
18	19	20	21	22	23	24
25	26	27	28	29	30	31

Exercise Use the calendars above to solve the problems.

1. The Biggo Company wants its lawn watered every three days and cut every fifth day in July. Watering is to start on July 3 and cutting on July 5. The fee is $20.00 for watering and $75.00 for cutting. What is the total cost for July?

2. Mrs. Jeno wants her lawn watered every three days and cut every seven days in July. She also wants it fertilized when the watering and cutting occur on the same day. Watering starts on July 3 and cutting starts on July 7. Watering costs $5.00, cutting costs $15.00, and fertilizing costs $25.00. What is the total cost for July?

Chapter 2 R E V I E W

Write the letter of the best answer to each question.

1. Which set shows the factors for the number 14?

   A {1, 14}

   B {1, 2, 7, 14}

   C {1, 4, 7, 14}

   D {1, 2, 4, 6, 8, 10, 12, 14}

2. Which number is a multiple of 7?

   A 21

   B 26

   C 34

   D 46

3. Which of the following is a prime number?

   A 9

   B 36

   C 63

   D 71

4. The number 36,321 is divisible by—

   A 2

   B 3

   C 4

   D 5

5. What is the prime factorization of the number 48?

   A $2 \times 3 \times 8$

   B $2 \times 2 \times 3 \times 4$

   C $2 \times 2 \times 2 \times 2 \times 3$

   D $2 \times 2 \times 2 \times 3 \times 3$

List the set of all factors of these numbers:

6. F_{18}

7. F_{28}

8. F_{30}

List the set of the first three multiples of these numbers:

9. M_8

10. M_{13}

11. M_{20}

Give the next three numbers in each pattern:

12. $\{0, 1, 3, 6, 10, \_\_\_, \_\_\_, \_\_\_, \ldots\}$

13. $\{1, 3, 5, 7, \_\_\_, \_\_\_, \_\_\_, \ldots\}$

14. $\{0, 1, 4, 9, \_\_\_, \_\_\_, \_\_\_, \ldots\}$

Answer the following questions:

15. Which of these are prime numbers?

45	37	16	53
117	2	57	19

16. Which of these are composite numbers?

4	57	31	59
9	49	101	27

17. Which number is divisible by 5?

2,431   4,307   2,503   1,760

18. Which number is divisible by 3?

2,871   4,303   9,286   4,009

Write these numbers as the sum of two prime numbers:

19. 42

20. 30

Give the prime factorization of these numbers:

21. 12

22. 24

23. 28

24. 36

Find the least common multiple (LCM) of each pair of numbers:

25. LCM (12, 16)

26. LCM (6, 8)

27. LCM (4, 12)

Find the greatest common factor (GCF) of each pair of numbers:

28. GCF (12, 16)

29. GCF (18, 25)

30. GCF (27, 36)

Test-Taking Tip

When learning math vocabulary, make flash cards with words and abbreviations on one side and definitions on the other side. Draw pictures next to the words, if possible. Then use the flash cards in a game to test your vocabulary skills.

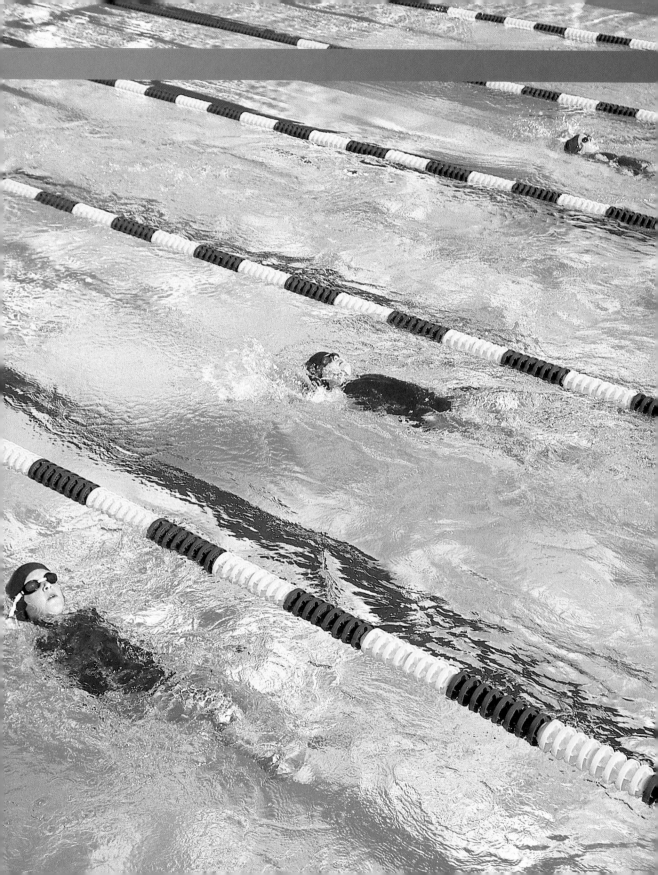

3 Fractions

Do you enjoy competing in sports? Think about the mathematics that are part of sports. Swimmers win races by fractions of a meter. Ice skaters win by fractions of a point, and runners win by fractions of a second. Sometimes we don't realize how often we use mathematics until we stop to think about it.

In Chapter 3, you will learn how to add, subtract, multiply, and divide fractions. Then, watch for the next time you use fractions while planning and enjoying your recreational activities.

Goals for Learning

◆ To compare fractions and determine which is more than or less than

◆ To simplify fractions

◆ To rename mixed numbers and improper fractions

◆ To compute with fractions and mixed numbers

Fraction

Part of a whole number

Numerator

The number of parts that are used; the number above the fraction bar

Denominator

The number of parts to the whole; the number below the fraction bar

This figure is divided into eight equal parts:

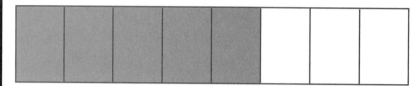

Five of the eight parts are shaded. $\frac{5}{8}$ of the figure is shaded. We call $\frac{5}{8}$ a **fraction.** A fraction has a **numerator** and a **denominator.** The numerator tells how many parts are shaded. The denominator tells how many parts there are to the whole.

$$\frac{5}{8} \begin{array}{l} \text{— Numerator} \\ \text{— Denominator} \end{array}$$

Exercise A Write a fraction to show what part of each figure is shaded.

1.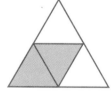

4.

7.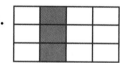

2.

5.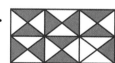

8.

3.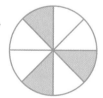

6.

9.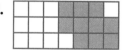

Cross product
The answer obtained by multiplying the denominator of one fraction by the numerator of another

Greater than, >

Larger than

Less than, <

Smaller than

The less than symbol points to the left. The greater than symbol points to the right.

You can tell which of two fractions is greater by using **cross products.**

 EXAMPLE Compare $\frac{3}{4}$ and $\frac{4}{7}$.

Step 1 21

  The product of 3 and 7 is 21. $3 \times 7 = 21$

Step 2 21   16

 The product of 4 and 4 is 16. $4 \times 4 = 16$

Step 3 21 > 16

$\frac{3}{4}$ $\frac{4}{7}$ 21 is **greater than** 16, therefore,

Step 4 $\frac{3}{4} > \frac{4}{7}$ $\frac{3}{4}$ is greater than $\frac{4}{7}$.

The symbol < means **less than.**

Exercise B Tell whether the first fraction is less than (<) or greater than (>) the second fraction in each pair.

1. $\frac{2}{3}$ $\frac{3}{4}$ **8.** $\frac{6}{8}$ $\frac{5}{6}$ **15.** $\frac{5}{15}$ $\frac{2}{3}$ **22.** $\frac{5}{17}$ $\frac{1}{3}$

2. $\frac{7}{8}$ $\frac{5}{6}$ **9.** $\frac{2}{3}$ $\frac{4}{7}$ **16.** $\frac{11}{15}$ $\frac{16}{17}$ **23.** $\frac{6}{11}$ $\frac{1}{5}$

3. $\frac{2}{7}$ $\frac{3}{9}$ **10.** $\frac{2}{9}$ $\frac{3}{10}$ **17.** $\frac{7}{8}$ $\frac{14}{18}$ **24.** $\frac{2}{13}$ $\frac{1}{6}$

4. $\frac{4}{7}$ $\frac{3}{8}$ **11.** $\frac{5}{8}$ $\frac{4}{7}$ **18.** $\frac{12}{17}$ $\frac{3}{4}$ **25.** $\frac{18}{19}$ $\frac{17}{18}$

5. $\frac{3}{11}$ $\frac{4}{6}$ **12.** $\frac{7}{8}$ $\frac{6}{7}$ **19.** $\frac{2}{16}$ $\frac{1}{5}$ **26.** $\frac{4}{30}$ $\frac{2}{8}$

6. $\frac{2}{5}$ $\frac{3}{7}$ **13.** $\frac{5}{12}$ $\frac{2}{3}$ **20.** $\frac{3}{18}$ $\frac{2}{3}$ **27.** $\frac{5}{19}$ $\frac{2}{7}$

7. $\frac{5}{7}$ $\frac{4}{8}$ **14.** $\frac{5}{6}$ $\frac{6}{7}$ **21.** $\frac{5}{17}$ $\frac{3}{5}$ **28.** $\frac{16}{17}$ $\frac{15}{16}$

You might need to express a fraction in higher terms before you can do an addition or a subtraction problem. You can raise a fraction to higher terms by multiplying the numerator and the denominator by the same number.

EXAMPLE Express $\frac{5}{6}$ as a fraction with a denominator of 24.

Step 1 $\frac{5}{6} = \frac{\blacksquare}{24}$

Step 2 Divide 24 by 6. $24 \div 6 = 4$

Step 3 Multiply $\frac{5}{6}$ by $\frac{4}{4}$. $\frac{5 \times 4}{6 \times 4} = \frac{20}{24}$

Step 4 $\frac{5}{6} = \frac{20}{24}$

Exercise A Express these fractions in higher terms.

1. $\frac{2}{3} = \frac{\blacksquare}{6}$

2. $\frac{5}{7} = \frac{\blacksquare}{35}$

3. $\frac{7}{8} = \frac{\blacksquare}{32}$

4. $\frac{5}{6} = \frac{\blacksquare}{60}$

5. $\frac{11}{17} = \frac{\blacksquare}{51}$

6. $\frac{13}{14} = \frac{\blacksquare}{42}$

7. $\frac{5}{18} = \frac{\blacksquare}{72}$

8. $\frac{6}{13} = \frac{\blacksquare}{39}$

9. $\frac{17}{32} = \frac{\blacksquare}{64}$

10. $\frac{9}{32} = \frac{\blacksquare}{96}$

11. $\frac{11}{15} = \frac{\blacksquare}{45}$

12. $\frac{7}{9} = \frac{\blacksquare}{99}$

13. $\frac{11}{12} = \frac{\blacksquare}{36}$

14. $\frac{15}{23} = \frac{\blacksquare}{92}$

15. $\frac{12}{17} = \frac{\blacksquare}{34}$

16. $\frac{6}{19} = \frac{\blacksquare}{57}$

17. $\frac{11}{13} = \frac{\blacksquare}{52}$

18. $\frac{21}{32} = \frac{\blacksquare}{160}$

19. $\frac{9}{41} = \frac{\blacksquare}{123}$

20. $\frac{11}{33} = \frac{\blacksquare}{132}$

21. $\frac{10}{16} = \frac{\blacksquare}{48}$

22. $\frac{1}{7} = \frac{\blacksquare}{49}$

23. $\frac{1}{10} = \frac{\blacksquare}{100}$

24. $\frac{2}{8} = \frac{\blacksquare}{56}$

25. $\frac{19}{65} = \frac{\blacksquare}{130}$

26. $\frac{21}{70} = \frac{\blacksquare}{280}$

27. $\frac{221}{500} = \frac{\blacksquare}{4,000}$

28. $\frac{9}{375} = \frac{\blacksquare}{1,500}$

When you are doing problems with fractions, you will often need to rename the answer in lowest terms. This is called **simplest form.** To **simplify** a fraction, divide the numerator and the denominator by the largest number that divides into both evenly.

Simplest form

A fraction in which the numerator and denominator have no common factor greater than one

Simplify

To express in simplest form

EXAMPLES $\frac{15}{20} = \frac{15 \div 5}{20 \div 5} = \frac{3}{4}$ $\frac{24}{30} = \frac{24 \div 6}{30 \div 6} = \frac{4}{5}$

$\frac{28}{30} = \frac{28 \div 2}{30 \div 2} = \frac{14}{15}$ $\frac{42}{44} = \frac{42 \div 2}{44 \div 2} = \frac{21}{22}$

Exercise A Rename these fractions in simplest form.

1. $\frac{4}{18}$ 9. $\frac{12}{42}$ 17. $\frac{27}{81}$ 25. $\frac{80}{100}$

2. $\frac{6}{18}$ 10. $\frac{16}{48}$ 18. $\frac{8}{16}$ 26. $\frac{28}{64}$

3. $\frac{8}{12}$ 11. $\frac{13}{39}$ 19. $\frac{8}{20}$ 27. $\frac{63}{72}$

4. $\frac{15}{20}$ 12. $\frac{26}{39}$ 20. $\frac{42}{60}$ 28. $\frac{16}{22}$

5. $\frac{16}{32}$ 13. $\frac{45}{50}$ 21. $\frac{38}{57}$ 29. $\frac{72}{81}$

6. $\frac{18}{24}$ 14. $\frac{28}{42}$ 22. $\frac{80}{120}$ 30. $\frac{75}{250}$

7. $\frac{24}{32}$ 15. $\frac{32}{64}$ 23. $\frac{12}{50}$ 31. $\frac{200}{3,000}$

8. $\frac{12}{15}$ 16. $\frac{42}{64}$ 24. $\frac{10}{16}$ 32. $\frac{55}{121}$

Exercise B Rename these fractions in simplest form.

1. $\frac{16}{28}$ 4. $\frac{48}{56}$ 7. $\frac{14}{26}$ 10. $\frac{36}{90}$

2. $\frac{26}{52}$ 5. $\frac{52}{62}$ 8. $\frac{39}{42}$ 11. $\frac{44}{132}$

3. $\frac{18}{26}$ 6. $\frac{120}{130}$ 9. $\frac{78}{81}$ 12. $\frac{118}{220}$

Mixed number

Number composed of a whole number and a fraction

Improper fraction

Fraction with its numerator equal to or greater than its denominator

When you multiply or divide with **mixed numbers,** you will need to change the mixed numbers to **improper fractions.** An improper fraction has a numerator that is greater than or equal to the denominator.

EXAMPLE   Write $4\frac{2}{3}$ as an improper fraction.

Step 1   Multiply the whole number by the denominator.
$4 \times 3 = 12$

Step 2   Add the numerator.
$12 + 2 = 14$

Step 3   Write the answer over the original denominator. $\frac{14}{3}$
$4\frac{2}{3} = \frac{14}{3}$ — New Numerator
        — Original Denominator

Exercise A Rename these mixed numbers as improper fractions.

1. $2\frac{3}{4}$

2. $5\frac{1}{2}$

3. $6\frac{2}{3}$

4. $5\frac{4}{5}$

5. $6\frac{2}{7}$

6. $3\frac{2}{5}$

7. $8\frac{3}{7}$

8. $7\frac{3}{8}$

9. $11\frac{2}{3}$

10. $5\frac{6}{8}$

11. $4\frac{1}{3}$

12. $5\frac{2}{7}$

13. $9\frac{8}{9}$

14. $1\frac{2}{3}$

15. $2\frac{1}{3}$

16. $16\frac{5}{6}$

17. $13\frac{1}{3}$

18. $23\frac{2}{5}$

19. $6\frac{1}{9}$

20. $17\frac{1}{7}$

21. $2\frac{4}{5}$

22. $19\frac{1}{2}$

23. $13\frac{3}{4}$

24. $6\frac{2}{9}$

Exercise B Rename these mixed numbers as improper fractions.

1. $7\frac{1}{6}$

2. $5\frac{2}{3}$

3. $8\frac{1}{9}$

4. $11\frac{1}{3}$

5. $10\frac{2}{5}$

6. $1\frac{1}{2}$

7. $18\frac{1}{2}$

8. $13\frac{2}{3}$

9. $25\frac{3}{4}$

10. $21\frac{2}{7}$

11. $66\frac{2}{3}$

12. $50\frac{1}{2}$

Use your calculator to help rename mixed numbers as improper fractions.

EXAMPLE Rename $2\frac{4}{5}$ as an improper fraction. $2\frac{4}{5} = \frac{\blacksquare}{5}$

Step 1 Multiply the whole number by the denominator.
Press 2 $\times$ 5 $=$
The display reads 10.

Step 2 Add the product to the numerator.
Press $+$ 4 $=$

Step 3 Write the sum over the denominator.
$2\frac{4}{5} = \frac{14}{5}$

Calculator Exercise Use a calculator to rename these mixed numbers as improper fractions.

1. $12\frac{2}{5}$

2. $33\frac{10}{11}$

3. $15\frac{6}{13}$

4. $22\frac{3}{4}$

5. $21\frac{5}{6}$

6. $31\frac{9}{11}$

7. $9\frac{11}{12}$

8. $12\frac{5}{13}$

9. $12\frac{7}{12}$

10. $13\frac{2}{7}$

11. $28\frac{12}{13}$

12. $18\frac{5}{21}$

13. $44\frac{6}{7}$

14. $48\frac{2}{3}$

15. $55\frac{11}{12}$

16. $73\frac{13}{15}$

17. $78\frac{3}{8}$

18. $81\frac{12}{17}$

19. $90\frac{21}{29}$

20. $150\frac{39}{51}$

When an answer to a problem is an improper fraction, you may need to rename it. To do this, divide the numerator by the denominator. Write any remainder over the divisor. Some improper fractions may equal whole numbers.

EXAMPLES   Rename $\frac{45}{8}$.   Rename $\frac{48}{6}$.

$$8\overline{)45} \;\; 5\tfrac{5}{8}$$
$$\underline{-\,40}$$
$$5$$

$$6\overline{)48} \;\; 8$$
$$\underline{-\,48}$$
$$0$$

Exercise A   Rename each improper fraction. Simplify when needed.

1. $\frac{18}{5}$ **8.** $\frac{32}{6}$ **15.** $\frac{61}{4}$ **22.** $\frac{125}{5}$

2. $\frac{16}{6}$ **9.** $\frac{48}{7}$ **16.** $\frac{51}{8}$ **23.** $\frac{128}{7}$

3. $\frac{17}{4}$ **10.** $\frac{56}{6}$ **17.** $\frac{102}{10}$ **24.** $\frac{231}{9}$

4. $\frac{18}{2}$ **11.** $\frac{47}{7}$ **18.** $\frac{121}{11}$ **25.** $\frac{162}{3}$

5. $\frac{19}{2}$ **12.** $\frac{43}{6}$ **19.** $\frac{99}{11}$ **26.** $\frac{121}{20}$

6. $\frac{23}{4}$ **13.** $\frac{21}{2}$ **20.** $\frac{89}{2}$ **27.** $\frac{235}{4}$

7. $\frac{42}{9}$ **14.** $\frac{38}{2}$ **21.** $\frac{79}{5}$ **28.** $\frac{178}{16}$

Exercise B   Rename these improper fractions as mixed numbers.

1. $\frac{18}{5}$ **4.** $\frac{42}{3}$ **7.** $\frac{32}{7}$ **10.** $\frac{155}{10}$

2. $\frac{26}{3}$ **5.** $\frac{38}{2}$ **8.** $\frac{77}{10}$ **11.** $\frac{75}{5}$

3. $\frac{23}{10}$ **6.** $\frac{56}{12}$ **9.** $\frac{81}{8}$ **12.** $\frac{140}{80}$

Often, the answers to fraction problems will be mixed numbers that are not in their simplest form. You will need to rename these mixed numbers in their simplest form, a whole number and a reduced proper fraction.

Look for improper fractions and proper fractions with a common factor in the numerator and denominator.

EXAMPLES

$2\frac{8}{14} = 2 + \frac{8}{14} = 2 + \frac{4}{7} = 2\frac{4}{7}$

$3\frac{7}{3} = 3 + \frac{7}{3} = 3 + 2\frac{1}{3} = 5\frac{1}{3}$

$5\frac{16}{8} = 5 + \frac{16}{8} = 5 + 2 = 7$

$8\frac{12}{10} = 8 + \frac{12}{10} = 8 + 1\frac{2}{10} = 9\frac{2}{10}$ or $9\frac{1}{5}$

Exercise A Write these mixed numbers in their simplest form.

1. $6\frac{5}{15}$

2. $7\frac{6}{3}$

3. $8\frac{7}{14}$

4. $6\frac{15}{24}$

5. $9\frac{8}{6}$

6. $6\frac{4}{3}$

7. $11\frac{11}{22}$

8. $12\frac{16}{18}$

9. $17\frac{13}{10}$

10. $12\frac{8}{24}$

11. $23\frac{16}{48}$

12. $21\frac{24}{20}$

13. $19\frac{11}{33}$

14. $32\frac{5}{3}$

15. $42\frac{9}{7}$

16. $30\frac{24}{48}$

17. $52\frac{17}{51}$

18. $17\frac{18}{54}$

19. $44\frac{12}{72}$

20. $31\frac{36}{29}$

21. $19\frac{42}{7}$

22. $7\frac{36}{9}$

23. $10\frac{25}{6}$

24. $53\frac{17}{16}$

25. $36\frac{24}{96}$

26. $51\frac{12}{60}$

27. $33\frac{22}{26}$

28. $35\frac{17}{5}$

29. $41\frac{13}{13}$

30. $42\frac{26}{13}$

31. $10\frac{250}{1,000}$

32. $29\frac{45}{405}$

Exercise B Rename each mixed number in its simplest form.

1. $3\frac{7}{21}$

2. $6\frac{9}{8}$

3. $4\frac{4}{8}$

4. $8\frac{2}{6}$

5. $9\frac{7}{21}$

6. $6\frac{12}{4}$

7. $14\frac{15}{13}$

8. $13\frac{18}{38}$

9. $42\frac{18}{5}$

10. $12\frac{14}{10}$

11. $18\frac{20}{6}$

12. $14\frac{27}{12}$

You multiply fractions by multiplying the numerators together and then multiplying the denominators together.

EXAMPLES

$\frac{3}{5} \times \frac{4}{7} = \blacksquare$

$\frac{3}{5} \times \frac{4}{7} = \frac{3 \times 4}{5 \times 7} = \frac{12}{35}$

$5 \times \frac{2}{3} = \blacksquare$

$5 \times \frac{2}{3} = \frac{5}{1} \times \frac{2}{3} = \frac{5 \times 2}{1 \times 3} = \frac{10}{3} = 3\frac{1}{3}$

Exercise A Multiply. Write your answers in simplest form.

1. $\frac{2}{3} \times \frac{4}{5}$

2. $\frac{4}{7} \times \frac{3}{6}$

3. $\frac{2}{9} \times \frac{1}{2}$

4. $\frac{4}{7} \times \frac{2}{3}$

5. $\frac{6}{7} \times \frac{2}{5}$

6. $\frac{5}{9} \times \frac{1}{4}$

7. $\frac{5}{11} \times \frac{2}{3}$

8. $\frac{4}{5} \times \frac{7}{9}$

9. $\frac{5}{11} \times \frac{4}{6}$

10. $\frac{4}{13} \times \frac{2}{3}$

11. $\frac{6}{8} \times \frac{7}{8}$

12. $\frac{5}{16} \times \frac{8}{9}$

13. $\frac{1}{6} \times \frac{11}{12}$

14. $\frac{5}{11} \times 2$

15. $\frac{6}{13} \times 26$

16. $6 \times \frac{3}{5}$

17. $\frac{15}{16} \times \frac{6}{7}$

18. $\frac{11}{13} \times \frac{26}{33}$

19. $\frac{6}{7} \times 3$

20. $\frac{1}{3} \times 8$

21. $\frac{5}{18} \times \frac{9}{13}$

22. $\frac{7}{15} \times \frac{30}{42}$

23. $\frac{6}{7} \times \frac{5}{12}$

24. $9 \times \frac{7}{12}$

Often, you can simplify the problem before multiplying. See if numerators and the denominators have any common factors. If they do, divide both the numerator and the denominator by their common factor before you multiply.

If you can simplify before multiplying, you will have smaller numbers to multiply.

EXAMPLE $\frac{12}{14} \times \frac{7}{16} = \blacksquare$

Step 1 12 and 16 have a common factor of 4.
Divide 12 and 16 by 4.

$$\frac{\overset{3}{\cancel{12}}}{14} \times \frac{7}{\underset{4}{\cancel{16}}}$$

Step 2 14 and 7 have a common factor of 7.
Divide 14 and 7 by 7.

$$\frac{\overset{3}{\cancel{12}}}{\underset{2}{\cancel{14}}} \times \frac{\overset{1}{\cancel{7}}}{\underset{4}{\cancel{16}}}$$

Step 3 Multiply the numerators.
Multiply the denominators.

$$\frac{3 \times 1}{2 \times 4} = \frac{3}{8}$$

Sometimes the multiplication sign, $\times$, is replaced by the word *of*. Think of the word *of* as meaning "times." For example, one half of one half of a pizza is one-fourth pizza.

Exercise B Find the answers. Simplify the problem before multiplying, if you can.

1. $\frac{3}{5}$ of $\frac{7}{8}$

2. $\frac{5}{7}$ of $\frac{2}{7}$

3. $\frac{6}{7}$ of $\frac{5}{6}$

4. $\frac{5}{9}$ of $\frac{7}{8}$

5. $\frac{4}{15}$ of $\frac{5}{12}$

6. $\frac{4}{9}$ of $\frac{7}{12}$

7. $\frac{11}{12}$ of $\frac{4}{11}$

8. $\frac{6}{13}$ of $\frac{5}{12}$

9. $\frac{4}{13}$ of $\frac{5}{11}$

10. $\frac{6}{12}$ of $\frac{2}{12}$

11. $\frac{3}{7}$ of $\frac{1}{2}$

12. $\frac{3}{7}$ of $\frac{14}{15}$

13. $\frac{6}{18}$ of $\frac{36}{55}$

14. $\frac{3}{16}$ of $\frac{8}{9}$

15. $\frac{7}{10}$ of $\frac{5}{28}$

Before you multiply mixed numbers, change them to improper fractions. Then, multiply the numerators and the denominators. Next, write your answers in simplest form.

Remove factors of 1 before you multiply.

EXAMPLES

$3\frac{1}{2} \times 1\frac{4}{5} = \blacksquare$

$3\frac{1}{2} \times 1\frac{4}{5} = \frac{7}{2} \times \frac{9}{5}$

$= \frac{63}{10} = 6\frac{3}{10}$

$6 \times 2\frac{3}{4} = \blacksquare$

$6 \times 2\frac{3}{4} = \frac{6}{1} \times \frac{11}{4}$

$= \frac{\overset{3}{6}}{1} \times \frac{11}{\underset{2}{4}}$

$= \frac{33}{2} = 16\frac{1}{2}$

Exercise A Multiply. Write your answers in simplest form.

1. $1\frac{1}{2} \times 2\frac{3}{5}$

2. $2\frac{1}{6} \times \frac{2}{3}$

3. $4\frac{1}{3} \times \frac{1}{6}$

4. $4\frac{2}{7} \times 14$

5. $5\frac{1}{3} \times 2\frac{1}{2}$

6. $3\frac{2}{3} \times 5$

7. $\frac{15}{16} \times 2\frac{2}{5}$

8. $2\frac{1}{7} \times \frac{19}{30}$

9. $3\frac{5}{6} \times \frac{3}{8}$

10. $7\frac{2}{3} \times \frac{3}{4}$

11. $6\frac{3}{5} \times 2\frac{2}{9}$

12. $4\frac{9}{10} \times 1\frac{3}{7}$

13. $1\frac{1}{2} \times 1\frac{1}{3}$

14. $4\frac{3}{8} \times 2\frac{3}{7}$

15. $\frac{5}{6} \times 2\frac{3}{10}$

16. $\frac{1}{2} \times 3\frac{3}{7}$

17. $\frac{7}{8} \times 1\frac{3}{7}$

18. $5\frac{1}{5} \times 3\frac{1}{8}$

Exercise B Find the answers. Write them in simplest form.

1. $\frac{5}{6}$ of $1\frac{1}{2}$

2. $\frac{4}{7}$ of $1\frac{1}{1}$

3. $3\frac{2}{3} \times 1\frac{1}{2}$

4. $\frac{3}{8}$ of $2\frac{1}{3}$

5. $\frac{3}{4}$ of $2\frac{1}{6}$

6. $2\frac{1}{3}$ of 5

7. $6 \times 1\frac{1}{3}$

8. $\frac{3}{5}$ of 9

9. $2\frac{3}{8} \times \frac{12}{19}$

10. $5\frac{2}{7} \times 1\frac{5}{37}$

11. $\frac{7}{8}$ of $3\frac{2}{7}$

12. $\frac{9}{19}$ of $4\frac{2}{9}$

13. $\frac{6}{19}$ of $6\frac{1}{3}$

14. $5\frac{4}{5} \times \frac{25}{29}$

PROBLEM SOLVING

Exercise C Solve these word problems.

1. Jason wants to build 5 shelves, each measuring $3\frac{3}{4}$ feet long. How many feet of shelving board will he need?

2. If it takes $2\frac{1}{4}$ cups of flour to make a cake, then how much flour will you need to make $\frac{1}{2}$ of the recipe?

3. Shateel weighs 112 pounds. His sister, Alma, weighs $\frac{3}{4}$ as much. How much does Alma weigh?

4. Omar wants to fence his property. Each side of his square lot is $14\frac{1}{2}$ feet long. How much fencing does Omar need?

Invert

Change positions of a fraction; for example, $\frac{2}{3}$ inverted is $\frac{3}{2}$

When you divide fractions, you really just multiply after inverting the divisor. The inverted divisor is called the reciprocal.

The easiest way to divide fractions is to **invert,** or change positions of, the divisor and then multiply.

EXAMPLES $\quad \frac{7}{8} \div \frac{2}{3} = \blacksquare$

The divisor is $\frac{2}{3}$. When you invert $\frac{2}{3}$, it becomes $\frac{3}{2}$.

$$\frac{7}{8} \div \frac{2}{3} = \frac{7}{8} \times \frac{3}{2}$$
$$= \frac{7 \times 3}{8 \times 2}$$
$$= \frac{21}{16} = 1\frac{5}{16}$$

$$\frac{4}{7} \div \frac{2}{3} = \blacksquare$$

$$\frac{4}{7} \div \frac{2}{3} = \frac{4}{7} \times \frac{3}{2}$$

$$= \frac{\overset{2}{\cancel{4}}}{7} \times \frac{3}{\underset{1}{\cancel{2}}}$$

$$= \frac{2 \times 3}{7 \times 1}$$

$$= \frac{6}{7}$$

Exercise A Divide. Write your answers in simplest form.

1. $\frac{2}{7} \div \frac{5}{6}$

2. $\frac{3}{8} \div \frac{3}{4}$

3. $\frac{4}{7} \div \frac{5}{7}$

4. $\frac{2}{3} \div \frac{5}{6}$

5. $5 \div \frac{1}{6}$

6. $\frac{5}{6} \div \frac{5}{6}$

7. $\frac{5}{8} \div \frac{5}{6}$

8. $\frac{4}{7} \div \frac{2}{3}$

9. $\frac{5}{11} \div \frac{15}{22}$

10. $\frac{3}{13} \div \frac{7}{39}$

11. $\frac{8}{9} \div 4$

12. $\frac{6}{13} \div \frac{1}{26}$

13. $\frac{7}{8} \div \frac{3}{8}$

14. $\frac{3}{13} \div \frac{5}{6}$

15. $\frac{7}{15} \div \frac{14}{25}$

Exercise B Find the answers. Write them in simplest form.

1. $\frac{6}{7} \div \frac{8}{9}$

2. $\frac{3}{5} \div \frac{5}{8}$

3. $\frac{7}{8} \div 4$

4. $\frac{7}{12} \div 7$

5. $6 \div \frac{5}{7}$

6. $12 \div \frac{6}{13}$

7. $9 \div \frac{9}{10}$

8. $\frac{4}{5} \div \frac{3}{5}$

9. $\frac{6}{11} \div \frac{3}{5}$

10. $\frac{7}{13} \div \frac{5}{13}$

11. $\frac{8}{9} \div \frac{4}{9}$

12. $\frac{4}{9} \div \frac{8}{9}$

13. $\frac{12}{14} \div \frac{24}{28}$

14. $\frac{5}{9} \div \frac{3}{7}$

15. $\frac{4}{7} \div \frac{2}{11}$

16. $\frac{5}{6} \div \frac{3}{13}$

17. $\frac{7}{9} \div \frac{1}{3}$

18. $\frac{4}{13} \div \frac{3}{26}$

19. $\frac{5}{12} \div \frac{25}{36}$

20. $\frac{9}{10} \div \frac{4}{5}$

21. $\frac{2}{3} \div \frac{2}{5}$

22. $\frac{2}{5} \div \frac{1}{5}$

23. $\frac{6}{11} \div \frac{5}{8}$

24. $\frac{5}{13} \div \frac{5}{16}$

25. $\frac{3}{11} \div \frac{9}{22}$

26. $\frac{3}{8} \div \frac{8}{3}$

27. $\frac{8}{12} \div \frac{8}{11}$

 PROBLEM SOLVING

Exercise C Solve these word problems.

1. A group of home economics students needs to divide $\frac{3}{4}$ pound of sugar 4 ways. What fraction of a pound will each student get?

2. How many pieces of pipe can be cut from a 12-foot piece of pipe if each is to be $\frac{2}{3}$ of a foot long?

3. Gina can walk a mile in $\frac{1}{4}$ hour. At this rate, how far can she walk in 4 hours?

To divide mixed numbers, you first change the mixed numbers to improper fractions. Then, you invert the divisor and multiply.

EXAMPLE $2\frac{1}{3} \div 5\frac{2}{3} = \blacksquare$

$$2\frac{1}{3} \div 5\frac{2}{3} = \frac{7}{3} \div \frac{17}{3}$$

$$= \frac{7}{3} \times \frac{3}{17}$$

$$= \frac{7}{\overset{}{\underset{1}{3}}} \times \frac{\overset{1}{3}}{17} = \frac{7 \times 1}{1 \times 17} = \frac{7}{17}$$

Exercise A Find the quotients. Write them in simplest form.

1. $2\frac{3}{4} \div \frac{5}{6}$

2. $1\frac{1}{3} \div \frac{1}{4}$

3. $\frac{2}{5} \div 1\frac{2}{5}$

4. $\frac{5}{7} \div 3\frac{1}{5}$

5. $2\frac{2}{7} \div 2\frac{2}{7}$

6. $4\frac{1}{5} \div 2\frac{3}{5}$

7. $7\frac{1}{2} \div 6\frac{2}{3}$

8. $6\frac{1}{2} \div \frac{1}{2}$

9. $1\frac{1}{5} \div 1\frac{2}{5}$

10. $1\frac{2}{3} \div 5$

11. $6 \div 1\frac{1}{5}$

12. $5\frac{2}{5} \div 1\frac{1}{5}$

 PROBLEM SOLVING

Exercise B Solve these word problems.

1. Kim buys $3\frac{1}{3}$ pounds of potato salad for her birthday party. There are to be 20 people at the party. How much potato salad does each person get?

2. A mathematics class makes a giant turkey sandwich that measures $7\frac{1}{2}$ feet long. If 15 students share the sandwich equally, how long is each student's serving?

3. Jim loses $12\frac{1}{2}$ pounds over a 5-week period. What is his average weekly weight loss?

4. Anna needs $1\frac{2}{3}$ yards of fabric to make a dress. If she has $6\frac{2}{3}$ yards of fabric, then how many dresses can she make?

Like denominators

Having the same denominators

Adding fractions and mixed numbers with **like denominators** is much like adding whole numbers. You add the whole numbers, add the numerators, and keep the same denominator.

You need common denominators when you add fractions.

EXAMPLES

$$4 \frac{3}{11}$$
$$+ 6 \frac{4}{11}$$
$$10 \frac{7}{11}$$

$$3 \frac{5}{7}$$
$$+ 2 \frac{6}{7}$$
$$5 \frac{11}{7} = 6 \frac{4}{7}$$

Exercise A Add. Write your answers in simplest form.

1. $2 \frac{5}{8}$
$+ 1 \frac{3}{8}$

6. $\frac{5}{18}$
$+ \frac{7}{18}$

11. $\frac{7}{19}$
$+ \frac{14}{19}$

16. $4 \frac{17}{20}$
$+ \frac{3}{20}$

2. $2 \frac{5}{11}$
$+ 3 \frac{4}{11}$

7. $\frac{9}{17}$
$+ 2 \frac{8}{17}$

12. $\frac{7}{25}$
$+ \frac{16}{25}$

17. $\frac{23}{40}$
$+ \frac{7}{40}$

3. $2 \frac{5}{16}$
$+ 5 \frac{1}{16}$

8. $3 \frac{9}{10}$
$+ 1 \frac{3}{10}$

13. $\frac{13}{15}$
$+ \frac{8}{15}$

18. $\frac{5}{6}$
$+ \frac{5}{6}$

4. $3 \frac{2}{19}$
$+ 4 \frac{3}{19}$

9. $\frac{11}{16}$
$+ \frac{3}{16}$

14. $\frac{9}{11}$
$+ \frac{5}{11}$

19. $\frac{7}{11}$
$+ \frac{9}{11}$

5. $1 \frac{6}{7}$
$+ \frac{2}{7}$

10. $5 \frac{13}{16}$
$+ 6 \frac{1}{16}$

15. $12 \frac{11}{25}$
$+ 11 \frac{9}{25}$

20. $6 \frac{4}{15}$
$+ 2 \frac{14}{15}$

Exercise B Add. Write your answers in simplest form.

1. $3\frac{6}{13}$
$+ \; 4\frac{6}{13}$

4. $\frac{7}{20}$
$+ \; \frac{13}{20}$

7. $\frac{11}{12}$
$+ \; \frac{5}{12}$

10. $\frac{9}{17}$
$+ \; \frac{3}{17}$

2. $\frac{5}{12}$
$+ \; \frac{1}{12}$

5. $2\frac{17}{21}$
$+ \; 6\frac{5}{21}$

8. $4\frac{5}{17}$
$+ \; 9\frac{12}{17}$

11. $7\frac{14}{45}$
$+ \; \frac{7}{45}$

3. $4\frac{7}{25}$
$+ \; \frac{21}{25}$

6. $8\frac{15}{22}$
$+ \; \frac{3}{22}$

9. $\frac{7}{15}$
$+ \; \frac{11}{15}$

12. $\frac{5}{42}$
$+ \; \frac{11}{42}$

Exercise C Add. Write your answers in simplest form.

1. $2\frac{13}{34} + \frac{9}{34}$

4. $2\frac{3}{5} + 1\frac{2}{5}$

2. $\frac{23}{24} + \frac{5}{24}$

5. $\frac{7}{12} + \frac{9}{12} + \frac{6}{12}$

3. $\frac{5}{31} + \frac{2}{31}$

6. $2\frac{1}{15} + 4\frac{11}{15} + 7\frac{8}{15}$

PROBLEM SOLVING

Exercise D Solve these word problems. Write your answers in simplest form.

1. Leon, a plumber, joins two pieces of pipe. They measure $7\frac{3}{16}$ inches and $4\frac{7}{16}$ inches. How long is the new piece of pipe?

2. Justin works part-time after school. One week he works $3\frac{1}{4}$ hours on Monday, $2\frac{3}{4}$ hours on Wednesday, and $1\frac{1}{4}$ hours on Friday. How many hours does he work that week?

Common denominators

Common multiples of two or more denominators

Least common denominator (LCD)

Smallest denominator that is a multiple of two denominators

Raising a fraction to higher terms is really multiplying it by 1.

Before you can add fractions, they must have **common denominators,** or denominators that are alike. If the denominators are not alike, you will need to raise the fractions to higher terms so that the denominators are the same. This new denominator is called the **least common denominator (LCD).**

  EXAMPLE   Add $\frac{1}{8}$ and $\frac{5}{6}$.

Step 1   Find the least common multiple of the denominators.
The least common multiple of 8 and 6 is 24.

Step 2   Use 24 as a new denominator.
24 is the least common denominator or LCD.

$$\frac{1}{8} = \frac{\blacksquare}{24}$$
$$+\frac{5}{6} = \frac{\blacksquare}{24}$$

Step 3   Raise the fractions to higher terms.

$$\frac{1}{8} = \frac{3}{24}$$
$$+\frac{5}{6} = \frac{20}{24}$$

Step 4   Add the new fractions.

$$\frac{3}{24}$$
$$+\frac{20}{24}$$
$$\overline{\frac{23}{24}}$$

Technology Connection

Fractions help us understand numbers by comparing one group to the whole. You might hear phrases like "four out of five," "half of all," or "two out of three." Look on the Internet or in a newspaper for phrases such as these. Write the phrase and the fraction. Use a computer to draw a picture or make a chart to show what you found.

Exercise A Add these fractions. Write your answers in simplest form.

1. $\dfrac{2}{7}$ **2.** $\dfrac{3}{8}$ **3.** $\dfrac{2}{9}$ **4.** $\dfrac{1}{8}$ **5.** $\dfrac{5}{12}$ **6.** $\dfrac{9}{16}$ **7.** $2\dfrac{3}{5}$ **8.** $13\dfrac{1}{5}$

$+\dfrac{3}{4}$ $\quad+\dfrac{2}{3}$ $\quad+\dfrac{2}{3}$ $\quad+\dfrac{2}{5}$ $\quad+\dfrac{2}{3}$ $\quad+\dfrac{3}{8}$ $\quad+3\dfrac{2}{9}$ $\quad+2\dfrac{3}{10}$

Exercise B Find the answers. Write them in simplest form.

1. $\dfrac{3}{4}+\dfrac{5}{6}$

2. $\dfrac{1}{8}+\dfrac{1}{5}$

3. $\dfrac{3}{7}+\dfrac{5}{21}$

4. $\dfrac{5}{11}+\dfrac{5}{22}$

5. $\dfrac{3}{8}+\dfrac{2}{11}$

6. $5\dfrac{1}{3}+4\dfrac{1}{6}$

7. $6\dfrac{3}{7}+3\dfrac{1}{3}$

8. $5\dfrac{1}{6}+2\dfrac{3}{5}$

9. $5\dfrac{1}{6}+4\dfrac{4}{9}$

10. $7\dfrac{1}{11}+2\dfrac{2}{33}$

11. $5\dfrac{3}{8}+2\dfrac{1}{6}+\dfrac{1}{4}$

12. $12\dfrac{1}{8}+3\dfrac{1}{6}+2\dfrac{1}{3}$

13. $5\dfrac{5}{6}+3\dfrac{1}{7}$

14. $4\dfrac{5}{8}+3\dfrac{1}{4}$

15. $6\dfrac{7}{10}+3\dfrac{2}{5}$

16. $2\dfrac{3}{8}+6\dfrac{3}{10}$

17. $7\dfrac{1}{9}+2\dfrac{1}{6}$

18. $11\dfrac{5}{8}+13$

PROBLEM SOLVING

Exercise C Solve these word problems.

1. Guido buys $2\dfrac{1}{4}$ pounds of tomatoes and $3\dfrac{2}{3}$ pounds of lettuce. How many pounds of vegetables does he buy?

2. Miss Watts is building a bookshelf. She needs a piece of wood measuring $3\dfrac{1}{2}$ feet long and a piece of wood $5\dfrac{1}{4}$ feet long. What is the total length of the wood she needs?

3. Paolo needs to replace three sections of damaged pipe. They measure $2\dfrac{1}{2}$ feet, $4\dfrac{3}{4}$ feet, and $3\dfrac{1}{8}$ feet. What length of pipe must he buy to cut these three pieces?

You need like denominators to subtract fractions or mixed numbers. If the denominators are alike, then you subtract the whole numbers and the numerators. You keep the same common denominator for your answer. You may need to rename your answer in simplest form.

Look at your answers to see if fractions can be simplified.

EXAMPLES

$$\begin{array}{r} \frac{9}{13} \\ -\ \frac{4}{13} \\ \hline \frac{5}{13} \end{array}$$

$$\begin{array}{r} 20\frac{11}{18} \\ -\ 4\frac{5}{18} \\ \hline 16\frac{6}{18} = 16\frac{1}{3} \end{array}$$

$$\begin{array}{r} 10\frac{7}{12} \\ -\ 4\frac{5}{12} \\ \hline 6\frac{2}{12} = 6\frac{1}{6} \end{array}$$

Exercise A Subtract these fractions. Write your answers in simplest form.

1. $\quad 9\frac{7}{8}$
$\quad -\ 2\frac{3}{8}$

5. $\quad 8\frac{11}{12}$
$\quad -\ \frac{1}{12}$

9. $\quad \frac{19}{20}$
$\quad -\ \frac{11}{20}$

13. $\quad 18\frac{19}{21}$
$\quad -\ 7\frac{1}{21}$

2. $\quad 25\frac{4}{5}$
$\quad -\ 6\frac{3}{5}$

6. $\quad 10\frac{3}{4}$
$\quad -\ 2\frac{1}{4}$

10. $\quad 46\frac{2}{9}$
$\quad -\ 6\frac{1}{9}$

14. $\quad 13\frac{3}{13}$
$\quad -\ 5\frac{2}{13}$

3. $\quad 29\frac{5}{12}$
$\quad -\ 3\frac{1}{12}$

7. $\quad 19\frac{19}{21}$
$\quad -\ 5\frac{5}{21}$

11. $\quad 11\frac{7}{9}$
$\quad -\ 7\frac{4}{9}$

15. $\quad 26\frac{7}{10}$
$\quad -18\frac{7}{10}$

4. $\quad 57\frac{7}{8}$
$\quad -\ 48$

8. $\quad \frac{15}{16}$
$\quad -\ \frac{3}{16}$

12. $\quad 12\frac{10}{11}$
$\quad -\ 5\frac{5}{11}$

16. $\quad 39\frac{15}{16}$
$\quad -\ 8\frac{5}{16}$

Exercise B Subtract. Write your answers in simplest form.

1. $12\frac{6}{7} - 3\frac{4}{7}$

2. $13\frac{7}{8} - 10\frac{3}{8}$

3. $15\frac{9}{10} - \frac{3}{10}$

4. $19\frac{7}{8} - 11$

5. $\frac{11}{13} - \frac{9}{13}$

6. $15\frac{7}{10} - 8\frac{7}{10}$

7. $28\frac{5}{12} - 19$

8. $32\frac{8}{9} - 3\frac{1}{9}$

9. $23\frac{4}{5} - 22\frac{4}{5}$

10. $19\frac{13}{21} - 15\frac{10}{21}$

11. $105\frac{3}{4} - 42$

12. $18\frac{7}{8} - 9\frac{7}{8}$

13. $8\frac{11}{12} - 6\frac{5}{12}$

14. $92\frac{5}{9} - 48\frac{1}{9}$

15. $109\frac{4}{5} - 86\frac{3}{5}$

16. Take $18\frac{7}{19}$ from $20\frac{12}{19}$

17. From $35\frac{12}{35}$ take $\frac{9}{35}$

18. Subtract $2\frac{5}{13}$ from $5\frac{12}{13}$

19. Subtract $42\frac{1}{8}$ from $42\frac{7}{8}$

20. Take $\frac{7}{18}$ from $\frac{11}{18}$

21. Subtract $27\frac{7}{8}$ from $27\frac{7}{8}$

22. Subtract $32\frac{5}{12}$ from $38\frac{11}{12}$

23. Take $\frac{8}{21}$ from $53\frac{11}{21}$

24. From $32\frac{15}{16}$ subtract $8\frac{7}{16}$

25. Subtract $8\frac{1}{8}$ from $15\frac{3}{8}$

26. From $13\frac{8}{17}$ subtract $8\frac{6}{17}$

27. Subtract $13\frac{2}{11}$ from $16\frac{5}{11}$

28. From $18\frac{5}{16}$ take $15\frac{3}{16}$

29. From $18\frac{7}{8}$ subtract $6\frac{3}{8}$

30. Subtract $3\frac{2}{9}$ from $5\frac{7}{9}$

Try This

Check your answers to problems 1–30 by using addition. Add each answer to the number that was subtracted from the larger number. Compare this sum to the larger number. If the numbers are not the same, your answer is incorrect. Try solving the problem again.

If the denominators in a subtraction problem are not alike, then you need to rename the fractions to higher terms, just as you did with addition problems. After you have like denominators, you subtract the whole numbers. Then subtract the numerators.

You need common denominators when you subtract fractions.

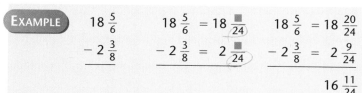

EXAMPLE

$$18 \frac{5}{6} \qquad 18 \frac{5}{6} = 18 \frac{\blacksquare}{24} \qquad 18 \frac{5}{6} = 18 \frac{20}{24}$$
$$-2 \frac{3}{8} \qquad -2 \frac{3}{8} = 2 \frac{\blacksquare}{24} \qquad -2 \frac{3}{8} = 2 \frac{9}{24}$$
$$\overline{} \qquad \qquad \qquad 16 \frac{11}{24}$$

If you cannot find the least common denominator, use the product of the denominators for a common denominator. You will get the same answer after you reduce.

EXAMPLE

$$18 \frac{5}{6} \qquad 18 \frac{5}{6} = 18 \frac{\blacksquare}{48} \qquad 18 \frac{5}{6} = 18 \frac{40}{48}$$
$$-2 \frac{3}{8} \qquad -2 \frac{3}{8} = 2 \frac{\blacksquare}{48} \qquad -2 \frac{3}{8} = 2 \frac{18}{48}$$
$$\overline{} \qquad \qquad \qquad 16 \frac{22}{48} = 16 \frac{11}{24}$$

You may need to add or subtract fractions when cooking or baking.

Exercise A Find a common denominator for each problem. Subtract.

1.
$$\frac{8}{9}$$
$$-\frac{1}{3}$$

2.
$$\frac{2}{3}$$
$$-\frac{2}{5}$$

3.
$$18 \frac{15}{16}$$
$$-2 \frac{1}{4}$$

4.
$$25 \frac{6}{7}$$
$$-4 \frac{2}{3}$$

5.
$$22 \frac{7}{8}$$
$$-4 \frac{2}{3}$$

6.
$$13 \frac{11}{13}$$
$$-\frac{1}{39}$$

7.
$$13 \frac{4}{5}$$
$$-2 \frac{1}{3}$$

8.
$$\frac{7}{8}$$
$$-\frac{3}{4}$$

9.
$$19 \frac{5}{6}$$
$$-3 \frac{1}{4}$$

10.
$$16 \frac{7}{10}$$
$$-16 \frac{1}{2}$$

11.
$$10 \frac{9}{10}$$
$$-\frac{3}{20}$$

12.
$$26 \frac{5}{6}$$
$$-3 \frac{5}{18}$$

Exercise B Subtract. Write your answers in simplest form.

1. $27\frac{5}{9}$

$-5\frac{1}{3}$
_____

4. $11\frac{4}{5}$

$-\frac{7}{25}$
_____

7. $72\frac{11}{12}$

$-3\frac{5}{8}$
_____

10. $\frac{11}{36}$

$-\frac{1}{6}$
_____

2. $16\frac{4}{5}$

$-4\frac{7}{10}$
_____

5. $12\frac{9}{10}$

$-6\frac{4}{5}$
_____

8. $52\frac{1}{2}$

$-3\frac{1}{6}$
_____

11. $21\frac{9}{10}$

$-4\frac{1}{2}$
_____

3. $28\frac{7}{9}$

$-5\frac{1}{6}$
_____

6. $19\frac{13}{16}$

$-2\frac{3}{8}$
_____

9. $23\frac{16}{27}$

$-4\frac{1}{3}$
_____

12. $35\frac{11}{20}$

$-34\frac{2}{5}$
_____

Exercise C Subtract. Write your answers in simplest form.

1. From $13\frac{8}{13}$ subtract $8\frac{3}{26}$

2. From $19\frac{2}{3}$ subtract $3\frac{4}{7}$

3. From $18\frac{5}{16}$ subtract $2\frac{1}{16}$

4. Subtract $6\frac{8}{15}$ from $12\frac{5}{6}$

5. Subtract $3\frac{6}{7}$ from $8\frac{7}{8}$

6. Subtract $2\frac{4}{11}$ from $9\frac{21}{44}$

7. From the sum of $6\frac{2}{3}$ and $5\frac{2}{5}$ subtract $2\frac{1}{15}$

8. From the product of $2\frac{1}{2}$ and $3\frac{1}{2}$ subtract $2\frac{1}{3}$

You can subtract a mixed number from a whole number.
First you rename the whole number as a mixed number.
Then subtract.

EXAMPLE

$$14 \quad = \quad 13\frac{9}{9}$$
$$-3\frac{7}{9} \quad = \quad 3\frac{7}{9}$$
$$\overline{\qquad\qquad = \quad 10\frac{2}{9}}$$

$$14 \quad = \quad 13 + 1$$
$$= \quad 13 + \frac{9}{9}$$
$$= \quad 13\frac{9}{9}$$

After you change to common denominators, you may find that
the top fraction is less than the bottom fraction. Then you will
need to rename the top mixed number before you can subtract.

EXAMPLE

$$19\frac{2}{5} = 19\frac{16}{40} = 18\frac{56}{40}$$
$$-4\frac{7}{8} = 4\frac{35}{40} = 4\frac{35}{40}$$
$$\overline{\qquad\qquad\qquad 14\frac{21}{40}}$$

$$19\frac{16}{40} = 18 + 1 + \frac{16}{40}$$
$$= 18 + \frac{40}{40} + \frac{16}{40}$$
$$= 18 + \frac{56}{40}$$
$$= 18\frac{56}{40}$$

Renaming in
subtraction is like
making change
with money.

Exercise A Subtract. You may need to rename.

1. $\begin{array}{r} 23 \\ -14\frac{3}{7} \\ \hline \end{array}$

3. $\begin{array}{r} 18\frac{2}{9} \\ -4\frac{3}{9} \\ \hline \end{array}$

5. $\begin{array}{r} 6\frac{2}{11} \\ -4\frac{5}{11} \\ \hline \end{array}$

7. $\begin{array}{r} 8\frac{2}{7} \\ -4\frac{2}{3} \\ \hline \end{array}$

2. $\begin{array}{r} 25 \\ -4\frac{2}{11} \\ \hline \end{array}$

4. $\begin{array}{r} 27\frac{4}{5} \\ -2\frac{5}{6} \\ \hline \end{array}$

6. $\begin{array}{r} 4\frac{2}{9} \\ -1\frac{5}{6} \\ \hline \end{array}$

8. $\begin{array}{r} 15 \\ -2\frac{11}{15} \\ \hline \end{array}$

Exercise B Subtract. Write your answers in simplest form.

1. $12\frac{2}{9}$ $-\;6\frac{3}{8}$

3. $8\frac{1}{8}$ $-\;2\frac{7}{8}$

5. $12\frac{5}{8}$ $-\;5\frac{3}{4}$

7. 98 $-\;7\frac{11}{16}$

9. $25\frac{5}{7}$ $-\;2\frac{4}{5}$

11. $7\frac{5}{12}$ $-\;3\frac{7}{8}$

2. $5\frac{3}{14}$ $-\;3\frac{6}{7}$

4. $5\frac{2}{13}$ $-\;3\frac{5}{26}$

6. 16 $-\;1\frac{7}{8}$

8. $22\frac{7}{8}$ $-\;9\frac{5}{6}$

10. $31\frac{1}{10}$ $-\;3\frac{9}{20}$

12. $4\frac{7}{24}$ $-\;2\frac{5}{6}$

Exercise C Subtract. Write your answers in simplest form.

1. $15\frac{1}{3} - 6\frac{7}{11}$

2. $19 - 5\frac{9}{13}$

3. $15\frac{1}{3} - 5\frac{7}{8}$

4. $13\frac{1}{6} - 3\frac{9}{10}$

5. Subtract $5\frac{2}{9}$ from 20

6. Subtract $3\frac{7}{18}$ from $6\frac{1}{9}$

7. From $8\frac{1}{12}$ subtract $6\frac{5}{8}$

8. From $4\frac{1}{2}$ subtract $2\frac{7}{10}$

PROBLEM SOLVING

Exercise D Solve these word problems.

1. Brandon uses $7\frac{3}{4}$ yards of material from a bolt of cloth that is 18 yards long. How many yards of material are left on the bolt?

2. Julio opens a 10-pound bag of sugar. He uses $\frac{5}{8}$ of a pound for cookies. How much sugar is left?

3. If $2\frac{3}{8}$ yards of fabric on a bolt are irregular and the bolt contains $6\frac{1}{3}$ yards of fabric, then how much regular fabric remains?

4. If Renée and Geraldo combine their wood scraps, then they can try to make another doghouse. Renée has $1\frac{1}{5}$ feet of scrap and Geraldo has $9\frac{2}{7}$ feet of scrap. Do they have enough scrap to build another doghouse, if it requires $12\frac{1}{2}$ feet?

Exercise E Practice working with fractions. Solve these word problems.

1. Jodhi opens a $6\frac{1}{2}$-pound bag of nuts. She uses $\frac{7}{8}$ pound for cookies. How many pounds of nuts does she have left?

2. Tina purchases $2\frac{3}{4}$ yards of material. She uses $\frac{2}{3}$ of the material to make a blouse. How many yards of material are left?

3. Doug works at home for $5\frac{3}{4}$ hours on Monday, $2\frac{1}{2}$ hours on Tuesday, and $4\frac{1}{4}$ hours on Friday. How many hours does he work?

4. Miranda buys $3\frac{1}{2}$ pounds of flour. She uses $2\frac{1}{8}$ pounds to bake cakes. How many pounds of flour does she have left?

5. Jim rides $15\frac{7}{10}$ miles on his bike over a two-day period. If he rides $8\frac{2}{5}$ miles the first day, how far does he ride the second day?

6. Brian lives $\frac{4}{5}$ mile from school. He jogs $\frac{1}{2}$ of this distance daily. How far does he jog every day?

7. A recipe calls for $\frac{3}{4}$ cup sugar. How much sugar is needed if you make only $\frac{1}{2}$ of the recipe?

8. Bhaktir lost $\frac{6}{7}$ pound during the first week of his diet. During the second week, he lost $\frac{2}{3}$ of what he lost the first week. How much did he lose the second week?

It Pays to Know Your Paycheck

Some workers earn a regular lump sum called a salary. Others earn an hourly wage. The rate of pay is determined by multiplying the number of hours by the hourly rate of pay.

 EXAMPLE   Julio works part-time at a fast food restaurant. Look at his time card below. How many hours did he work last week? If his hourly wage is $6.00, how much money did he earn last week?

Step 1   Calculate the number of hours worked.

$$2 \quad + 3\frac{1}{2} = 5\frac{1}{2} \text{ hours}$$
$$3\frac{1}{2} + 2\frac{3}{4} = 6\frac{1}{4} \text{ hours}$$
$$4\frac{1}{2} + 1\frac{1}{4} = 5\frac{3}{4} \text{ hours}$$
$$3\frac{3}{4} + 2\frac{1}{2} = 6\frac{1}{4} \text{ hours}$$

Total $23\frac{3}{4}$ hours

Step 2   Calculate the amount of money earned.

$$23\frac{3}{4} \times \$6.00 = (23 + \tfrac{3}{4}) \times \$6.00$$
$$= (23 \times \$6) + (\tfrac{3}{4} \times \$6.00)$$
$$= \$138.00 + \$4.50$$
$$= \$142.50$$

Time Clock Entries	
Day	**Times**
Monday	3:00–5:00 P.M., 5:30–9:00 P.M.
Tuesday	9:30 A.M.–1:00 P.M., 1:30–4:15 P.M.
Thursday	3:00–7:30 P.M., 7:45–9:00 P.M.
Friday	9:30 A.M.–1:15 P.M., 1:45–4:15 P.M.

Julio worked $23\frac{3}{4}$ hours and earned $142.50 last week.

Exercise   Solve each problem.

1. Megan works from 12:30 to 5:15 P.M. every day on Monday through Friday. She earns $7.00 an hour. How many hours per week does she work? How much money does she earn per week?

2. Alan worked the hours to the right for a week. At $7.00 per hour, how much money did he earn?

Day	Hours
Monday	$7\frac{1}{2}$
Tuesday	$6\frac{3}{4}$
Wednesday	$5\frac{1}{6}$
Thursday	$7\frac{1}{3}$
Friday	$5\frac{1}{4}$

Chapter 3   R E V I E W

Write the letter of the best answer to each question.

1. Choose the answer that correctly compares the fractions $\frac{3}{8}$ and $\frac{9}{16}$.

    A $<$

    B $>$

    C $=$

2. Choose the answer that shows the fraction $\frac{75}{125}$ in simplest form.

    A $\frac{2}{5}$

    B $\frac{3}{5}$

    C $\frac{4}{5}$

    D $\frac{15}{25}$

3. Choose the answer that shows the mixed number $48\frac{3}{8}$ renamed as an improper fraction.

    A $\frac{43}{8}$

    B $\frac{59}{8}$

    C $\frac{384}{8}$

    D $\frac{387}{8}$

4. Choose the correct answer to the problem below.

$$3\frac{1}{8}$$
$$+\ 4\frac{1}{2}$$

    A $7\frac{1}{16}$

    B $7\frac{1}{5}$

    C $7\frac{1}{4}$

    D $7\frac{5}{8}$

Compare the fractions in each pair. Write $<$ or $>$.

5. $\dfrac{4}{5}$ $\dfrac{6}{7}$

6. $\dfrac{5}{6}$ $\dfrac{3}{4}$

7. $\dfrac{2}{11}$ $\dfrac{5}{12}$

Write these in simplest form.

8. $\dfrac{9}{21}$

9. $15\dfrac{8}{12}$

10. $\dfrac{50}{125}$

11. $\dfrac{11}{88}$

Rename these mixed numbers as improper fractions.

12. $3\dfrac{6}{7}$

13. $1\dfrac{1}{3}$

14. $5\dfrac{3}{8}$

Rename these improper fractions as whole numbers or mixed numbers.

15. $\dfrac{26}{7}$

16. $\dfrac{12}{3}$

17. $\dfrac{38}{6}$

Find the answers. Write them in simplest form.

18. $\frac{2}{3} \times \frac{4}{5}$

19. $1\frac{1}{3} \div 3\frac{2}{3}$

20. $1\frac{1}{2} \times 2\frac{3}{4}$

21. $2\frac{8}{11} + 3\frac{2}{11}$

22. $\frac{2}{3} \div \frac{7}{8}$

23. $3\frac{5}{16} - 1\frac{1}{8}$

24. $15 - 4\frac{7}{8}$

25. $\begin{array}{r} 3\frac{8}{9} \\ + 2\frac{1}{9} \\ \hline \end{array}$

28. $\begin{array}{r} 6\frac{5}{8} \\ + 2\frac{7}{8} \\ \hline \end{array}$

26. $\begin{array}{r} 5\frac{3}{7} \\ + 2\frac{7}{8} \\ \hline \end{array}$

29. $\begin{array}{r} 20\frac{3}{4} \\ - 4\frac{7}{8} \\ \hline \end{array}$

27. $\begin{array}{r} 19\frac{5}{6} \\ - 3\frac{1}{4} \\ \hline \end{array}$

30. $\begin{array}{r} 14\frac{1}{3} \\ - 5\frac{3}{5} \\ \hline \end{array}$

Test-Taking Tip

When taking a mathematics test, complete the problems that you know before solving more difficult problems.

Decimals

Numbers can be very large, such as the distance from the sun to the planet Pluto. It is 3,600,000,000 miles from the sun. Numbers can also be very small. A house dust mite is about 0.0001 meter, but it can be magnified to more than 2,500 times its size. Both of these numbers tell you something about the dust mite. Mathematics allows us to write numbers in more than one way. These other ways are helpful when we solve problems with very large or very small numbers.

In Chapter 4, you will learn about place value and scientific notation, which help us make sense out of numbers.

Goals for Learning

◆ To write numbers in word form and in standard notation

◆ To order numbers

◆ To round decimals

◆ To compute with decimals and whole numbers

◆ To express fractions as decimals

◆ To express numbers in scientific notation

The planet Jupiter makes one trip around the sun every 11.8613 years. We read this numeral as "eleven and eight thousand six hundred thirteen ten-thousandths." The concept of place value helps us to understand the meaning of long numbers like this one.

Ten-thousands	Thousands	Hundreds	Tens	Ones		Tenths	Hundredths	Thousandths	Ten-thousandths
			1	1	.	8	6	1	3

Exercise A Write the name of the place for each underlined digit.

1. 867.4̲3
2. 6.239̲5
3. 14̲8.37
4. 66̲.875
5. 9.376̲5

6. 1̲42.876
7. 0.875̲6
8. 12̲84
9. 92̲.8
10. 6857.3̲

11. 72.8̲597
12. 0.47̲6
13. 7̲8.94
14. 6.37̲892
15. 6̲789.03

Exercise B Write the name of the place for the last digit in each numeral.

1. 0.38
2. 427.389
3. 0.4678

4. 92.386
5. 76.8436
6. 16.0004

7. 200.307
8. 392.05
9. 867.384

Exercise C Copy each number. Underline the digit that is in the place name in italics.

1. 46.3826 *hundredths*
2. 35.0038 *ten-thousandths*
3. 148.296 *tenths*
4. 6758.23 *hundreds*
5. 91.4082 *thousandths*
6. 204.37 *tens*
7. 14.0079 *ones*
8. 208.097 *hundredths*
9. 5.23981 *thousandths*

10. 502.967 *tenths*
11. 587.029 *ones*
12. 0.298 *hundredths*
13. 329.768 *tens*
14. 52.694 *thousandths*
15. 498.276 *tenths*
16. 0.5296 *ten-thousandths*
17. 468.539 *hundreds*
18. 324.06 *tenths*

Decimal places

Positions to the right of a decimal point

Place value helps us to read decimal numerals. To read a decimal numeral, use the following steps. If there is a zero or no number to the left of the decimal point, then skip Steps 1 and 2.

Step 1 Read the digits to the left of the decimal point as a whole number.

Step 2 Say "and" for the decimal point.

Step 3 Read the digits to the right of the decimal point as a whole number. These are the **decimal places.**

Step 4 Say the place name of the last digit.

The decimal point separates the whole number from the fraction.

EXAMPLES

23.415

Step 1 twenty-three

Step 2 and

Step 3 four hundred fifteen

Step 4 thousandths

Say, "twenty-three and four hundred fifteen thousandths."

0.62

No number

Step 3 sixty-two

Step 4 hundredths

Say, "sixty-two hundredths."

Technology Connection

Decimals are used to represent very large and very small numbers. Pick a subject area that interests you and that uses measurements. Some subjects include astronomy, microbiology, economics, or medicine. Use the Internet to search using key words that are used in the subject area you selected. Print any pages that use decimals for measurements. Make a poster using your printouts. Write each measurement in numerals and words.

Exercise A Read the words. Then write the numeral that means the same as the words.

1. Sixteen and twelve-hundredths   16.012   16.12   16.0012

2. Nine-hundredths   0.0009   900   0.09

3. One hundred and six-thousandths   0.106   100.06   100.006

4. Seventy and eight-hundredths   70.08   70.008   0.78

5. Seventy-nine thousandths   70.009   0.079   0.79

6. Twenty-eight and six-tenths   28.06   0.286   28.6

7. One thousand and six-thousandths   1006   1000.006   0.1006

8. Forty-eight ten-thousandths   0.0048   0.048   40.008

PROBLEM SOLVING

Exercise B Write the numeral that means the same as the bold words.

1. Large hailstones can weigh **thirty-five hundredths** of a pound.

2. The average annual rainfall is **one hundred twenty-three and thirty-seven hundredths** inches.

3. The rainfall in one minute is **three and twelve-hundredths** inches.

4. Barnard's Star is **four ten-thousandths** times as bright as our sun.

5. The star Sirius B is **seventeen ten-thousandths** times as bright as our sun.

6. Lydia weighs **ninety-two and eight-tenths** pounds.

7. Normal body temperature is **ninety-eight and six-tenths** degrees Fahrenheit.

8. Jupiter weighs **three hundred eighteen and three-tenths** times as much as Earth.

9. Jupiter is only **twenty-four hundredths** times as dense as Earth.

10. Paul weighs **one hundred forty and twenty-five hundredths** pounds.

11. Lydia weighs **forty-seven and forty-five hundredths** pounds less than Paul.

You can tell which of two decimals is greater if you add zeros to one of them. You can easily compare them when both have the same number of decimal places to the right of the decimal point.

EXAMPLE   Compare 24.428 and 24.43
24.428 and 24.430
24.430 is larger.
24.428 < 24.430

Exercise A Compare these pairs of decimals. Write > or < to show whether the first decimal is greater or less than the second.

1.	16.837	16.9	**18.**	6.205	6.25
2.	3.6	3.486	**19.**	5.304	5.403
3.	15.487	15.7	**20.**	7.62	7.6203
4.	0.43	0.3	**21.**	8.34	8.304
5.	12.377	12.41	**22.**	9.36	9.036
6.	70.396	68.9	**23.**	17.228	17.28
7.	8.446	8.45	**24.**	3.62	3.598
8.	6.39	6.392	**25.**	2.25	0.225
9.	5.7	5.4	**26.**	8.00	0.0800
10.	0.5	0.49	**27.**	2.01	0.398
11.	0.946	1.712	**28.**	0.023	0.00981
12.	4.68	4.71	**29.**	1.11	0.112
13.	12.348	12.2	**30.**	89.1	88.9
14.	4.72	4.724	**31.**	12.23	13
15.	3.537	3.536	**32.**	4.01	10.1
16.	2.04	2.40	**33.**	101.10	98.0231
17.	17.003	17.03	**34.**	2.2201	4

Exercise B Tell which numeral in each set is greatest.

1. 5.332	5.359	5.317		**9.** 3.056	3.56	3.506
2. 2.076	2.07	2.077		**10.** 8.009	8.1	8.079
3. 0.392	0.39	0.4		**11.** 2.708	2.69	2.7
4. 1.404	1.44	1.441		**12.** 11.398	11.2	11.36
5. 3.9	3.178	3.79		**13.** 4.228	4.2	4.293
6. 14.04	14.198	14.2		**14.** 9.308	9.3	9.299
7. 11.361	11.35	11.3		**15.** 26.3	26.198	26.228
8. 72.8	72.29	71.96		**16.** 7.9	7.902	7.829

Exercise C Write each set of numerals in order from least to greatest.

1. 3.06	3.219	3.058	**13.** 5.82	5.2	5.8
2. 12	11.98	12.006	**14.** 3.09	4	3.1
3. 0.9	0.872	0.903	**15.** 7.086	7.2	7.15
4. 4.08	4.19	4.079	**16.** 0.903	0.95	0.921
5. 2.209	2.229	2.902	**17.** 8	7.09	8.2
6. 11.36	11	11.209	**18.** 5.31	5.031	5.1
7. 4.368	4.3	4.319	**19.** 6.08	6.8	6.76
8. 14.508	14.39	14.47	**20.** 3.2	32	0.32
9. 8.902	8.9	8.91	**21.** 5.091	5.19	5.6
10. 72.008	72.01	72.0	**22.** 3.08	3.1	3.092
11. 6.128	6.2	6.0091	**23.** 7.06	7.6	7.612
12. 3.876	3.869	3.87	**24.** 6.534	6.5	6.098

Sometimes you may want to round a decimal numeral so that you have fewer digits.

EXAMPLE Round 3.247 to hundredths.

Step 1 Find the place that you are rounding to.
3.247 (hundredths)

Step 2 If the digit to the right is 5 or more, then add 1 to the place that you are rounding to. If it is less than 5, then do not add anything.

3.247 (7 is five or more: add one)

Step 3 Drop all of the digits to the right of the place that you are rounding to.

3.25_ (digit dropped)

Therefore, 3.247 $\doteq$ 3.25.

The symbol, $\doteq$, means "is about equal to."

Exercise D Round these decimals to the nearest tenth.

1. 2.34

2. 42.25

3. 14.6458

4. 4.16

5. 6.05

6. 0.829

Exercise E Write the choice that is the decimal correctly rounded to the nearest tenth.

1. 0.03 :   0.1   0.04   0.0

2. 2.98 :   2.9   3.0   2.99

3. 5.06 :   5   5.11   5.1

4. 1.18 :   1.19   1.1   1.2

5. 0.08 :   0.1   0.0   0

Exercise F Write the choice that is the decimal correctly rounded to the nearest hundredth.

1. 5.823 :   5.82   5.8   5.83

2. 5.095 :   5.10   5.096   5

3. 2.1239 :   2.12   2.124   2.2

4. 0.065 :   0.06   0.07   0.066

5. 0.499 :   5   0.489   0.50

Exercise G Round these decimals to the nearest:

Tenth	Hundredth	Thousandth
1. 2.36	**6.** 14.023	**11.** 5.0618
2. 4.23	**7.** 0.067	**12.** 8.8397
3. 2.06	**8.** 1.089	**13.** 8.0552
4. 4.109	**9.** 0.4209	**14.** 5.0168
5. 0.072	**10.** 73.9029	**15.** 78.0999

Exercise H Complete the chart by rounding to the placed named.

		Tenth	Hundredth	Thousandth
1.	2.8354	2.8		
2.	4.6215			
3.	0.2918			0.292
4.	0.2065			
5.	0.1853		0.19	
6.	5.6356			
7.	2.1523			
8.	4.6652			

PROBLEM SOLVING

Exercise I Follow the directions for rounding in each problem.

1. The average lap speed in the Oceanside 500 auto race is 352.627 km/h. Round to the nearest tenth.

2. Sound travels about 0.336 km/s. Round this to the nearest hundredth.

3. Light travels about 2.997925×10^8 m/s. Round 2.997925 to the nearest thousandth.

4. A centimeter is about 0.3937 inches. Round this to the nearest hundredth.

When you add decimals, it is important to keep the places in the same column, so that you will not add tenths to hundredths. You can do this easily if you line up the decimal points. You may also want to include zeros to avoid confusion.

Keep the decimal points aligned. This will help you keep the columns straight.

EXAMPLE   4.3 + 2 + 0.79

```
    4.3              4.30
    2.       or      2.00
  + 0.79           + 0.79
  ──────           ──────
    7.09             7.09
```

Exercise A Find the sums.

1.
```
    4.57
    3.9
   26.
 +  3.298
 ────────
```

5.
```
   17.
    0.352
    6.7
 + 42.06
 ───────
```

9.
```
    0.663
   48.
    0.43
 + 37.
 ───────
```

2.
```
    0.304
   42.8
    3.08
 +  0.007
 ────────
```

6.
```
    8.
   35.
    0.837
 +  0.6684
 ─────────
```

10.
```
    3.207
   52.
    0.868
 + 48.02
 ───────
```

3.
```
    7.
    0.346
   12.8
 +  4.036
 ────────
```

7.
```
    5.025
   64.4
    0.62
 +  1.013
 ────────
```

11.
```
    7.08
   36.341
    0.2034
 + 52.
 ────────
```

4.
```
    0.007
    5.03
   38.
 +  0.963
 ────────
```

8.
```
    0.304
    8.9
   34.447
 +  0.003
 ────────
```

12.
```
    5.058
    0.7
    9.006
 +  0.49
 ───────
```

Exercise B Write these addition problems in vertical form and then add.

1. $2.35 + 6 + 0.42$
2. $4.83 + 7.6 + 2.41$
3. $5.2 + 0.62 + 2.5$
4. $56 + 2.5 + 0.93$
5. $4.6 + 2 + 0.05$
6. $5 + 6.3 + 0.413$

7. $5.1 + 0.12 + 0.53 + 0.116$
8. $4 + 1.5 + 0.023 + 1$
9. $2.5 + 6.25 + 0.63 + 1$
10. $0.03 + 0.5 + 0.006 + 2$
11. $9 + 1.2 + 0.26 + 0.711$
12. $4 + 51.1 + 0.23 + 0.026$

Exercise C Find the sums.

1. 2.5, 6.25, 8.31, and 6
2. 3.6, 2, 0.53, and 0.06
3. 5, 0.23, 2.8, and 0.06
4. 5.2, 4.35, 0.83, and 2.1
5. 61, 0.27, 2.3, and 2
6. 4.3, 0.52, 0.6, and 0.203

7. 5.5, 0.23, 4.16, and 2
8. 0.201, 0.6, 2, and 1.1
9. 5.9, 2.35, and 0.004
10. 3.2, 9.42, and 0.002
11. 25, 2.5, 5.02, and 5
12. 0.602, 0.35, 0.4, and 5

PROBLEM SOLVING

Exercise D Solve these addition problems.

1. Juan delivers newspapers after school. He walks 2.3 miles on Monday, 2.45 miles on Tuesday, and 5 miles on Wednesday. What is the total distance that Juan walks in these three days?

2. One rainy week, it rains 2.5 inches on Monday, 1.63 inches on Tuesday, and 3 inches on Wednesday. What is the total rainfall for these three days?

3. Laura goes to the store and buys apples costing $1.52, tomatoes for $0.95, and candy for $2.50. How much does Laura spend at the store?

4. Corey's dog, Max, has three puppies. Their weights are 8.2 ounces, 5.12 ounces, and 6 ounces. What is the total weight?

Exercise E Add the following:

1. $\$2.56 + \$10.03 + \$4.60$
2. $\$1.55 + \$4.67 + \$15.00$
3. $2.574 + 4.3 + 2.23$

4. $4.3 + 5 + 6.2 + 7.35$
5. $7 + 8.7 + 2.03 + 0.08$
6. $0.34 + 0.2 + 0.007 + 0.1$

You must also line up the decimal points when you subtract decimals. It is important to include zeros to help you subtract. Remember to rewrite the problem in vertical form and line up the decimals.

Fill in zeros to help you line up the numbers and to hold places of the digits.

EXAMPLES

$76.4 - 0.13 = \blacksquare$ $39 - 3.84 = \blacksquare$

$$\begin{array}{r} 76.40 \\ -\ 0.13 \\ \hline 76.27 \end{array}$$ $$\begin{array}{r} 39.00 \\ -\ 3.84 \\ \hline 35.16 \end{array}$$

Exercise A Rewrite these subtraction problems in vertical form and then subtract. Remember to include the zeros.

1. $12.5 - 4.2$

2. $15.6 - 2.34$

3. $5.8 - 2.14$

4. $12.6 - 0.42$

5. $4.7 - 0.62$

6. $0.54 - 0.23$

7. $0.43 - 0.023$

8. $5.2 - 0.423$

9. $6.2 - 4.31$

10. $14.6 - 0.25$

11. $5.04 - 1.2$

12. $23.1 - 0.9$

13. $0.8 - 0.088$

14. $0.1 - 0.035$

15. $5.6 - 0.6$

16. $2 - 0.16$

17. $5 - 0.16$

18. $4.6 - 4.14$

19. $13.2 - 1.1$

20. $14.6 - 12$

A salesclerk subtracts decimals when giving change back on a purchase.

Exercise B Find the answers to these problems.

1. From 3.5 subtract 0.52

2. From 3.83 subtract 0.83

3. From 23 subtract 4.3

4. From 3 take away 2.8

5. From 2.3 take away 0.34

6. From 13 take away 0.83

7. Take away 2.3 from 8

8. Take away 0.08 from 2.3

9. Subtract 5 from 16.5

10. Subtract 0.35 from 13.7

11. Take away 3 from 15.3

12. From 0.93 take away 0.834

PROBLEM SOLVING

Exercise C Solve these word problems.

1. Marco weighs 135 pounds before he goes on his candy-free diet. He loses 5.6 pounds. How much does he weigh after his diet?

2. Marnie purchases a pair of skates for $68.23, including tax. She gives the salesperson $70.00. How much change does she receive?

3. Frank wants to have a party at the end of the school year. He buys sodas, candy, and chips for a total of $16.95. How much change does he receive from the $20.00 he gives the clerk?

4. Kim Lee buys potatoes for $2.98, tomatoes for $1.53, steak for $5.65, and a peach pie for $2.50. What is her change from $20.00?

5. Michael earns $15.00 on Saturday cutting grass. His expenses are: $1.50, bus fare; $2.75, laundry; and $7.00, lunches. How much money does Michael have left after he pays all of his expenses?

When multiplying decimals, count the number of decimal places in the problem to determine where to place the decimal point in the answer.

Hundredths times tenths is thousandths. Hundredths times hundredths is ten-thousandths.

EXAMPLES $6.32 \times 3.2 = \blacksquare$ $0.45 \times 3.31 = \blacksquare$

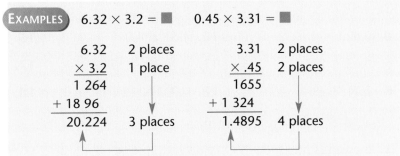

6.32	2 places		3.31	2 places
× 3.2	1 place		× .45	2 places
1 264			1655	
+ 18 96			+ 1 324	
20.224	3 places		1.4895	4 places

A zero is placed before the decimal point if there is not a whole number. However, zeros before the decimal point are not necessary when multiplication problems are written in vertical form.

Exercise A Write the decimal point in the proper place.

1.   2.35
   × 4.2
   9870

2.   5.34
   × .56
   29904

3.   7.07
   × 1.12
   79184

4.   7.23
   × 4.22
   305106

5.   .23
   × .85
   1955

6.   6.1
   × .72
   4392

7.   .45
   × .58
   2610

8.   4.73
   × .123
   58179

9.   7.8
   × .02
   156

10.   781
   × .23
   17963

11.   2.61
   × 31.2
   81432

12.   .48
   × .68
   3264

Exercise B Multiply to find the products.

1.   2.3
   × 4.6

2.   2.96
   × .17

3.   .43
   × 1.7

4.   5.62
   × .17

Exercise C Rewrite these multiplication problems in vertical form.
Multiply to find the products. Count the decimal places in each problem
before you place the decimal point.

1. 2.3 × 4.5

2. 3.34 × 2.1

3. 4.61 × 0.35

4. 0.423 × 2.1

5. 0.62 × 2.3

6. 8.71 × 2.6

7. 11.3 × 0.27

8. 26.7 × 0.04

9. 9.37 × 0.07

10. 4.63 × 4.02

11. 0.961 × 0.35

12. 0.023 × 12

13. 23.45 × 1.8

14. 14.6 × 4.21

15. 37.15 × 4.35

16. 3.51 × 4.35

17. 355 × 2.78

18. 14.6 × 0.03

Exercise D Solve these problems.

1. 6 pounds potatoes, 89¢ per pound,
cost $_____.

2. 1.2 pounds nuts, $4.75 per pound,
cost $_____.

3. 7 dozen eggs, $0.98 per dozen, cost
$_____.

4. 3.4 mph for 6.2 hours =
_____ miles.

5. 13.2 mph for 4.6 hours =
_____ miles.

6. 2.3 hours, 45.2 mph =
_____ miles.

7. 3.2 times 6.2

8. 0.73 times 2.8

9. 12.3 times 0.1

10. The product of 18.3 and 0.64
is _____.

Sometimes, your answer will not have enough digits for the
number of decimal places that you need. Then you must add
some zeros to your answer.

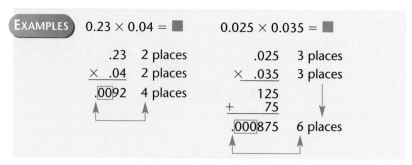

EXAMPLES   0.23 × 0.04 = ■   0.025 × 0.035 = ■

.23   2 places   .025   3 places
× .04   2 places   × .035   3 places
.0092   4 places   125
+   75

.000875   6 places

Exercise E Write the decimal point in the proper place. You may need to include zeros.

1. .23
× .03

69

3. 4.3
× .07

301

5. .025
× .07

175

7. .62
× .09

558

2. .006
×.023

138

4. 1.035
× .002

2070

6. .012
× 1.1

132

8. .62
× .45

2790

Exercise F Multiply to find the products.

1. .483
× .026

2. 5.6
× .98

3. .403
× .063

4. 2.73
× .069

Exercise G Rewrite these multiplication problems in vertical form and then find the products.

1. 4.3 × 0.06
2. 0.03 × 0.02
3. 0.183 × 0.44
4. 0.027 × 0.31
5. 0.034 × 0.06
6. 1.83 × 0.09

7. 1.05 × 0.004
8. 2.31 × 0.08
9. 0.006 × 0.02
10. 0.31 × 0.07
11. 0.09 × 0.09
12. 0.006 × 0.023

13. 32 × 0.004
14. 0.015 × 0.012
15. 2.6 × 0.002
16. 0.024 × 1.02
17. 26 × 0.021
18. 0.036 × 1.2

PROBLEM SOLVING

Exercise H Solve these word problems.

1. What is the total length of 6 pieces of ribbon each 0.012 foot long?

2. If the deli scale shows that 0.36 pound of hummus is packaged at $2.63 per pound, then what is the cost of the package?

3. What is the total cost of 12 washers at $0.03 each?

4. What is the total length of 7 pieces of pipe each 0.04 foot long?

5. What is the total distance traveled at 1.3 mph for 0.6 hour?

6. What is the cost of 0.6 pound of grapes at $0.93 per pound?

Lesson 7   Scientific Notation

Scientific notation

A number between one and ten, including one, multiplied by a power of ten

Power of ten

A product of multiplying ten by itself one or more times

Negative exponent

Shows the opposite of a power of a number; used to express smaller numbers

A number is rewritten in **scientific notation** if it is a number between one and ten (including one) multiplied by a **power of ten,** written with an exponent.

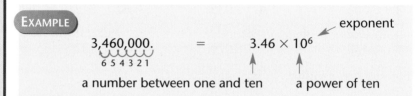

EXAMPLE

$$3{,}460{,}000. \quad = \quad 3.46 \times 10^6$$

6 5 4 3 2 1

a number between one and ten   a power of ten

exponent

Exercise A Write these numbers in scientific notation.

1. 26,000

2. 425,000

3. 630,000

4. 2,000,000

5. 21,000

6. 231,000

7. 43,000,000

8. 2,612,000

9. 500,000,000

10. 32,300

11. 52,000

12. 10,000,000

13. 21,000,000,000

14. 2,300,000,000

Decimals can also be rewritten in scientific notation. Move the decimal point to the *right.* The exponent is negative. It is called a **negative exponent.**

A number written with a positive exponent is a whole number. A negative exponent is a mixed number, a fraction, or a decimal.

EXAMPLES

$$0.0345 = 3.45 \times 10^{-2}$$

1 2

a number between one and ten   a power of ten

negative exponent

$$0.0000463 = 4.63 \times 10^{-5}$$

1 2 3 4 5

a number between one and ten   a power of ten

negative exponent

Exercise B Write these decimals in scientific notation.
Remember, if you move the decimal point to the left, then you
find the exponent. If you move the decimal point to the right,
then you find the negative exponent.

1. 0.0037
2. 0.0000286
3. 0.471
4. 0.058
5. 40.8
6. 2.34
7. 14.8
8. 0.00000000057

9. 0.0000000671
10. 0.00000834
11. 0.0000056
12. 0.000128
13. 0.0063
14. 0.00309
15. 0.0012
16. 416.8

Exercise C Express these numbers in scientific notation.
Remember, if you move the decimal point to the left, then you
find the exponent. If you move the decimal point to the right,
then you find the negative exponent.

1. 0.345
2. 0.000051
3. 482,000
4. 0.00026
5. 0.000000377
6. 0.65
7. 0.00279
8. 0.0530
9. 0.00000007
10. 1,720,000
11. 0.000000250

12. 0.0820
13. 0.00305
14. 0.206
15. 41,200
16. 0.00018
17. 0.023
18. 0.0000841
19. 602,000,000
20. 51,000,000
21. 351,000
22. 0.0000064

Exercise D Copy each problem and fill in the correct exponent.

1. $0.0026 = 2.6 \times 10$—
2. $0.000045 = 4.5 \times 10$—
3. $0.0006 = 6 \times 10$—
4. $0.092 = 9.2 \times 10$—
5. $0.6 = 6 \times 10$—
6. $0.7 = 7 \times 10$—
7. $0.0069 = 6.9 \times 10$—
8. $0.002 = 2 \times 10$—

9. $0.000000031 = 3.1 \times 10$—
10. $0.00000001 = 1 \times 10$—
11. $0.00000351 = 3.51 \times 10$—
12. $0.00915 = 9.15 \times 10$—
13. $0.0000000851 = 8.51 \times 10$—
14. $0.637 = 6.37 \times 10$—
15. $0.00000000007 = 7 \times 10$—
16. $0.000081 = 8.1 \times 10$—

When you divide a decimal by a whole number, you divide as though you were dividing whole numbers. After you find the quotient, then you bring the decimal point straight up into the quotient.

EXAMPLES

$$
\begin{array}{r}
5.2 \\
6\overline{)31.2} \\
-30 \\
\hline
1\,2 \\
-1\,2 \\
\hline
0
\end{array}
\qquad
\begin{array}{r}
5.6 \\
8\overline{)44.8} \\
-40 \\
\hline
4\,8 \\
-4\,8 \\
\hline
0
\end{array}
$$

$$
\begin{array}{r}
0.14 \\
23\overline{)3.22} \\
-2\,3 \\
\hline
92 \\
-92 \\
\hline
0
\end{array}
\qquad
\begin{array}{r}
0.012 \\
14\overline{)0.168} \\
-14 \\
\hline
28 \\
-28 \\
\hline
0
\end{array}
$$

Exercise A Find the quotients.

1. $5\overline{)1.40}$

2. $8\overline{)1.52}$

3. $9\overline{)2.439}$

4. $7\overline{)4.69}$

5. $6\overline{)34.2}$

6. $5\overline{)11.15}$

7. $21\overline{)13.083}$

8. $35\overline{)143.15}$

9. $9\overline{)19.26}$

10. $4\overline{)0.304}$

11. $13\overline{)0.546}$

12. $12\overline{)14.424}$

13. $36\overline{)37.584}$

14. $16\overline{)0.912}$

15. $18\overline{)0.2016}$

16. $17\overline{)0.204}$

17. $19\overline{)0.2033}$

18. $23\overline{)1.012}$

Exercise B Copy each problem. Place a decimal point in the proper place in the quotient.

1.   825
      9) 74.25

2.   236
      8) 1.888

3.   450
      18) 0.8100

4.   623
      6) 37.38

5.   0723
      9) 0.6507

6.   415
      19) 788.5

7.   523
      4) 209.2

8.   391
      15) 58.65

9.   501
      23) 11,523

10.   325
      11) 35.75

Exercise C Find the quotients.

1. 8) 21.04

2. 28) 141.4

3. 11) 584.1

4. 32) 66.24

5. 16) 4.656

6. 25) 15.575

PROBLEM SOLVING

Exercise D Solve these word problems.

1. Behram earns $235.15 a week delivering newspapers. If he works 5 mornings a week, then what are his daily earnings?

2. Mrs. Brennan wants to pay her bill of $162.75 to the local food market over a 7-week period. How much will she pay each week?

3. Ray has to cut a 2.3-foot-long pipe into 4 equal pieces. How long is each piece?

4. Ronald buys some ground beef for $17.43. How much does the ground beef cost per pound if he buys 7 pounds?

5. If three dozen pencils cost $6.48, then what does one pencil cost?

If the divisor is a decimal, then follow these steps:

Step 1 Move the decimal point in the divisor to the right of the number to make it a whole number.

Step 2 Move the decimal point in the dividend the same number of places.

Step 3 Divide and then bring the decimal point straight up into the quotient.

Moving the decimal point one place is really multiplying the divisor and dividend by 10.

EXAMPLES

$$\begin{array}{r} 13.4 \\ 0.7\,\overline{)9.38} \\ -7 \\ \hline 2\,3 \\ -2\,1 \\ \hline 28 \\ -28 \\ \hline 0 \end{array}$$

$$\begin{array}{r} 0.017 \\ 0.5\,\overline{)0.0085} \\ -5 \\ \hline 35 \\ -35 \\ \hline 0 \end{array}$$

Exercise E Find the quotients.

1. $0.5\,\overline{)6.85}$

2. $0.6\,\overline{)9.36}$

3. $0.7\,\overline{)8.26}$

4. $0.8\,\overline{)21.28}$

5. $0.9\,\overline{)13.95}$

6. $0.12\,\overline{)1.416}$

7. $2.6\,\overline{)3.12}$

8. $1.6\,\overline{)5.76}$

9. $1.7\,\overline{)7.65}$

10. $2.3\,\overline{)9.453}$

11. $4.1\,\overline{)21.73}$

12. $5.2\,\overline{)5.824}$

13. $0.18\,\overline{)0.0828}$

14. $0.16\,\overline{)0.3696}$

15. $0.21\,\overline{)0.01323}$

16. $0.32\,\overline{)1.152}$

17. $0.47\,\overline{)0.4794}$

18. $0.39\,\overline{)1.5717}$

19. $0.06\,\overline{)0.1896}$

20. $0.07\,\overline{)0.1435}$

21. $0.08\,\overline{)0.3216}$

22. $0.09\,\overline{)0.1053}$

23. $0.08\,\overline{)0.1688}$

24. $0.07\,\overline{)0.2205}$

Exercise F Copy each problem. Write a decimal point in the proper place in the quotient.

1.
$$0.6 \overline{)2.022} \quad 337$$

6.
$$0.09 \overline{)3.519} \quad 391$$

2.
$$0.7 \overline{)0.0441} \quad 63$$

7.
$$0.09 \overline{)0.0315} \quad 35$$

3.
$$7.8 \overline{)90.48} \quad 116$$

8.
$$2.9 \overline{)9.077} \quad 313$$

4.
$$8 \overline{)47.76} \quad 597$$

9.
$$0.6 \overline{)0.0042} \quad 7$$

5.
$$1.8 \overline{)93.6} \quad 52$$

10.
$$3.3 \overline{)28.05} \quad 85$$

Exercise G Find the quotients.

1. $0.06 \overline{)0.798}$

4. $0.19 \overline{)40.85}$

2. $0.002 \overline{)0.1624}$

5. $8.6 \overline{)215.86}$

3. $0.13 \overline{)0.728}$

6. $0.008 \overline{)0.2832}$

PROBLEM SOLVING

Exercise H Solve these word problems.

1. Melinda's part-time job pays her $118.65. How many hours does she work if she earns $5.65 per hour?

2. Nina pays Randy $55.25 for cleaning her basement. If the job takes Randy 8.5 hours, then what are his hourly wages?

3. John buys steaks for $45.14. If he buys 7.4 pounds of steaks, what is the price per pound?

4. At $1.65 per pound, how many pounds of potatoes can you buy for $13.20?

5. Larry drives 261.56 miles in 5.2 hours. What is his average speed?

You may need to include one or more zeros after the decimal point in the dividend so that the division will work out evenly. If there is no decimal point in the dividend, then place a decimal point and the zeros to the right of the dividend.

4 divided by 8

$$
\begin{array}{r}
0.5 \\
8\overline{)4.0} \\
-4\,0 \\
\hline
0
\end{array}
$$

4 divided by 0.5

$$
\begin{array}{r}
8. \\
0.5\overline{)4.0} \\
-4\,0 \\
\hline
0
\end{array}
$$

$0.06 \div 0.5$

$$
\begin{array}{r}
0.12 \\
0.5\overline{)0.060} \\
-5 \\
\hline
10 \\
-10 \\
\hline
0
\end{array}
$$

$0.18 \div 3.6$

$$
\begin{array}{r}
0.05 \\
3.6\overline{)0.180} \\
-180 \\
\hline
0
\end{array}
$$

Exercise I Find the quotients.

1. $5\overline{)1}$

2. $4\overline{)6}$

3. $8\overline{)6}$

4. $0.5\overline{)2}$

5. $0.4\overline{)36}$

6. $0.12\overline{)7.2}$

7. $0.19\overline{)3.8}$

8. $0.18\overline{)7.2}$

9. $0.12\overline{)0.156}$

10. $1.4\overline{)112}$

11. $0.15\overline{)4.545}$

12. $4.3\overline{)473}$

13. $0.63\overline{)6.93}$

14. $0.025\overline{)0.0525}$

15. $0.014\overline{)0.00532}$

Exercise J Copy each problem. Write a decimal point in the proper place in the quotient.

1. $0.32\overline{)17.6}$ quotient 55

2. $0.4\overline{)5}$ quotient 125

3. $15\overline{)0.465}$ quotient 31

4. $4.5\overline{)432}$ quotient 96

5. $0.004\overline{)0.09}$ quotient 225

6. $0.005\overline{)0.235}$ quotient 47

Exercise K Find the quotients. Round answers to the nearest hundredth.

1. $0.17\overline{)34}$

2. $1.03\overline{)2.7}$

3. $0.28\overline{)45}$

4. $0.016\overline{)4.3}$

5. $0.18\overline{)5.9}$

6. $1.8\overline{)0.37}$

PROBLEM SOLVING

Exercise L Solve these word problems.

1. Jeffrey buys some picture frame wire for $3.30. If the wire costs 60¢ per foot, then how many feet of wire does he buy?

2. Carla buys a 7.4-pound roast for $22.57. What is the cost of the roast per pound?

3. A plane flies 858.2 miles in 2.8 hours. What is the plane's average speed?

4. A plane flies 958.2 miles in 3 hours. What is the plane's average speed?

Exercise M Solve these problems.

1. Divide the sum of 8.5 and 5.3 by 2.
2. Divide 76.02 by 3 and add 4.374 to the answer.
3. Divide the difference of 14.3 and 9.28 by 4.
4. Divide the sum of 8.4 and 7.47 by 2.3.
5. Divide the product of 0.21 and 2.5 by 3.5.

Calculator Practice Dividing decimals can be easy with your calculator. Use the decimal point and the division key. Check each entry to make sure the decimal point is correct.

> **EXAMPLE** 72.3 ÷ 81.78
>
> Press 72.3 ÷ 81.78 =
>
> The display reads 0.8840792.
> Round to the nearest thousandth.
>
> 72.3 ÷ 81.78 = 0.884

Calculator Exercise Use a calculator to find these quotients. Round these answers to the nearest thousandth.

1. 61.5 ÷ 72.85
2. 8.36 ÷ 9.453
3. 72.4 ÷ 83.59
4. 5.8 ÷ 63.32
5. 702.7 ÷ 835.29
6. 906 ÷ 1,740.2

A decimal numeral may be renamed as a common fraction by using the digits in the numeral for the numerator. The denominator is the value of the last place name at the right of the numeral. You may need to simplify the fraction.

EXAMPLES $0.08 = \blacksquare$ $0.012 = \blacksquare$

$0.08 = \frac{8}{100} = \frac{2}{25}$ $0.012 = \frac{12}{1,000} = \frac{3}{250}$

Exercise A Rename each decimal as a fraction or a mixed number. Give your answers in simplest form.

1. 0.82	**16.** 0.36	**31.** 0.0198	**46.** 0.00004
2. 0.5	**17.** 0.705	**32.** 0.00002	**47.** 0.1425
3. 0.208	**18.** 0.1	**33.** 0.55	**48.** 0.625
4. 0.75	**19.** 0.505	**34.** 0.006	**49.** 0.40
5. 0.888	**20.** 0.068	**35.** 0.3275	**50.** 0.488
6. 0.7	**21.** 0.0008	**36.** 16.375	**51.** 8.75
7. 0.240	**22.** 0.48	**37.** 50.05	**52.** 0.0384
8. 0.19	**23.** 0.00075	**38.** 0.000002	**53.** 3.84
9. 0.3425	**24.** 0.386	**39.** 0.0296	**54.** 0.0800
10. 0.45	**25.** 0.182	**40.** 0.101	**55.** 0.0075
11. 0.128	**26.** 4.8	**41.** 0.33	**56.** 0.3279
12. 0.60	**27.** 0.9000	**42.** 0.0015	**57.** 0.0099
13. 0.06	**28.** 0.298	**43.** 5.84	**58.** 0.39
14. 0.875	**29.** 0.345	**44.** 0.009	**59.** 0.0045
15. 0.0004	**30.** 0.63	**45.** 0.57	**60.** 0.365

Some fractions may be renamed as decimals by changing the denominator to a power of ten — like 10, 100, or 1,000.

EXAMPLES $\frac{9}{25} = \frac{9 \times 4}{25 \times 4} = \frac{36}{100} = 0.36$

$\frac{3}{40} = \frac{3 \times 25}{40 \times 25} = \frac{75}{1,000} = 0.075$

Exercise A Rename each fraction as a decimal.

1. $\frac{3}{10}$

2. $\frac{17}{100}$

3. $\frac{125}{1,000}$

4. $\frac{7}{10}$

5. $\frac{16}{25}$

6. $\frac{17}{1,000}$

7. $\frac{3}{50}$

8. $\frac{2}{5}$

9. $\frac{5}{8}$

10. $\frac{15}{16}$

11. $\frac{377}{2,000}$

12. $\frac{7}{80}$

13. $\frac{17}{20}$

14. $\frac{23}{40}$

15. $\frac{1}{2}$

16. $\frac{19}{200}$

17. $\frac{117}{10,000}$

18. $\frac{18}{250}$

19. $\frac{13}{16}$

20. $\frac{13}{25}$

21. $\frac{9}{16}$

22. $\frac{72}{125}$

23. $\frac{9}{100}$

24. $\frac{3}{16}$

PROBLEM SOLVING

Exercise B Earth is the densest of all of the planets in our solar system. Change the fraction in each of these problems to a decimal by first changing the denominator to a power of ten.

1. Mercury is $\frac{239}{250}$ as dense as Earth.

2. Mars is $\frac{359}{500}$ as dense as Earth.

3. Pluto is only $\frac{1}{4}$ as dense as Earth.

4. Venus, our closest neighbor, is $\frac{119}{125}$ as dense as Earth.

5. Saturn is $\frac{1}{8}$ as dense as Earth.

6. Neptune is $\frac{19}{50}$ as dense as Earth.

7. The largest planet, Jupiter, is $\frac{121}{500}$ as dense as Earth.

8. Uranus is $\frac{29}{100}$ as dense as Earth.

9. Which of the planets listed is the least dense?

10. Except for Earth, which planet is the densest?

Repeating decimal

A decimal where the same series of digits repeats

All fractions will repeat decimal places if you divide to enough places.

Some fractions cannot be changed to a decimal by raising the fraction to higher terms. They can be changed to a decimal only by dividing. Continue placing zeros in the dividend until the digits in the quotient begin repeating. Draw a bar over the digits to show which digits repeat. This is a **repeating decimal.**

EXAMPLE

$$\frac{5}{11} = 11\overline{)5.0000}\qquad 0.4545 = 0.\overline{45}$$

$$
\begin{array}{r}
0.4545 \\
11\overline{)5.0000} \\
\underline{-44} \\
60 \\
\underline{-55} \\
50 \\
\underline{-44} \\
60 \\
\underline{-55} \\
5
\end{array}
$$

Exercise A Change these fractions to repeating decimals.

1. $\frac{3}{11}$ **5.** $\frac{7}{15}$ **9.** $\frac{2}{3}$

2. $\frac{4}{9}$ **6.** $\frac{10}{11}$ **10.** $\frac{5}{6}$

3. $\frac{7}{12}$ **7.** $\frac{2}{33}$ **11.** $\frac{1}{9}$

4. $\frac{19}{22}$ **8.** $\frac{1}{3}$ **12.** $\frac{5}{7}$

Try This

Sevenths are special fractions. Use a calculator to help you write $\frac{1}{7}, \frac{2}{7}, \frac{3}{7}, \frac{4}{7}, \frac{5}{7},$ and $\frac{6}{7}$ as repeating decimals. Look closely at each one. Are all of the digits from 0 to 9 represented? Do you notice anything about the order of the digits?

Another way to express a fraction as a decimal is to round the decimal if it does not divide evenly.

$$\frac{5}{9} = 9 \overline{)5.000} \qquad 0.555 \doteq 0.56$$
$$\begin{array}{r} -4\,5 \\ \hline 50 \\ -45 \\ \hline 50 \\ -45 \\ \hline 5 \end{array}$$

$$\frac{1}{6} = 6 \overline{)1.000} \qquad 0.166 \doteq 0.17$$
$$\begin{array}{r} -6 \\ \hline 40 \\ -36 \\ \hline 40 \\ -36 \\ \hline 4 \end{array}$$

Exercise B Change these fractions to decimals. Divide to three places and then round to two places.

1. $\frac{8}{13}$

2. $\frac{3}{7}$

3. $\frac{5}{8}$

4. $\frac{2}{3}$

5. $\frac{9}{11}$

6. $\frac{8}{21}$

7. $\frac{7}{9}$

8. $\frac{5}{6}$

9. $\frac{1}{12}$

10. $\frac{7}{8}$

11. $\frac{10}{21}$

12. $\frac{7}{12}$

Decimals and fractions are used to express distances on some road signs.

Find the Best Buy

To be a smart consumer, many times you have to compare the price of two or more brands. Although some brands may be the same price, they may have a different weight or contain a different number of objects. By calculating the unit price for two or more brands, you can find the best buy for the amount of money spent. The unit price is the price for one unit of an item, such as an ounce of cereal in a box that holds 13 ounces.

EXAMPLE   Janelle is shopping for cereal. To find the best buy, she wants to buy the brand with the lowest unit price.

Brand A	Brand B	Brand C
13 ounces	20 ounces	25 ounces
$3.58	2 for $10.00	$5.96

Step 1   Divide to find the unit prices. (Round the costs.)
$3.58 ÷ 13 = $0.28 per ounce
$5.00 ÷ 20 = $0.25 per ounce
$5.96 ÷ 25 = $0.24 per ounce

Step 2   Compare the unit prices.
Brand C at $0.24 per ounce is the lowest unit price.

Exercise Find the best buy among each set of brands listed.

1. Brand A eggs: 12 eggs for $1.38
Brand B eggs: 18 eggs for $1.98

2. Brand A peanut butter: 20 ounces for $3.58
Brand B peanut butter: 28 ounces for $5.38

3. Brand A soda: 12 12-ounce cans for $3.50
Brand B soda: 6 20-ounce bottles for $3.09

4. Brand A milk: $\frac{1}{2}$ gallon for $1.98
Brand B milk: 1 gallon for $3.38

Chapter 4 REVIEW

Write the letter of the best answer to each question.

1. Write the name of the place of this underlined digit:
   1<u>2</u>8.924
   A ones
   B tens
   C hundreds
   D thousands

2. Select the answer that means the same as these words:
   Fifty-five and eight-tenths
   A 5.58
   B 55.008
   C 55.08
   D 55.8

3. Which answer shows this set of decimals listed from least to greatest?
   2.15 2.896 3.342 2.9
   A 2.15, 2.896, 2.9, 3.342
   B 2.15, 2.9, 2.896, 3.342
   C 2.9, 2.15, 2.896, 3.342
   D 2.9, 2.896, 2.15, 3.342

4. Which number shows 65.861 rounded to the nearest tenth?
   A 65.86
   B 65.87
   C 65.9
   D 66

5. Choose the correct answer to 0.87 subtracted from 94.
   A 9.313
   B 93.1
   C 93.13
   D 94.87

Write these numerals in words:

6. 162.057

7. 37.1008

Write a numeral for each:

8. Nine and forty-two hundredths

9. One hundred three and ninety-six thousandths

Arrange each set in order from least to greatest:

10. 0.3156   0.309   315

11. 0.0235   0.1   0.0209

Round each numeral:

12. 17.429 to the nearest tenth

13. 53.0819 to the nearest thousandth

Find the answers:

14. 25 + 0.7 + 0.29 + 3

15. 5 + 0.92 + 13.2 + 0.6

16. 5.8 × 36

17. 0.329 × 0.003

18. 1.7 − 0.236

19. 12 − 0.981

Divide:

20. $1.012 \div 23$

21. $1.152 \div 0.32$

22. $6.56 \div 0.016$

Express each fraction as a decimal rounded to 3 places:

23. $\dfrac{1}{6}$

24. $\dfrac{6}{7}$

25. $\dfrac{7}{9}$

26. $\dfrac{5}{11}$

Express these numerals in scientific notation:

27. 0.000835

28. 0.0000051

29. 0.0000009315

30. 0.000851

Test-Taking Tip

When you read decimal numbers, get in the habit of reading them as mathematical language. For example, read 0.61 as "sixty-one hundredths" instead of "point 61."

5 Ratio and Proportion

Whether you ride a bicycle, repair the gears in a large machine, prepare recipes, or paint a house, you use ratio and proportion to help you. Ratio and proportion can help you solve problems throughout your lifetime. You'll find yourself using the skills you learn in this chapter when you read maps, buy gasoline, or rearrange your bedroom.

In Chapter 5, you will learn some of the ways to use division and algebra to help you solve problems.

Goals for Learning

◆ To write a ratio as a fraction in simplest form
◆ To compare amounts using a ratio
◆ To identify ratios that form a proportion
◆ To find the missing term in a proportion
◆ To solve word problems using ratios and proportions

Ratio

Comparison of two numbers using division

Comparison

Examining two numbers to see which is larger

Fractional form

Expressed as a fraction

Order is important in a ratio. The first number is part of a set. The second number is the whole set.

A **ratio** is a **comparison** of two numbers that uses division. This division is usually written as a fraction.

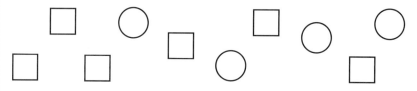

There are four circles and six squares above. The ratio of the number of circles to the number of squares is *four to six*. Three ways to write this ratio are:

$$4 \text{ to } 6 \qquad 4{:}6 \qquad \frac{4}{6}$$

The ratio of squares to circles is *six to four*. This ratio can also be written in three ways:

$$6 \text{ to } 4 \qquad 6{:}4 \qquad \frac{6}{4}$$

You can simplify a ratio by writing it as a fraction and then dividing both terms by their greatest common factor. Leave the ratio in **fractional form** even if you can change the fraction to a whole number or a mixed number.

EXAMPLES   12 to 14   18 to 12

$$\frac{12}{14} = \frac{12 \div 2}{14 \div 2} \qquad\qquad \frac{18}{12} = \frac{18 \div 6}{12 \div 6}$$

$$= \frac{6}{7} \qquad\qquad\qquad = \frac{3}{2}$$

Exercise A Write each ratio as a fraction in simplest form.

1. 12 to 20
2. 18 to 21
3. 12 to 8
4. 4 to 6
5. 12 to 15

6. 14 to 21
7. 21 to 14
8. 8 to 36
9. 15 to 19
10. 6 to 15

11. 8 to 2
12. 9 to 12
13. 20 to 24
14. 16 to 12
15. 8 to 19

A ratio may compare two amounts or two sets of objects. It may describe a rate. Use like units whenever possible.

EXAMPLES   5 pounds for \$1.40 $\frac{5}{1.40} = \frac{1}{0.28}$

($\frac{1}{0.28}$ means 1 pound for \$0.28)

$$\square\square\square \text{ to } \bigcirc\bigcirc \qquad \frac{9 \text{ squares}}{6 \text{ circles}} = \frac{3}{2}$$

15 minutes to 1 hour $\frac{15 \text{ minutes}}{60 \text{ minutes}} = \frac{1}{4}$

A ratio compares two amounts, such as two coins.

Exercise B Write a ratio to compare each of the following. Express it in simplest form.

1. 150 miles to 4 hours

2. 1 quarter to 1 nickel

3. 4 cans of soup for 85¢

4. 150 miles on 8 gallons

5. \$4.35 per hour

6. 1 fifty-cent piece to 1 dime

7. 4 hits for 6 times at bat

8. 12 apples to 1 orange

9. 25 minutes to 2 hours

10. 4 days to 2 weeks

Technology Connection

Use the Internet or an almanac to find the total area and population of your state. Then find the per capita income and the number of members of the House of Representatives in your state. Write the ratio of the population to the number of House members. Write the ratio of the population to the area. Write the ratio of per capita income to area. Change these ratios to decimals. Do the same thing for four more states. Make a chart on a computer to organize these numbers. Do you see any numbers that are similar? Can you draw any conclusions?

Proportion

Two equal ratios

When two ratios are equal, we say that they form a **proportion.**
You can tell if two ratios are equal by comparing the cross products.

EXAMPLES Do $\frac{4}{5}$ and $\frac{7}{8}$ form a proportion?

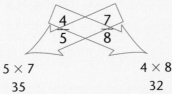

$5 \times 7 \qquad\qquad 4 \times 8$

$35 \qquad\qquad\qquad 32$

The cross products are 35 and 32. The cross products
are not equal. Therefore, the ratios do not form a
proportion. This inequality can be shown with a
symbol, ≠, which means "is not equal to."

$\frac{4}{5} \neq \frac{7}{8}$

Do $\frac{1\frac{1}{2}}{4}$ and $\frac{3}{8}$ form a proportion?

$$\frac{1\frac{1}{2}}{4} = \frac{3}{8}$$

$4 \times 3 \qquad\qquad 1\frac{1}{2} \times 8 = \frac{3}{2} \times \frac{8}{1} = \frac{24}{2}$

$12 \qquad\qquad\qquad 12$

The cross products are 12 and 12. The cross products
are equal. Therefore, the ratios do form a proportion.

$$\frac{1\frac{1}{2}}{4} = \frac{3}{8}$$

Exercise A Use cross products to see if the ratios are equal.
Write an equal sign to show which ratios form a proportion.
Write an inequality symbol (≠) to show which ratios do not
form a proportion.

1. $\frac{10}{16}$ $\qquad$ $\frac{5}{8}$ $\qquad$ **4.** $\frac{12}{20}$ $\qquad$ $\frac{3}{5}$ $\qquad$ **7.** $\frac{10}{12}$ $\qquad$ $\frac{2}{3}$

2. $\frac{4}{8}$ $\qquad$ $\frac{2}{3}$ $\qquad$ **5.** $\frac{10}{12}$ $\qquad$ $\frac{15}{18}$ $\qquad$ **8.** $\frac{5}{9}$ $\qquad$ $\frac{15}{27}$

3. $\frac{6}{8}$ $\qquad$ $\frac{9}{12}$ $\qquad$ **6.** $\frac{\frac{2}{3}}{6}$ $\qquad$ 32 $\qquad$ **9.** $\frac{1\frac{1}{2}}{3}$ $\qquad$ $\frac{3}{6}$

Use your calculator to find cross products. If the cross products are equal, the ratios form a proportion.

EXAMPLES $\frac{2}{3}$ and $\frac{4}{6}$

Press $3 \times 4 =$ The display reads *12*.

Press $2 \times 6 =$ The display reads *12*.

12 = 12 Therefore the ratios are equal and form a proportion.

$\frac{5}{6}$ and $\frac{7}{8}$

Press $6 \times 7 =$ The display reads *42*.

Press $5 \times 8 =$ The display reads *40*.

40 ≠ 42 Therefore the ratios do not form a proportion.

Calculator Exercise Use a calculator to find the cross products. Compare the cross products and determine if the ratios form a proportion.

1. $\frac{3}{12}$ and $\frac{10}{30}$

2. $\frac{7}{16}$ and $\frac{42}{66}$

3. $\frac{13}{70}$ and $\frac{39}{200}$

4. $\frac{16}{34}$ and $\frac{80}{170}$

5. $\frac{11}{12}$ and $\frac{66}{72}$

6. $\frac{14}{17}$ and $\frac{112}{134}$

7. $\frac{2}{3}$ and $\frac{120}{190}$

8. $\frac{23}{99}$ and $\frac{115}{495}$

Try This

Take two dice numbered from 1 to 6. There are 36 possible totals that can result from rolling the dice. The totals could be as low as 2 or as high as 12. List all 36 possible dice totals. Include sets of like numbers such as 1 and 2 and 2 and 1. Write a ratio to compare the number of possible outcomes for each total to the total possible outcomes of 36. Simplify your answers. Which number has the highest ratio? the lowest?

You can use cross products to find an **unknown term** in a proportion. The letter **n** stands for the missing number.

EXAMPLES

$$\frac{6}{n} = \frac{3}{12}$$

$$3 \times n = 6 \times 12$$

$$3n = 72$$

$$\frac{3n}{3} = \frac{72}{3}$$

$$n = 24$$

$$\frac{1\frac{1}{2}}{4} = \frac{n}{8}$$

$$4 \times n = 1\frac{1}{2} \times 8$$

$$4n = 12$$

$$\frac{4n}{4} = \frac{12}{4}$$

$$n = 3$$

$n \times 3$ is the same as $3 \times n$. The numeral is written first, as in $3n$.

Exercise A Solve for the missing number.

1. $\frac{12}{n} = \frac{20}{25}$

2. $\frac{5}{8} = \frac{n}{24}$

3. $\frac{2}{3} = \frac{16}{n}$

4. $\frac{12}{14} = \frac{n}{21}$

5. $\frac{n}{10} = \frac{6}{15}$

6. $\frac{12}{3} = \frac{10}{n}$

7. $\frac{\frac{1}{2}}{4} = \frac{n}{20}$

8. $\frac{5}{n} = \frac{10}{16}$

9. $\frac{12}{8} = \frac{4\frac{1}{2}}{n}$

10. $\frac{30}{20} = \frac{n}{15}$

11. $\frac{3}{n} = \frac{51}{17}$

12. $\frac{1\frac{1}{2}}{3} = \frac{n}{8}$

13. $\frac{9}{n} = \frac{27}{33}$

14. $\frac{8}{10} = \frac{n}{25}$

15. $\frac{6}{8} = \frac{7}{n}$

16. $\frac{3}{7} = \frac{n}{25}$

17. $\frac{4}{n} = \frac{12}{15}$

18. $\frac{n}{10} = \frac{8}{11}$

Mixture
Combination of two or more items

Proportions can be used to solve problems involving **mixtures.** You must be careful that the two ratios are written in the same order.

Always include units of measure in your answer.

EXAMPLE Sunburst Gold paint is made by mixing 2 parts yellow to 1 part red. How many pints of red paint should be mixed with 3 pints of yellow paint?

$$\frac{Yellow}{Red} \qquad \frac{2}{1} = \frac{3}{n} \qquad 3 = 2n$$

$$\frac{3}{2} = \frac{2n}{2}$$

$$1\frac{1}{2} = n$$

You should use $1\frac{1}{2}$ pints of red paint.

PROBLEM SOLVING

Exercise A Use proportions to help you solve these word problems.

1. Apple Green paint is made by mixing 7 parts yellow to 3 parts blue. How much yellow should be mixed with 9 pints of blue?

2. A snack is 5 parts peanuts and 2 parts raisins. How many pounds of peanuts should be mixed with one-half pound of raisins?

3. Peach paint is 1 part yellow to 3 parts red. How much yellow should be mixed with 4 quarts of red?

4. Mix 3 quarts of water with 2 lemons to make lemonade. How many quarts of water are mixed with 1 lemon?

5. Mix 6 parts cornstarch to 1 part water to make Glop. How much water should be used with 2 cups cornstarch?

6. Purple paint is 5 parts blue to 1 part red. How much red should be mixed with 2 quarts of blue?

7. Mix 4 parts yellow to 2 parts red to get orange. How much red and yellow should be mixed to get 2 gallons of orange?

Sprocket
A wheel with teeth that pulls a chain

A five-speed bicycle has a chain that is attached to a pedal **sprocket** in the front and to five gears in the back. The ratio of pedal turns to rear wheel turns for each gear is:

$$\frac{\text{Pedal Turns}}{\text{Rear Wheel Turns}}$$

1st gear	2nd gear	3rd gear	4th gear	5th gear
$\dfrac{9}{14}$	$\dfrac{4}{7}$	$\dfrac{1}{2}$	$\dfrac{3}{7}$	$\dfrac{5}{14}$

You can use a proportion to help you find the number of times that the rear wheel turns for a given number of pedal turns.

Writing About Mathematics

Measure the length and height of a toy car, then measure a real car that is similar. Use the same units. Write ratios for each measure. Do the ratios form a proportion? Write your conclusions.

EXAMPLE In fourth gear, the pedal turned 21 times. How many times did the rear wheel turn?

$$\frac{\text{Pedal Turns}}{\text{Rear Wheel Turns}} \qquad \frac{3}{7} = \frac{21}{n}$$

$$147 = 3n$$
$$49 = n$$

The rear wheel turned 49 times.

You can also find the number of times that you must turn the pedal for a given number of rear wheel turns.

EXAMPLE In fifth gear, the rear wheel turned 42 times. How many pedal turns were there?

$$\frac{\text{Pedal Turns}}{\text{Rear Wheel Turns}} \qquad \frac{5}{14} = \frac{n}{42}$$

$$14n = 210$$
$$n = 15$$

The pedal turned 15 times.

	Gear	Pedal Turns	Rear Wheel Turns
1.	1st	270	
2.	2nd	270	
3.	3rd	270	
4.	4th	270	
5.	1st		42
6.	2nd		42
7.	3rd		42
8.	4th		42

EXAMPLE With one rear wheel turn, a 26-inch bicycle moves 82 inches along the ground. If someone makes 270 pedal turns in first gear, then how many inches does the bike travel?

Step 1 Solve a proportion for pedal turns to rear wheel turns in first gear.

$$\frac{9 \text{ Pedal turns}}{14 \text{ Rear wheel turns}} = \frac{270 \text{ Pedal turns}}{n \text{ Rear wheel turns}}$$

$n = 420$. There are 420 rear wheel turns in 270 pedal turns.

Step 2 Calculate how many inches are in 420 rear wheel turns.

$$\frac{1 \text{ Rear wheel turn}}{82 \text{ inches}} = \frac{420 \text{ Rear wheel turns}}{n \text{ Inches}}$$

$n = 34{,}440$. The bike will have traveled 34,440 inches with 420 pedal turns in first gear.

PROBLEM SOLVING

Exercise C Use the ratios on page 130 to solve the following word problems.

1. Shana makes 24 pedal turns in second gear with her 26-inch bicycle. About how many inches has her bicycle traveled?

2. A 24-inch bicycle travels about 75 inches with one rear wheel turn. How many inches will the bike go with 270 pedal turns in fifth gear?

Proportions may be used to make **conversions** between the **currencies** of different countries.

	Conversion
Conversion	
Change from one unit of measure to a different one	
Currency	
Money	

In January 2002, 11 European countries started to use the same currency: the Euro.

Country	Currency	1 U.S. Dollar =
Canada	Canadian dollar = 100 cents	1.57 CAD
Cayman Islands	Cayman Islands dollar = 100 cents	0.80 CID
China	Chinese yuan renminbi = 100 fen	8.28 CYR
11 European countries	Euro dollar = 100 cents	1.16 EUR
West Indies	East Carib dollar = 100 cents	2.70 ECD

EXAMPLES Change 50 U.S. dollars to East Carib dollars.

$$\frac{USD}{ECD} \qquad \frac{1}{2.70} = \frac{50}{n}$$

$135 = 1n$

135 dollars

$50.00 U.S. dollars = $135.00 East Carib dollars

Change 32 East Carib dollars to U.S. currency.

$$\frac{USD}{ECD} \qquad \frac{1}{2.70} = \frac{n}{32}$$

$2.70n = 32$

$n = 11.85$

11 dollars and 85 cents.

$32.00 East Carib dollars = $11.85 U.S. dollars

Exercise D Use a proportion to make these currency conversions. Refer to the chart above. Round your answers to the nearest cent.

1. Change 50 U.S. dollars to Canadian currency.

2. Change 74 East Carib dollars to U.S. currency.

3. Change 60 U.S. dollars to Chinese currency.

4. Change 40 yuan to U.S. currency.

5. Change 45 U.S. dollars to Euros.

Exercise E Use a proportion to help you solve each word problem.

1. A car travels 240 miles on 15 gallons of gas. How far can the car travel on 20 gallons of gas?

2. Three gallons of paint will cover 825 square feet of wall space. How many square feet will 4 gallons cover?

3. Mario can drive 250 miles in 4 hours. How far can he drive in 6 hours?

4. At Smythe College, there are 5 females for every 4 males. If there are 372 males, then how many females are there?

5. If 2 pounds of hamburger will serve 3 people, then how many pounds of hamburger will serve 7 people?

6. Kim Lu can mow 2 lawns in $1\frac{1}{2}$ hours. How long will it take him to mow 6 lawns?

7. At Camp Runabout, there are 2 counselors for every 15 campers. If 165 campers are at the camp, then how many counselors are there?

8. On a map, 1 inch equals 15 miles. How many miles apart are two towns that are 6.4 inches apart on the map?

9. A deluxe dollhouse is built to a 1:40 scale. If the dollhouse is 20 inches high, then how high is the actual house?

10. Oranges are selling at the rate of 12 oranges for a dollar. How much will 27 oranges cost?

11. Kevin's car gets 32 miles to one gallon of gas. How much gas will he use on a 475-mile trip?

Currency Exchange

When traveling in a foreign country, you need to exchange your money to the local currency. Before you travel, convert a small amount to foreign currency. You may need some pocket money upon arrival. Convert most of your money when you reach the foreign country to get a better exchange rate. Before leaving the country, try to spend all foreign coins and small bank notes. Many countries will not re-exchange amounts that are very small.

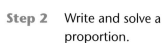

EXAMPLE   Jason is going to Japan. He is taking 300 United States dollars (USD). What is this amount converted to yen?

Step 1   Find the exchange rate in the table.
1 USD = 112.86 JPY

Step 2   Write and solve a proportion.

$$\frac{USD}{JPY} \quad \frac{1}{112.86} = \frac{300}{y}$$

$$y = 300 \times 112.86$$
$$= 33,858$$

$300.00 converts to 33,858 Japanese yen (JPY).

Selected Foreign Exchange Rates		
Country	**Foreign Currency in USD**	**USD in Foreign Currency**
Britain (pound)	1.4286	0.700 GBP
Canada (dollar)	0.6369	1.57 CAD
China (yuan renminbi)	0.1208	8.28 CYR
Japan (yen)	0.008139	112.86 JPY

Exercise Solve each problem. Round your answers to the nearest cent.

1. Convert $500.00 to English pounds.

2. Convert 5,000 Japanese yen to U.S. dollars.

3. Convert $400.00 to Canadian dollars.

4. Kayla exchanged some U.S. money in Japan, then exclaimed, "Now I'm rich! I have 11,286 yen." How much money did she exchange?

5. How can you quickly estimate USD to Canadian dollars mentally?

Chapter 5 R E V I E W

Write the letter of the best answer to each question.

1. How would 16 to 80 be written as a fraction in simplest form?

A $\frac{1}{5}$

B $\frac{4}{20}$

C $\frac{16}{80}$

D $\frac{1}{4}$

2. How would 3 days to 3 weeks be written as a ratio in simplest form?

A $\frac{3}{21}$

B $\frac{1}{7}$

C $\frac{1}{5}$

D $\frac{3}{3}$

3. Does $\frac{12}{15}$ and $\frac{10}{18}$ form a proportion? Use = or ≠.

A =

B ≠

4. Find the value of n in this proportion: $\frac{1}{10} = \frac{n}{50}$

A $\frac{1}{2}$

B 1

C 5

D 10

5. Alberto earns $12.75 per hour. How much does he earn if he works 4 hours?

A $31.90

B $32.00

C $50.00

D $51.00

Write each ratio as a fraction in simplest form:

6. 18 to 24

7. 48 to 32

8. 27 to 32

Write a ratio to compare the amounts below. Simplify
to the lowest terms.

9. 35 minutes to 1 hour

10. 15¢ to 25¢

Tell whether or not each pair of ratios forms a proportion.
Use = or ≠.

11. $\frac{12}{15}$ $\frac{8}{10}$

12. $\frac{12}{8}$ $\frac{4}{3}$

13. $\frac{6}{8}$ $\frac{9}{12}$

Solve for the missing number:

14. $\frac{n}{8} = \frac{6}{12}$

15. $\frac{4}{10} = \frac{n}{15}$

16. $\frac{7}{9} = \frac{5}{n}$

17. $\frac{\frac{2}{3}}{n} = \frac{7}{21}$

18. $\frac{4}{3} = \frac{n}{9}$

19. $\frac{378}{5.4} = \frac{n}{3.1}$

Solve these word problems:

20. Sunset Gold paint is made by mixing 3 parts yellow to 1 part red. How much red is to be mixed with 2 quarts of yellow?

21. Four oranges cost $3.00. How much will 1 orange cost?

22. John's car gets 36 miles to one gallon of gas. How much gas will he use to travel 81 miles?

23. The scale on a map is 1 inch to 20 miles. How many miles apart are two towns that are $8\frac{2}{5}$ inches apart on the map?

24. Paula drives 252 miles and uses 8 gallons of gas. How far does she drive on one gallon of gas?

25. If one dollar equals 80¢ in Cayman Islands currency, then what would $8.40 in Cayman Islands currency be in U.S. currency?

Test-Taking Tip

Learn from your mistakes. Review corrected homework and tests to identify your errors.

6

Percent

List the places where you have seen percents used to communicate an idea to people. Does your list include baseball statistics on trading cards, or grades on reports, projects, and tests? How about money off at sales? Tips for good service are usually based on a percent. Some jobs such as car sales pay based on a percent of sales. When you think about it and look around you, you see that we use percent many ways in our daily lives.

In Chapter 6, you will learn about the mathematics involved in working with percents. Next time you and your friends go out to eat, you can be the one who calculates the tip!

Goals for Learning

◆ To rename a percent as a decimal and a fraction in simplest form

◆ To rename a decimal and a fraction as a percent

◆ To find the missing terms in a percent sentence

◆ To use a proportion to find the missing term in a percent sentence

◆ To solve word problems involving percents and tax, commissions, interest, and tips

◆ To calculate monthly payments on an installment plan

Percent, %
Part per one hundred

The symbol "%" is read as "percent." **Percent** means "per hundred" or "out of one hundred." Therefore, 82% means 82 per hundred, or 82 out of one hundred. In the example below, 82 squares out of the 100 squares are shaded. We say that 82% of the figure is shaded.

EXAMPLE

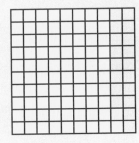

Exercise A Tell what percent of each figure is shaded.

1.
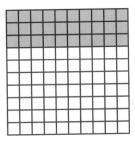

3.
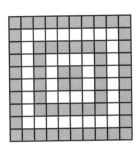

5.
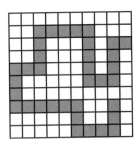

2.
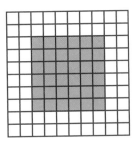

4.
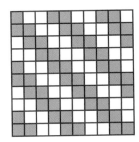

6.
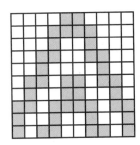

Twenty-seven percent means 27 per hundred or 27 hundredths. We can write 27 hundredths as 0.27 or as $\frac{27}{100}$. By writing the percent as hundredths, we can write a percent as a decimal or a fraction. You may need to simplify the fraction to lowest terms.

EXAMPLES   Write 35% as a decimal and as a fraction.

35% = 0.35

$35\% = \frac{35}{100} = \frac{7}{20}$

Write 8% as a decimal and as a fraction.

8% = 0.08

$8\% = \frac{8}{100} = \frac{2}{25}$

Exercise A Write each percent as a decimal and as a fraction.

1. 13%

2. 7%

3. 68%

4. 20%

5. 45%

6. 8%

7. 1%

8. 10%

9. 3%

10. 97%

11. 36%

12. 40%

13. 50%

14. 75%

15. 120%

Percent is often used to advertise sales in retail stores.

You may see a percent that is not a whole number. You still move the decimal point two places to the left to change to a decimal. Do not count any fractions in the two places.

EXAMPLES Change 2.3% to a decimal.
$$2.3\% = 0.023$$

Change $6\frac{2}{3}\%$ to a decimal.

$$6\frac{2}{3}\% = 0.06\frac{2}{3} = 0.0\overline{6}$$

Exercise B Change each percent to a decimal.

1. 46.3%
2. $8\frac{1}{3}\%$
3. 0.8%

4. $22\frac{1}{3}\%$
5. 3.62%
6. 4.45%

7. 1.04%
8. 0.27%
9. $5\frac{1}{3}\%$

10. $128\frac{1}{2}\%$
11. $\frac{4}{5}\%$
12. 0.075%

You can easily change a percent that contains a fraction to a fraction if you think of "percent" as meaning "times one-hundredth."

Simplify your answer if possible.

EXAMPLES Change $7\frac{1}{2}\%$ to a fraction.

$$7\frac{1}{2}\% = 7\frac{1}{2} \times \frac{1}{100}$$

$$= \frac{15}{2} \times \frac{1}{100}$$

$$= \frac{15}{200} \text{ or } \frac{3}{40}$$

Change $5\frac{4}{7}\%$ to a fraction.

$$5\frac{4}{7}\% = 5\frac{4}{7} \times \frac{1}{100}$$

$$= \frac{39}{7} \times \frac{1}{100}$$

$$= \frac{39}{700}$$

Exercise C Change each percent to a fraction in simplest form.

1. $2\frac{1}{2}\%$
2. $17\frac{1}{2}\%$
3. $3\frac{1}{3}\%$

4. $42\frac{1}{2}\%$
5. $20\frac{1}{2}\%$
6. $2\frac{1}{5}\%$

7. $37\frac{1}{2}\%$
8. $8\frac{1}{3}\%$
9. $16\frac{2}{3}\%$

10. $22\frac{2}{9}\%$
11. $14\frac{2}{7}\%$
12. $20\frac{1}{5}\%$

You can rename a decimal as a percent by moving the decimal point two places to the right and adding the percent symbol. You would not write the decimal point if it occurs at the end of the number.

Moving the decimal point two places to the right is really multiplying the number by 100.

EXAMPLES   Change 0.237 to a percent.

$0.237 = 23.7\%$

Change 0.4 to a percent.

$0.40 = 40\%$

Exercise A   Rename these decimals as percents.

1. 0.46   **5.** 0.003   **9.** 0.253

2. 0.102   **6.** 1.28   **10.** 0.0461

3. 0.9   **7.** 0.0042   **11.** 12.3

4. 0.046   **8.** 3.4   **12.** 0.068

You can change a fraction to a percent by dividing the denominator into the numerator. Add a decimal point and two zeros to the numerator. Divide. This gives you a two-place decimal for a quotient. Rename the decimal as a percent.

EXAMPLES   Change $\frac{3}{5}$ to a percent.

$$\begin{array}{r} 0.60 = 60\% \\ 5\overline{)3.00} \end{array}$$

Change $\frac{4}{7}$ to a percent.

$$\begin{array}{r} 0.57\frac{1}{7} = 57\frac{1}{7}\% \\ 7\overline{)4.00} \end{array}$$

Exercise B   Rename these fractions as percents.

1. $\frac{3}{4}$ **4.** $\frac{5}{9}$ **7.** $\frac{1}{15}$ **10.** $\frac{3}{16}$

2. $\frac{1}{20}$ **5.** $\frac{7}{13}$ **8.** $\frac{2}{3}$ **11.** $\frac{7}{8}$

3. $\frac{5}{8}$ **6.** $\frac{3}{50}$ **9.** $\frac{17}{20}$ **12.** $\frac{20}{13}$

You may not want a fractional percent for an answer. Then you would round to the nearest whole percent. This is done by dividing to three places instead of two. Round the three-place decimal to a two-place decimal and then change this decimal to a percent.

EXAMPLE Rename $\frac{6}{7}$ as a percent.

$$0.857 \doteq 0.86 = 86\%$$
$$7\overline{)6.000}$$

Exercise C Rename each fraction as a percent. Round to the nearest whole percent, if necessary.

1. $\frac{7}{8}$	**11.** $\frac{6}{8}$	**21.** $\frac{3}{8}$	**31.** $\frac{6}{20}$
2. $\frac{4}{5}$	**12.** $\frac{4}{9}$	**22.** $\frac{5}{8}$	**32.** $\frac{18}{48}$
3. $\frac{6}{7}$	**13.** $\frac{8}{10}$	**23.** $\frac{6}{9}$	**33.** $\frac{16}{48}$
4. $\frac{5}{11}$	**14.** $\frac{14}{20}$	**24.** $\frac{2}{3}$	**34.** $\frac{13}{20}$
5. $\frac{8}{9}$	**15.** $\frac{14}{16}$	**25.** $\frac{3}{4}$	**35.** $\frac{11}{15}$
6. $\frac{7}{10}$	**16.** $\frac{9}{12}$	**26.** $\frac{3}{12}$	**36.** $\frac{35}{40}$
7. $\frac{8}{12}$	**17.** $\frac{8}{22}$	**27.** $\frac{3}{24}$	**37.** $\frac{42}{50}$
8. $\frac{12}{24}$	**18.** $\frac{16}{20}$	**28.** $\frac{52}{100}$	**38.** $\frac{78}{100}$
9. $\frac{33}{40}$	**19.** $\frac{8}{14}$	**29.** $\frac{6}{12}$	**39.** $\frac{38}{50}$
10. $\frac{4}{10}$	**20.** $\frac{2}{7}$	**30.** $\frac{22}{25}$	**40.** $\frac{32}{64}$

Exercise D Rename the fractions described in these word problems as percents. Round any remainders.

1. Manuel receives $\frac{7}{8}$ of the votes cast. What percent of the votes does he receive?

2. Jason correctly answers 32 problems out of 35 problems on a test. What percent of the problems does he get correct?

3. An advertisement claims that 7 out of 10 doctors recommend Brand A vitamins. What percent of the doctors recommend the vitamins?

4. Kennedy Middle School wins 12 of their 20 football games. What percent of their games do they win? What percent of their games do they lose?

5. The ninth-grade class sells 16 tickets on Monday, 17 tickets on Tuesday, and 19 tickets on Wednesday. What percent of 135 tickets have they sold?

6. Suki can make 18 out of 25 shots from the foul line. What percent of the shots can she make?

7. Two-thirds of a neighborhood attend a meeting. What percent of the neighborhood attends the meeting?

8. Four members of the class are absent. What percent of the class of 35 is absent?

9. The Stateliners win 5 out of their 12 games. What percent of their games do they win?

10. Katie gets 38 of 45 problems correct. What percent of the problems does she get correct?

Exercise E Fill in this chart.

	Fraction	Decimal	Percent
1.	$\frac{3}{8}$		
2.			84%
3.		0.48	
4.			9%
5.		$0.2\overline{6}$	
6.	$\frac{3}{40}$		
7.			$6\frac{2}{3}\%$
8.		0.8	

PROBLEM SOLVING

Exercise F Make the conversions asked for in these word problems.

1. "55% cotton." What fraction is cotton?

2. The Bluebirds win 0.625 of their games. What percent do they win?

3. 48% are girls. What fraction are girls?

4. 87% pass the test. What fraction passes?

5. "$\frac{1}{4}$ off all prices." What is the percent off?

6. Joe is batting .408. What percent is this?

7. "22% down on a car." What fraction is this?

8. Sales are up 6.4%. What is this as a decimal?

9. "16% unemployed." What fraction are unemployed?

10. "4 out of 5 doctors recommend…" What percent is this?

Calculator Practice

Use your calculator to rename fractions as decimals and then you can change decimals to percents. Round decimals to two places.

EXAMPLE Express $\frac{6}{17}$ as a percent.

Press 6 $\div$ 17 $=$

The display reads 0.352941176.

Round the decimal to two places, then move the decimal point two places to the right and add the percent symbol.

The answer is 35%.

Calculator Exercise Use a calculator to rename these fractions as percents.

1. $\frac{5}{13}$

2. $\frac{6}{17}$

3. $\frac{8}{22}$

4. $\frac{5}{17}$

5. $\frac{6}{19}$

6. $\frac{5}{11}$

7. $\frac{9}{11}$

8. $\frac{15}{21}$

9. $\frac{34}{50}$

10. $\frac{8}{13}$

11. $\frac{45}{49}$

12. $\frac{9}{13}$

13. $\frac{13}{15}$

14. $\frac{9}{10}$

15. $\frac{14}{18}$

16. $\frac{19}{21}$

17. $\frac{22}{32}$

18. $\frac{41}{60}$

19. $\frac{78}{93}$

20. $\frac{89}{90}$

Rate

Percent

Base

The amount you are
taking a part or
percent of

Percentage

Result obtained by
multiplying a number
by a percent

Three elements are in any percent sentence—the rate, the base, and the percentage. The **rate** is the percent in the problem. The **base** is the whole amount, the number from which you are taking a percentage. The **percentage** is the part, the number that you get when you take the percent of the base.

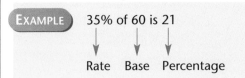

EXAMPLE   35% of 60 is 21

Rate   Base   Percentage

Exercise A In the problems below, identify the rate, the base, and the percentage. If one of these elements is not given, write *n* for that unknown element. It is not necessary to work any of the problems.

1. 35% of 40 is 14
2. 4.5 is 18% of 25
3. *x*% of 82 is 6
4. What is 29% of 103?
5. 18 is what percent of 82?
6. 9% of what number is 14?
7. What percent of 82 is 36?
8. 12% of 106 is what number?
9. 35 is 72% of what number?
10. 20% of 82
11. She got 82% of the 50 questions correct.
12. 4 out of 5 dentists recommend Brand A toothbrushes.
13. 25% off the regular price of $52.00
14. The 15% tip amounts to $1.75
15. 8% of the 52,000 parts are defective.

Lesson 5 | Finding the Percentage

You can find the percentage, or part, in a percent problem by expressing the rate as a decimal and multiplying it by the base.

EXAMPLES   34% of 38 is what number?
$$0.34 \times 38 = n$$
$$12.92 = n$$

6% of 48 is what number?
$$0.06 \times 48 = n$$
$$2.88 = n$$

Exercise A Find the percentage in each of these percent sentences.

1. 22% of 36 is ___.
2. 52% of 50 is ___.
3. 7% of 48 is ___.
4. 2% of 16 is ___.
5. 29% of 3 is ___.
6. 45% of 23 is ___.
7. 3.2% of 42 is ___.

8. 43% of 3.2 is ___.
9. 39% of 0.7 is ___.
10. 3% of 0.6 is ___.
11. 86% of 72 is ___.
12. 9.2% of 15 is ___.
13. 2% of 18 is ___.
14. 16% of 19 is ___.

15. 35% of 15 is ___.
16. 3.2% of 25 is ___.
17. 9% of 23 is ___.
18. 26% of 23 is ___.
19. 0.5% of 100 is ___.
20. 82% of 200 is ___.
21. 36% of 36 is ___.

Exercise B Solve for the percentage.

1. What number is 23% of 8?
2. What number is 15% of 30?
3. What number is 28% of 8?
4. What number is 19% of 0.6?
5. What number is 10% of 16?
6. What number is 2% of 0.7?
7. What number is 0.8% of 0.3?
8. What number is 1.9% of 2?
9. n is 0.02% of 1.7
10. n is 1.6% of 100
11. n is 25% of 50
12. n is 75% of 80
13. 82% of 50.2 is n
14. n is 92% of 92

15. n is 6.5% of 23
16. 0.8% of 50 is n
17. n is 6.5% of 60
18. 0.1% of 100 is n
19. n is 0.3% of 24
20. n is 2.2% of 10
21. 23% of 51 is n
22. n is 31% of 2.1
23. 0.9% of 34 is n
24. 25% of 72 is n
25. n is 39% of 10
26. 10% of 10 is n
27. 18% of 200 is n
28. n is 75% of 250

Andre earns $380.00. He spends 70%. How much does he spend?

70% of $380.00 is what number?
$0.70 \times \$380.00 = n$
$\$266.00 = n$

PROBLEM SOLVING

Exercise C Solve these word problems. Write a percent sentence first.

1. A test has 50 questions. Al gets 90% correct. How many questions does he get correct?

2. The team plays 60 games. They win 30%. How many do they win?

3. 35 students are in class. 60% are girls. How many are girls? How many are boys?

4. 25 students are tested. 20% do very well. How many do very well?

5. There are 960 tenth-grade students. 85% participate in extracurricular activities. How may students participate?

6. Raoul weighs 130 pounds. He loses 10% on a diet. How many pounds does he lose?

7. Cassie earns $150.00 per week. She receives a 20% raise. How much money is the raise?

8. Selena finds $32,000.00. There is a 15% reward. How much is the reward?

Try This

Look for ads in the front section of a newspaper. Estimate the percent of space that each ad takes up. If an ad takes up the whole page, the percent is 100%; $\frac{1}{2}$ of a page is 50%; $\frac{1}{3}$ of a page would be about 33%. Record your estimates in a chart. Then estimate the percent of the whole front section that is devoted to ads.

You can find the base in a percent problem by dividing the percentage by the rate. Rename the rate as a decimal first.

> The base is the number you are taking a percent of.

EXAMPLES

38% of what number is 19?
$$0.38 \times n = 19$$
$$n = 19 \div 0.38$$
$$n = 50$$

2.3% of what number is 1.725?
$$0.023 \times n = 1.725$$
$$n = 1.725 \div 0.023$$
$$n = 75$$

Writing About Mathematics

A deck of playing cards has 52 cards of four suits. Select a card from a deck and write down the suit. Replace the card. Do this 20 times. Find the percent of suits selected. Write a summary of your results.

Exercise A Find the base in each of these percent sentences.

1. 22% of ___ is 17.6

2. 45% of ___ is 80.55

3. 60% of ___ is 120

4. 75% of ___ is 42.6

5. 80% of ___ is 32

6. 30% of ___ is 18

7. 20% of ___ is 18

8. 10% of ___ is 8

9. 20% of ___ is 6.4

10. 12% of ___ is 7.2

11. 45% of ___ is 27

12. 60% of ___ is 42

13. 24% of ___ is 36

14. 15% of ___ is 60

15. 84% of ___ is 63

16. 48% of ___ is 78

17. 20% of ___ is 37

18. 5% of ___ is 92

19. 16% of ___ is 32

20. 19% of ___ is 57

21. 25% of ___ is 60

22. 42% of ___ is 84

23. 65% of ___ is 195

24. 85% of ___ is 595

Exercise B Solve for the base.

1. 5.75 is 23% of what number?
2. 35 is 35% of what number?
3. 45 is 25% of what number?
4. 64 is 32% of what number?
5. 21.6 is 48% of what number?
6. 6.5 is 13% of what number?
7. 12.6 is 28% of what number?
8. 190 is 95% of what number?
9. 2.2 is 40% of n
10. 1.62 is 60% of n
11. 22% of n is 21.56
12. 27 is 30% of n
13. 40% of n is 22
14. 57 is 95% of n

15. 21 is 35% of n
16. 26% of n is 13
17. 4.2 is 12% of n
18. 85% of n is 56.1
19. 20% of n is 1.7
20. 7.2 is 8% of n
21. 0.21 is 6% of n
22. 18% of n is 36
23. 30 is 60% of n
24. 10% of n is 0.55
25. 4.5 is 25% of n
26. 18% of n is 9
27. 85% of n is 680
28. 14.4 is 90% of n

EXAMPLE   20% of the class are girls. 6 girls are in the class.
How many students are in the class?

20% of what number is 6?
$0.20 \times n = 6$
$n = 6 \div 0.20$
$n = 30$

PROBLEM SOLVING

Exercise C Solve these word problems. Write a percent sentence first.

1. 75% of the buses have arrived. 48 have arrived. How many buses are there in all?

2. 80% of the students vote. 48 students vote. How many students are there in all?

3. Marit loses 32% of her beads. Marit loses 24 beads. How many beads did she have to begin with?

4. 8 students did not go on a trip. 16% did not go on the trip. How many students are there in all?

5. John saves 20% of his salary. He saves $16.00 per week. What is his weekly salary?

6. Susan spends 80% of her earnings. She spends $40.00. How much does she earn?

You can find the rate by dividing the percentage by the base.
Remember that the rate is a percent. This means that the answer
that you get is the rate times 100. One way to ensure that you
get the correct answer is to mark off two decimal places in the
base before dividing.

EXAMPLES What percent of 18 is 0.54?

$n\% \times 18 = 0.54$ $n \times 18 = 0.54$

$n \times 0.18 = 0.54$ $n = \frac{0.54}{18}$

$n = 0.54 \div 0.18$ $n = 0.03 = 3\%$

$n = 3\%$

What percent of 30 is 21?

$n\% \times 30 = 21$ $n \times 30 = 21$

$n \times 0.30 = 21$ $n = \frac{21}{30}$

$n = 21 \div 0.30$ $n = 0.7 = 70\%$

$n = 70\%$

Exercise A Find the rate in each of these percent sentences.

1. ___% of 18 is 2.7

2. ___% of 45 is 9

3. ___% of 200 is 120

4. ___% of 50 is 17.5

5. ___% of 80 is 65.6

6. ___% of 70 is 10.5

7. ___% of 48 is 24.48

8. ___% of 40 is 0.8

9. ___% of 70 is 2.45

10. ___% of 57 is 5.13

11. ___% of 50 is 11.5

12. ___% of 70 is 64.4

13. ___% of 80 is 3.6

14. ___% of 62 is 12.4

15. ___% of 35 is 34.3

16. ___% of 35 is 14.7

17. ___% of 96 is 35.52

18. ___% of 20 is 8.4

19. ___% of 2.6 is 0.221

20. ___% of 3.2 is 1.344

Exercise B Solve for the rate.

1. 6.5 is what percent of 50?

2. 1 is what percent of 20?

3. 6.8 is what percent of 85?

4. 1.5 is what percent of 75?

5. 19.8 is what percent of 60?

6. 450 is what percent of 500?

7. 117 is what percent of 90?

8. 42 is what percent of 56?

9. 24 is $n\%$ of 30

10. 0.11 is $n\%$ of 2.5

11. $n\%$ of 53 is 12.19

12. 18.2 is $n\%$ of 35

13. $n\%$ of 600 is 150

14. 8.1 is $n\%$ of 45

15. 1 is $n\%$ of 40

16. $n\%$ of 60 is 3

17. 3.2 is $n\%$ of 80

18. $n\%$ of 70 is 8.4

19. $n\%$ of 90 is 5.4

20. 40 is $n\%$ of 50

21. $n\%$ of 500 is 375

22. 15.6 is $n\%$ of 130

23. $n\%$ of 67 is 6.7

24. 54 is $n\%$ of 180

25. $n\%$ of 70 is 63

26. 2 is $n\%$ of 80

27. $n\%$ of 50 is 4

28. 43.2 is $n\%$ of 270

29. 110.4 is $n\%$ of 920

30. $n\%$ of 143 is 24.31

Technology Connection

Look at the stock exchange report on the Internet or in a newspaper. Find the stock name. Find the columns for the closing price and change. The stock's opening price is the closing price minus the change. Be careful. If the change shows a minus sign, the opening price was larger than the closing price. Calculate the rate of change as a percent of the opening price. Do this for three other stocks. Make a chart on a computer showing each stock and the rate of change for five days. How did the stocks you selected do during this time? Did the price of the stocks go up or down? Make a graph on a computer to show the rate of change for one of the stocks you chose.

EXAMPLE　Garcia has $450.00 to spend for school. He spends
$270.00 on clothes. What percent does he spend
on clothes?

What percent of $450.00 is $270.00?

n% of 450 is 270

$n \times 4.50 = 270$ 　　$n \times 450 = 270$

$n = 270 \div 4.50$ 　　$n = \frac{270}{450}$

$n = 60\%$ 　　　　$n = 0.6$ or 60%

PROBLEM SOLVING

Exercise C Solve these word problems. Write a percent sentence first.

1. 40 students are in the class. 18 students go on the field trip. What percent go on the field trip?

2. The total distance is 52 miles. Sue drives 13 miles. What percent of the distance does she drive?

3. Gary attempts 84 shots. He makes 63. What percent of the shots does he make?

4. Joe's allowance is $12.00. He spends $7.80. What percent does he spend?

5. 1,200 sandwiches are made for the picnic. 1,140 sandwiches are eaten. What percent are eaten?

6. The team plays 50 games. They win 35 games. What percent do they win?

7. 620 automobiles have to be inspected. 527 pass inspection. What percent do *not* pass?

8. There are 450 students. 90 are at home with the flu. What percent are absent?

All three types of percent problems can also be solved by using a proportion. The three major elements of a percent sentence are the rate, the base, and the percentage. Enter two of these elements in the proportion and solve for the third.

$$\frac{\text{RATE}}{100} = \frac{\text{PERCENTAGE}}{\text{BASE}}$$

Remember, place the rate over 100 and the percentage over the base.

EXAMPLE

80% of 55 is ___   ___% of 30 is 6   16% of ___ is 4

$\frac{80}{100} = \frac{n}{55}$ $\frac{n}{100} = \frac{6}{30}$ $\frac{16}{100} = \frac{4}{n}$

$100n = 80 \times 55$ $600 = 30n$ $400 = 16n$

$100n = 4,400$ $\frac{600}{30} = \frac{30n}{30}$ $\frac{400}{16} = \frac{16n}{16}$

$\frac{100n}{100} = \frac{4,400}{100}$

$n = 44$ $20 = n$ $25 = n$

You can write the correct proportion by following these steps:

Step 1   Write this: $\frac{\ \ }{100} = \frac{\ \ }{\ \ }$

Step 2   Write the percent over the 100.

Step 3   Find the phrase "percent of." The number after "percent of" goes on the bottom of the second fraction.

Step 4   The third number goes on the top of the second fraction.

Exercise A Use a proportion to help you find the missing number.

1. ___% of 30 is 6

2. 32% of 450 is ___

3. ___ is 40% of 9

4. 28% of ___ is 14

5. 16 is 8% of ___

6. 12 is 80% of ___

7. 6% of 15 is ___

8. ___% of 9 is 2

9. ___ is 45% of 200

10. 18 is ___% of 48

11. $4\frac{1}{2}$% of $3\frac{1}{3}$ is ___

12. 3.5% of ___ is 14

Exercise B Use a proportion to solve each of these percent problems.

1. Sampson gets 12 hits for 15 times at bat. What percent of the time does Sampson get a hit?

2. Sixty percent of the people sampled in a school survey prefer vanilla yogurt. If 84 of the people prefer vanilla, then how many people were surveyed?

3. If 70% is a passing grade, then how many questions do you need to answer correctly on a 40-question test to pass?

4. The fluid in your car's cooling system should be 40% antifreeze. If the cooling system holds 15 quarts of fluid, then how many quarts of antifreeze will you need?

5. Robin makes 85% of her shots from the foul line. How many foul shots will she make out of 60 attempts?

6. A tiger weighs 298 pounds. It has a 5% weight loss. How many pounds does the tiger lose?

7. 18 boys and 27 girls are in a class. What percent of the class are boys?

8. If iron ore is 15% iron, then how many tons of ore are needed to get 30 tons of iron?

9. Bagels used to sell for 30¢. Now they sell for 35¢. What is the percent of increase in the price of bagels?

10. Sharina buys a used car for $3,060.00. She pays $765.00 as a down payment. What percent of the total cost is her down payment?

List price
Regular price of an item

Sale price
Reduced price of an item

Discount
A reduction made from the regular price

Discount rate
Percent that the price is reduced

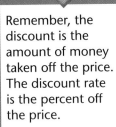

Remember, the discount is the amount of money taken off the price. The discount rate is the percent off the price.

Stores often have items for sale at a reduced cost. The usual price of an item is called the **list price.** The reduced cost is called the **sale price.** The **discount** is the amount that you save. The **discount rate** is the percent off the regular price. You can work discount problems if you remember these formulas:

Discount = List Price × Discount Rate
Sale Price = List Price − Discount
Discount Rate = Discount ÷ List Price

EXAMPLES   Find the sale price of a watch that lists for $25.50, if the discount rate is 20%.

Step 1   Identify formula
Sale price = List price − Discount

Step 2   Find discount
$ 25.50   List Price
×   .20   Discount Rate
$5.1000   Discount

Step 3   Apply formula for sale price
$ 25.50   List Price
−   5.10   Discount
$ 20.40   Sale Price

Find the discount rate if an item that sells for $34.20 is on sale for $29.07.

$ 34.20   List Price   0.15 = 15% Discount Rate
− 29.07   Sale Price   34.20) 5.1300
$ 5.13   Discount   − 3 420
                                          1 7100
                                       − 1 7100

Find the sale price of a book that usually sells for $5.98, if the discount rate is 15%. Round to the nearest cent.

$ 5.98   List Price $5.98   List Price
×   .15   Discount Rate   − 0.90   Discount
$0.8970   Discount $5.08   Sale Price

Exercise A Solve these discount problems.

1. $150.00 list price
   20% discount rate
   Discount _____
   Sale Price _____

2. Shirt usually costs $25.00
   30% discount rate
   Discount _____
   Sale Price _____

3. CD player costing $65.50
   45% discount rate
   Discount _____
   Sale Price _____

4. Shoes costing $45.50
   Discount rate is 20%
   Discount _____
   Sale Price _____

5. Television costs $450.00
   You pay only $360.00
   Discount _____
   Discount Rate _____

6. DVD usually costs $19.50
   You pay only $15.60
   Discount _____
   Discount Rate _____

7. Calculator costs $9.95
   10% discount rate
   Discount _____
   Sale Price _____

8. Computer game costs $46.50
   15% discount rate
   Discount _____
   Sale Price _____

9. Car costs $6,295.00
   10% discount rate
   Discount _____
   Sale Price _____

10. Bike costs $175.00
    On sale for $122.50
    Discount _____
    Discount Rate _____

PROBLEM SOLVING

Exercise B Solve these discount problems.

1. A pen usually sells for $5.75. It is on sale for 15% off. What is the sale price?

2. A CD player usually sells for $125.20. It is on sale for $100.16. Find the discount rate.

3. A dress shirt lists for $17.89. You can save 20% while it is on sale. Find the sale price.

Sales tax

Money paid as tax when you buy an item

Tax rate

The percent charged as tax

Always round up when calculating sales tax.

Most states in the U.S. charge a **sales tax** on items a consumer buys. The consumer pays this tax. The **tax rate** is a percent of the price to be added to the price. With sales tax, you round any part of a cent to the next cent.

EXAMPLES   Find the cost of a CD selling for $29.75 if the state sales tax is 6%.

Step 1	$ 29.75	Price
	× .06	Tax Rate
	$1.7850	Tax Rounds to $1.79

Step 2	$ 29.75	Price
	+ 1.79	Rounded tax
	$ 31.54	Price with tax

Find the cost of a calculator selling for $18.35 if the state sales tax is 6%.

Step 1	$ 18.35	Price
	× .06	Tax Rate
	$1.1010	Tax Rounds to $1.11

Step 2	$ 18.35	Price
	+ 1.11	Rounded tax
	$ 19.46	Price with tax

Exercise A Solve these tax problems. Remember to round up.

1. A poster costs $10.90. Tax rate 5%.
Tax _____
Price with tax _____

2. Tickets cost $15.00. Tax rate 6%.
Tax _____
Price with tax _____

3. A used car costs $4,000.00. Tax rate 8%.
Tax _____
Price with tax _____

4. A clock costs $7.50. Tax rate 3%.
Tax _____
Price with tax _____

5. A jacket costs $75.25. Tax rate 5%.
Tax _____
Price with tax _____

When you buy an item on sale, you pay the sales tax on the sale price rather than on the list price.

EXAMPLE Find the actual cost of a book that usually sells for $14.50, if you get a 10% rate of discount and the sales tax is 5%.

Step 1
$ 14.50	List Price
× .10	Discount Rate
$1.4500	Discount

Step 2
$14.50	List Price
− 1.45	Discount
$13.05	Sale Price

Step 3
$13.05	Sale Price
× .05	Tax Rate
$.6525	Tax

Step 4
$13.05	Sale Price
+ 0.66	Rounded tax
$13.71	Price with tax

Exercise B Complete the combination discount-tax table below.

	List Price	Discount Rate	Discount	Sale Price	Tax Rate	Tax	Amount Paid
1.	$14.50	10%	$1.45	$13.05	5%	$0.66	$13.71
2.	$18.00	20%			5%		
3.	$23.00	20%			6%		
4.	$48.00	35%			6%		
5.	$1.95	15%			7%		
6.	$245.00	10%			7%		
7.	$3,268.00	10%			6%		
8.	$0.85	20%			5%		
9.	$1,060.00	25%			5%		
10.	$38.95	12%			3%		

When you put money into a savings account, the bank pays you interest. You can solve interest problems if you remember this formula:

Principal

Amount borrowed or invested

Rate of interest

Percent paid or charged for the use of money

Interest = **Principal** × **Rate of Interest** × Time

You may need to round any part of a cent. You would follow the usual rules for rounding to two decimal places. If the time is not given in years, it must be changed to years before working the problem.

The interest is the amount of money. The interest rate is the percent of money.

EXAMPLES Compute the simple interest on a principal of $185.00 at a rate of interest of 5% for 3 years.

$185.00	Principal		$9.25	1 Year's Interest
× .05	Interest Rate		× 3	3 Years
$9.2500	1 Year's Interest		$27.75	3 Years' Interest

Compute the interest on a principal of $175.00 at a rate of interest of 6% for 6 months.

$ 175.00	Principal
× .06	Interest Rate
$10.5000	1 Year's Interest

$$6 \text{ months} = \frac{1}{2} \text{ year} = 0.5 \text{ year}$$

$$\$10.50 \times \frac{1}{2} = \$5.25 \text{ or } \$10.50 \times 0.5 = \$5.25$$

Exercise A Compute the interest. Round to the nearest cent.

1. $70.00 at 5% for 2 years

2. $172.00 at 4% for 3 years

3. $86.00 at 16% for 4 years

4. $227.00 at 11% for 3 years

5. $345.00 at 6% for 5 years

6. $945.00 at 7% for 1 year

7. $80.00 at 5% for 2 years

8. $85.00 at 12% for 3 years

9. $102.00 at 9% for 8 months

10. $286.00 at 12.5% for 2 years

11. $38.00 at 6% for 6 months

12. $45.00 at 9% for 4 months

13. $92.00 at 10% for 8 months

14. $48.00 at 15% for 4 years

Previous balance

Amount owed before a payment is made

Finance rate

Percent charged for borrowing money

Finance charge

Cost for borrowing money

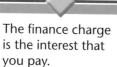

The finance charge is the interest that you pay.

Many stores have arrangements for buying expensive items on the installment plan. This means that you pay for the item over a period of months. Some stores charge a monthly finance charge of $1\frac{1}{2}\%$ of the unpaid balance.

EXAMPLE   Duane buys a TV set for $250.00 on the installment plan. He agrees to make monthly payments of $25.00 until the bill for the TV is paid in full.

Step 1 $250.000   **Previous Balance**
×   .015   **Finance Rate** ($1\frac{1}{2}\%$ = 0.015)
$3.75000   **Finance Charge** for first month

Step 2 $250.00   Previous Balance
+   3.75   Finance Charge
$253.75   Balance Before First Payment

Step 3 $253.75   Balance Before First Payment
− 25.00   First Month's Payment
$228.75   New Balance

The new balance becomes the previous balance for the next month.

Exercise A Fill in this chart to show how Duane will pay for his TV set.

Month	Previous Balance	Finance Charge	Before Payment	Monthly Payment	New Balance
April	$250.00	$3.75	$253.75	$25.00	$228.75
May	$228.75	$3.43	_____	$25.00	_____
June	_____	_____	_____	$25.00	_____
July	_____	_____	_____	$25.00	_____
Aug.	_____	_____	_____	$25.00	_____
Sept.	_____	_____	_____	$25.00	_____
Oct.	_____	_____	_____	$25.00	_____
Nov.	_____	_____	_____	$25.00	_____
Dec.	_____	_____	_____	$25.00	_____
Jan.	_____	_____	_____	$25.00	_____
Feb.	_____	_____	_____	_____	$0.00

Commission
Percentage of total sales

Rate of commission
The percent used to compute commissions

Salespeople are often paid a **commission** on their sales. A commission is a percent of the total amount of sales. You find the amount of the commission by multiplying the **rate of commission** by the total sales.

EXAMPLE   Mr. Ripley sold $8,950.00 worth of jewelry last week.
He is paid a 7% rate of commission.
How much is his commission?

$$\begin{array}{r} \$\ 8,950 \\ \times\quad .07 \\ \hline \$626.50 \end{array}$$ Mr. Ripley's commission is $626.50.

PROBLEM SOLVING

Exercise A Answer these word problems about commission.

1. Mary is paid an 11% rate of commission. What is her commission for selling $1,286.00 worth of merchandise?

2. A real estate agent receives 7% of the sale price of a house for commission. What is the commission for selling a house for $65,000.00?

3. Alberta receives an 8% rate of commission on all sales over $2,000.00. How much is her commission for $4,280.00 in sales?

4. Pedro gets a 2% rate of commission on the first $2,000.00 worth of sales and a 5% rate on all sales over $2,000.00. How much is his commission for sales totaling $13,283.00?

5. Li receives a different rate of commission for selling different items. Figure out his total commission for the sales in the chart below.

Item	Chains	Earrings	Tie Tacks	Rings	Pins
Total Sales	$10,428.00	$12,417.00	$6,453.00	$13,208.00	$348.00
Rate of Commission	4%	3%	6%	4%	2%

Tip

An amount of money paid for service

Tip rate

Percent left as a tip

The cost of the meal plus the tip equals the total cost.

It is customary to leave a **tip** for your server when you dine in a restaurant. The tip is usually 15% of the total cost of the meal.

EXAMPLE The meal costs $28.95. The tip should be 15% of $28.95.

Step 1

$ 28.95	Meal cost
× .15	**Tip rate**
$4.3425 = $4.34	Amount of tip

Step 2

$28.95	Meal
+ 4.34	Tip
$33.29	Total cost

Exercise A For each check, find the cost of the meal, the amount of a 15% tip, and the total cost.

1. Candle Hearth

1 salad	$1.90
1 soup	$1.00
1 chicken dinner	$5.25
1 fish dinner	$6.75
1 pie	$1.36
1 milk	$1.00

Meal cost _____

Tip _____

Total cost _____

2. Captain Jack's

1 spaghetti dinner	$5.25
1 fish dinner	$6.75
1 sundae	$1.45
1 lemonade	$0.50
1 root beer	$0.50

Meal cost _____

Tip _____

Total cost _____

3. Hilltop Inn Cafeteria

1 soup	$1.15
1 salad	$1.90
1 steak	$13.70
1 shrimp dinner	$6.50
1 pudding	$0.68
1 soft drink	$1.00
1 iced tea	$0.50

Meal cost _____

Tip _____

Total cost _____

4. Papa Nick's

1 salad	$2.30
1 soup	$1.20
1 chef special	$14.50
1 fish dinner	$6.75
1 iced tea	$1.50

Meal cost _____

Tip _____

Total cost _____

Some Tips on Tipping

One of the most common uses for percent is to estimate a tip for a service. Tips are usually 10%, 15%, or 20% of the total cost of the service.

EXAMPLE The cost of a pizza is $7.83 with tax. What is a reasonable estimated amount to give the pizza delivery person for a 15% tip?

Step 1 Estimate 10% of the cost first. Move the decimal point one place to the left. Then round the estimate. 10% of $7.83 = $0.783, or about $0.80.

Step 2 To estimate 5%, find half of the 10% estimate. Half of $0.80 = $0.40.

Step 3 To estimate a 15% tip, add the 10% and 5% estimates. $0.80 + $0.40 = $1.20

A 15% tip is about $1.20.

Exercise Estimate the amount of the tip in each problem.

1. Kevin got a haircut that costs $18.00. What is a reasonable amount to give the barber for a 10% tip?

2. The cost of a family meal in a restaurant came to $46.23 with tax. What is a reasonable amount to give the server for a 15% tip?

3. The cost of the shuttle ride from the airport to Mr. Zander's house was $29.00. Shuttle companies recommend a 10% tip and a baggage fee of $1.00 per bag. Mr. Zander has two bags. What is a reasonable amount to give the driver as a tip?

4. Marsha got her hair cut for $21.00 and a permanent for $65.00 at the hair salon. What is the reasonable amount to give the hairstylist for a 10% tip?

5. For dinner, Morris had a salad for $5.50, a steak for $17.00, a dessert for $4.50, and a soft drink for $2.75. The tax was 8%. What is a reasonable amount to give the server for a 20% tip?

Chapter 6 REVIEW

Write the letter of the best answer to each question.

1. 26% written as a decimal is—
   A   0.026
   B   0.26
   C   2.6
   D   26.0

2. The number 0.00489 written as a percent is—
   A   0.489%
   B   48.9%
   C   50%
   D   489%

3. $\frac{2}{5}$ written as a percent is—
   A   2.5%
   B   4%
   C   25%
   D   40%

4. 10% of __ is 6.8
   A   0.068
   B   0.68
   C   68
   D   680

5. For each computer Isabella sells, she earns a 5% commission. If she sells 3 computers for $985.00 each, what is her commission?
   A $14.78
   B $49.25
   C $98.50
   D $147.75

Rename each of the following as a decimal:

6. 8%

7. 42.6%

8. 5.2%

Rename each percent as a fraction in simplest form:

9. 45%

10. 79%

11. $12\frac{1}{2}$%

12. $5\frac{1}{3}$%

Rename each as a percent:

13. 0.4

14. 0.057

15. $\frac{3}{20}$

16. $\frac{8}{11}$

Find the missing numbers:

17. ____ is 30% of 82

18. 12 is 40% of ____

19. ____% of 32 is 8

20. 6% of 28 is ____

21. 0.6% of ____ is 9

22. 2.4 is ____% of 8

Find the missing numbers, using a proportion:

23. 15 is ___% of 300

24. 16% of ___ is 36

Find the answers to these word problems:

25. The bill for dinner comes to $45.30. How much is a 15% tip to the nearest cent?

26. Tracy buys a dress for $24.65, a belt for $6.85, and a scarf for $3.70. How much sales tax is due if the tax rate is 5%?

27. A coat usually sells for $48.60. It is on sale for 15% off. What is the sale price?

28. Yoshi is paid a 4% rate of commission on all sales over $600.00. How much commission does she get on $3,840.00 worth of sales?

29. How much interest is paid on $1,200.00 invested at 7% per year for 3 years?

30. Bill is going to buy a TV for $365.00. He makes a down payment of $50.00 and pays off the rest in 9 equal monthly payments. How much is each payment?

Test-Taking Tip

When you study for chapter tests, practice the step-by-step formulas and procedures.

Introduction to Geometry

Look around you. Think about the shapes you see. Notice the patterns that bricks make on the face of a building. Look closely at the angles made by the doors and windows in your room. Which angles are the same and which are different? All of these are examples of geometry in your world. Geometry is a form of mathematics that helps us construct safe and beautiful buildings. It also helps us in every part of our life.

In Chapter 7, you will learn more about the mathematics involved in measuring angles and describing shapes.

Goals for Learning

◆ To identify parallel lines

◆ To identify the point of intersecting lines

◆ To measure angles

◆ To name triangles by looking at angles and sides

◆ To name solid figures by looking at faces, vertices, and edges

Geometry

The study of points, lines, angles, surfaces, and solids

Line segment

Part of a line

Ray

A line that has a beginning point but no end

Angle

Two rays with the same endpoint

Vertex

The point where two rays meet

Plane

A flat surface that extends forever in all directions

Geometry is the study of points, lines, angles, surfaces, and solids. To study geometry, we need to define some geometric terms.

A *point* is a location in space. It is represented by a dot. Points are usually named with a letter. We say "point A" or "point M."

A *line* is a collection of points that extend forever in the same direction. A line does not have any endpoints. A line is named with any two points. We represent line *AB* like this: $\overleftrightarrow{AB}$.

A **line segment** is a part of a line. It has two endpoints. We represent line segment *AB* like this: $\overline{AB}$.

A **ray** is a collection of points that begin at one point and extend forever in one direction. A ray has one endpoint. We represent ray *AB* like this: $\overrightarrow{AB}$.

When two rays have the same endpoint, they form an **angle.** We call this angle ∠*ABC* or ∠*CBA*. The common endpoint *B* is in the middle of the symbol.

The common endpoint is called the angle's **vertex.**

We usually look at lines and points that are all on the same flat surface, like a piece of paper. A flat surface that extends forever in all directions is called a **plane.** We represent a plane with a lowercase letter like p.

P

Exercise A Give the best name for each drawing.

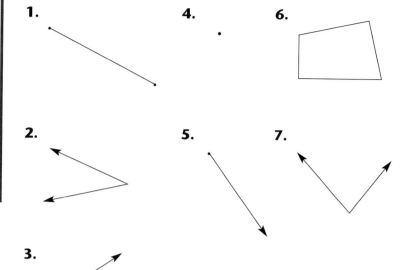

1.

4.

6.

2.

5.

7.

3.

Lines in a Plane If two lines are drawn in the same plane, then they might meet at a point or stay the same distance apart and never meet. Two lines that are always the same distance apart are called **parallel lines.** Lines that meet are called **intersecting lines.** Intersecting lines can meet in such a way that the four angles formed are all the same size. These lines are called **perpendicular lines.**

Exercise B Give the best name for each drawing.

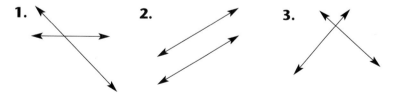

1.

2.

3.

Circle

A plane figure whose points are equally distant from the center

Degree

A measure of angles

An angle can be formed by the intersection of two rays. A ray is a line that has a beginning point but no end. Angular measure is based on the **circle.** The circle is divided into 360 equal parts, each called one **degree.**

If you divide a circle in half, then each part will contain 180 degrees. Therefore, the angular measure of a straight line, or a straight angle, is 180°. If you divide a circle into four equal parts with perpendicular lines, then each part will contain 90 degrees. Each 90° angle is called a right angle. Angles are classified by the number of degrees contained in them.

An angle can be classified as either an **acute angle,** a **right angle,** an **obtuse angle,** a **straight angle,** or a **reflex angle.** The chart below shows you how the different types of angles look. Once you see them it will be easier for you to remember their names.

Kind of Angle	Description	Degrees	Example
Acute	Less than a right angle	Between 0° and 90°	
Right	Formed by 2 perpendicular rays	90°	
Obtuse	Larger than a right angle but smaller than a straight angle	Between 90° and 180°	
Straight	2 rays form a straight line	180°	
Reflex	Larger than a straight angle	Between 180° and 360°	

Two angles which together measure 180° are called supplementary angles. Two angles which together measure 90° are called complementary angles.

Exercise A Give the correct name for each angle below.

1.

2.

3.

4.

5.

6.

Exercise B Use the diagram below to answer these questions.

1. Which two lines appear to be parallel?

2. What kind of angle is ∠DEF?

3. What kind of angle is ∠CGF?

4. What kind of lines are $\overleftrightarrow{AC}$ and $\overleftrightarrow{DG}$?

5. What kind of angle is ∠DGF?

6. Which two lines appear to be perpendicular?

7. What kind of angle is ∠DCA?

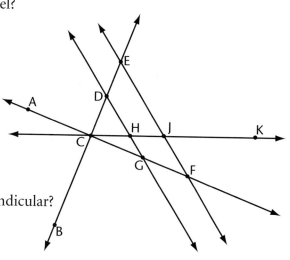

8. Two angles that together measure 180° are called supplementary angles. Name two supplementary angles.

9. Two angles that together measure 90° are complementary angles. Name two complementary angles.

Protractor

A tool used to draw or measure angles

An angle can be formed by the intersection of two rays. The rays are the sides of the angles. The point where the two rays intersect is called the vertex of the angle. The size of the angle is not affected by the length of the rays. The same number of degrees would be in the angle no matter how long you draw the rays. We use a **protractor** to measure angles. A protractor is a semicircle with the 180° marked off along its edge.

Center on the vertex and base line on one side. Read the measure of the angle where the other side crosses the scale.

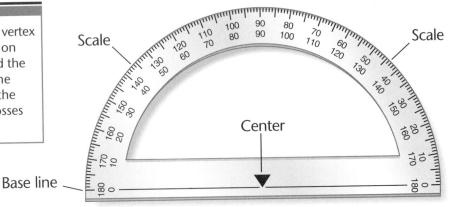

Follow these steps to measure an angle:

Step 1 Place the protractor on the angle to be measured so that the center is over the vertex of the angle and the base line is over one ray of the angle.

Step 2 Make sure that the second ray of the angle crosses the scale of the protractor. You may need to make the second ray longer.

Step 3 Read the number of degrees in the angle where the second ray of the angle crosses the scale.

If the first ray extends to the right of the vertex, then use the outside scale. If the first ray points left, then use the inside scale.

The following examples use these three steps to measure angles.

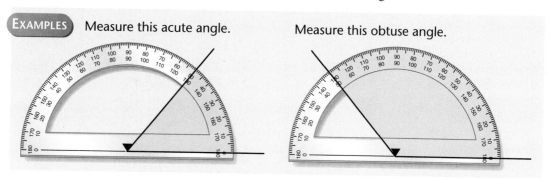

EXAMPLES Measure this acute angle.   Measure this obtuse angle.

The acute angle measures 50°. One line of the angle crosses 0 on the outer scale of the protractor. The other line crosses 50. You may notice a 130 at the same point. Since we are reading the outer scale for this angle, we do not use the 130.

The obtuse angle measures 130°. The outer scale of the protractor is used to measure this angle too.

Exercise A Measure these acute angles.

1.

3.

5.

2.

4.

6.

Exercise B Measure these obtuse angles. All of them will be more than 90 degrees.

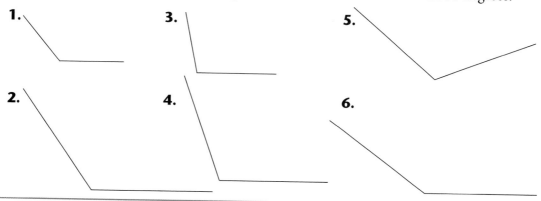

1.

3.

5.

2.

4.

6.

Use a protractor to measure angles of five objects in your classroom or at home. Record your results in a chart. List what each object is, the angle measurement in degrees, and whether the angle is acute, right, or obtuse.

Exercise C Use a protractor to help you measure these angles.

1.

6.

2.

7.

3.

8.

4.

9.

5.

10.

Constructing Angles Follow these steps to construct a 65° angle:

Step 1 Use the baseline of the protractor to draw one ray of the angle. Mark the vertex.

Step 2 Place the protractor on the ray so that the center is over the vertex of the angle to be drawn.

Step 3 On the scale of the protractor, find the number of degrees for the angle to be drawn. Make a mark (point) next to the number of degrees (65°).

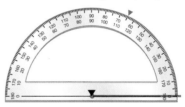

Step 4 Use the baseline of the protractor to connect the point and the vertex of the angle.

Step 5 Draw a ray from the vertex to the point.

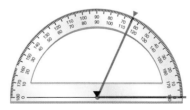

Exercise D Use a protractor to help you construct angles with the following measures:

1. 60°
2. 45°
3. 130°
4. 155°
5. 180°

6. 72°
7. 105°
8. 90°
9. 133°
10. 28°

<table>
<tr><td>

Polygon

A closed plane figure
with three or more sides
</td></tr>
</table>

A closed plane figure made of three or more line segments is called a **polygon.** Polygons are named according to the number of sides they have.

Number of Sides	Name of Polygon
3	triangle
4	quadrilateral
5	pentagon
6	hexagon
7	heptagon
8	octagon
9	nonagon
10	decagon
12	dodecagon

Writing About Mathematics

Polygons are all around you. Find an example of each polygon listed in the chart on this page. Write the name of the polygon and where you found an example. Describe each example.

Exercise A Count the number of sides on each polygon. Write the name for each polygon. Use the table above to help you.

1.
3.
5.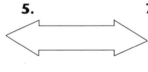
7.

2.
4.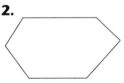
6.
8.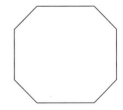

Types of Triangles **Triangles** may be classified by their angles.

 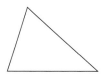

Right Triangle
One angle is 90°.

Obtuse Triangle
One angle is more than 90°.

Acute Triangle
All angles are less than 90°.

Triangles may be classified by their sides.

Scalene Triangle
No sides equal.

Isosceles Triangle
Two sides equal.

Equilateral Triangle
Three sides equal.

Exercise B Look at the sides of each triangle.
Tell what kind of triangle it is.

1.   **3.**   **5.**

2.   **4.**    **6.**

Exercise C Look at the angles of each triangle.
Tell what kind of triangle it is.

1. 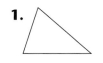   **3.**    **5.**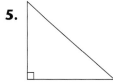

2. 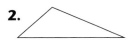   **4.**   **6.**

Quadrilateral
A polygon with four sides

Square
A polygon with four equal sides and four right angles

Rectangle
A four-sided polygon with four right angles and the opposite sides are equal

Rhombus
A polygon with four equal sides and the opposite angles are equal

Parallelogram
A four-sided polygon with two pairs of equal and parallel sides

Trapezoid
A four-sided polygon with one pair of parallel sides and one pair of sides that are not parallel

Types of Quadrilaterals

Quadrilaterals are classified by relationships of their sides and angles.

A **square** has four equal sides and four right angles.

A **rectangle** has four right angles and the opposite sides are equal.

A **rhombus** has four equal sides and the opposite angles are equal.

A **parallelogram** has two pairs of equal and parallel sides.

A **trapezoid** has one pair of parallel sides and one pair of sides that are not parallel.

Exercise D Give the best name for each quadrilateral.

1.   **3.**   **5.**

2. 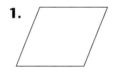 **4.**   **6.**

Measure of the Interior Angles of a Polygon

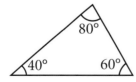
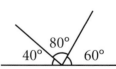

The sum of the measures of the angles in a triangle is 180°. We can show this by marking each angle of the triangle. If we arrange the angles so that they have the same vertex, then we see that the three angles form a straight angle. The measure of a straight angle is 180°.

Exercise E

1. Draw a quadrilateral. Select one vertex and draw a line segment to the opposite vertex. This line segment should divide the quadrilateral into two triangles. The sum of the angles of the quadrilateral is the same as the sum of the angles of the two triangles. How many degrees is the sum of the four angles of the quadrilateral?

2. Draw a pentagon. Select one vertex so that you can draw line segments to the other vertices without going outside of the pentagon. How many triangles are formed? What is the sum of the angles of a pentagon?

3. Draw a hexagon. Select one vertex and draw line segments to the other vertices to make triangles. How many triangles are formed? What is the sum of the angles of a hexagon?

 **Calculator Practice** The memory key on a calculator can store a number you want to use more than once in a set of problems. The repeated number is called a constant.

EXAMPLE Two angles in a triangle measure 70° and 80°. What is the measure of the third angle?

Step 1 Press *180* M+ . (The constant is 180°.)

Step 2 Press C to clear the display. The constant, 180°, is stored in the calculator's memory.

Step 3 Press MR (Memory Recall). The display reads *180*.

Step 4 Press − *70* − *80* =

The display reads 30.
The measure of the third angle is 30°.

Calculator Exercise Use your calculator's memory key to find the measure of the third angle in these triangles.

1.	124	48	**5.**	95	43	**9.**	85	15
2.	21	42	**6.**	45	45	**10.**	64	59
3.	18	113	**7.**	80	60	**11.**	15	145
4.	95	5	**8.**	60	60	**12.**	33	69

Solid geometric figures are three-dimensional. A solid figure with parallelograms for sides and two parallel faces of the same shape is called a **prism.** A prism is named for the shape of its faces. A prism with squares for sides and faces is called a **cube.**

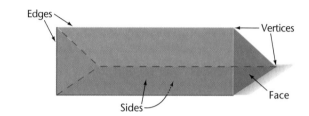

Edges — Vertices — Face — Sides

Prism

A solid figure with two parallel faces that are polygons of the same shape

Cube

A prism with square sides and faces

Pyramid

A solid figure with a base that is a polygon and triangular sides

Triangular Prism
A prism with triangular faces.

Hexagonal Prism
A prism with hexagonal faces.

Rectangular Prism
A prism with rectangular faces.

A **pyramid** has triangles for sides.

Some solid figures have curved surfaces.

  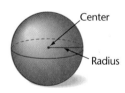

Circular bases — Vertex — Circular base — Center — Radius

Cylinder
A solid figure with two equal circular bases that are parallel.

Cone
A solid figure with a circular base connected to a vertex.

Sphere
A solid figure with a curved surface in which all points on the surface are equal distance from the center.

Exercise A Write the name of each solid figure. Look at the examples on page 184 to help you.

1.

3.

5.

2.

4.

6.

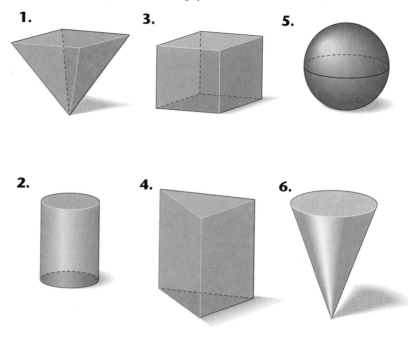

Technology Connection

Crystals are solid figures. They occur in many amazing shapes. Some of them can be found in nature, but many are made by scientists for use in industry. Collect samples or pictures of crystals. Many of the crystals have points and the edges suggest line segments. Identify any of the polygons or shapes that you studied in this chapter.

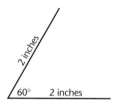
Shapely Angles

You can draw geometric figures using a protractor and a straightedge. Use the same processes you would use to construct angles and line segments. Combine angles and line segments to construct a polygon. To construct solid figures, remember how to construct parallel line segments. Use a ruler instead of a straightedge to draw sides of certain lengths.

EXAMPLE   Construct an equilateral triangle with 2-inch sides.

Step 1   Construct a 60° angle.

Step 2   Mark each side of the angle to be 2 inches long.

Step 3   Construct a 60° angle at the end of one 2-inch side. Draw the third side.

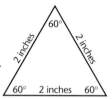

Exercise Use a protractor and a ruler to construct each figure.

1. Construct a 90° angle. Use the angle to construct a square with 3-inch sides. What is the sum of all of the angles?

2. Construct a rectangle that is 8 cm long and 5 cm wide. What is the sum of all of the angles?

3. Construct a right triangle. What is the sum of all of the angles?

4. Construct a 120° angle. Use the angle to construct a figure using 120° angles and each side measuring 10 cm. What is the name of the polygon you constructed? What is the sum of all of the angles?

5. Construct a rectangle. Use it to construct a rectangular prism. Label all the sides and angles with measurements. What size angle did you make to show perspective in this figure?

Chapter 7 R E V I E W

Write the letter of the best answer to each question.

1. What name is used to describe these lines?
    A intersecting
    B parallel
    C perpendicular
    D acute

2. A triangle with one 90° angle is called a(n)—
    A obtuse triangle
    B isosceles triangle
    C acute triangle
    D right triangle

3. Lines that cross in the same plane are called—
    A intersecting
    B parallel
    C perpendicular
    D straight

4. What is the measure of this angle?
    A 40°
    B 45°
    C 130°
    D 135°

5. What is the name of this solid figure?
    A prism
    B cone
    C cylinder
    D sphere

Chapter 7   R E V I E W - continued

Use the diagram to help you answer questions 6–10.

6. What line is parallel to line $\overleftrightarrow{GH}$?

7. Lines $\overleftrightarrow{AB}$ and $\overleftrightarrow{GE}$ intersect at what point?

8. What kind of angle is ∠FCB?

9. If $\overleftrightarrow{CE}$ is perpendicular to $\overleftrightarrow{BG}$, then what kind of angle is ∠BGC?

10. If ∠FBC is 26° and ∠CFB is 37°, then how many degrees is ∠FCB?

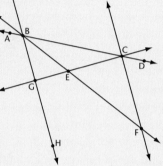

11. What triangle is formed by $\overleftrightarrow{GE}$, $\overleftrightarrow{AD}$, and $\overleftrightarrow{BF}$?

Write the name of each polygon.

12.

14.

13.

15.

16. What kind of triangle has two equal sides?

17. One angle of a triangle measures 135°. What kind of triangle is it?

Write the name of each quadrilateral.

18. **19.** **20.**

Write the name of each solid figure.

21. **22.** **23.** **24.**

25. What is the name of a prism that has squares for all of its faces?

Use your protractor to help you measure these angles:

26. 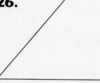 **27.**

28. What kind of angle is in question 26?

29. What kind of angle is in question 27?

Use a protractor to help you construct angles with these measurements:

30. 15°   **33.** 70°

31. 125°   **34.** 45°

32. 180°   **35.** 90°

Test-Taking Tip

When you prepare for a test that will require you to use tools such as a ruler or a protractor, practice with them before the test. Remember to bring the tools with you to the test.

Metric Measurement

Many countries use the metric system as their official standard of measurement. Americans are becoming more familiar with these units of measurement. People buy soda in liter bottles. Mechanics use metric tools to fix cars and equipment with metric measurements. Scientists use the metric system for doing experiments and measuring substances. In this age of worldwide communication and trade, understanding the metric system is useful.

In Chapter 8, you will learn how to make measurements using the metric system.

Goals for Learning

◆ To measure line segments to the nearest tenth of a centimeter (nearest millimeter)

◆ To estimate accurately the best unit for measuring a distance

◆ To change from one metric unit to another

◆ To find area measured in square units

◆ To find volume measured in cubic units

◆ To find volume, or capacity, measured in liters

Customary

Ordinary

Metric system

A system of measuring using the gram, liter, and meter as basic units

Meter, m

Measure of length about equal to the height of a doorknob

Liter, L

Measure of capacity about equal to the capacity of a coffee can

Gram, g

Measure of mass about equal to the weight of a paper clip

Prefix

Set of letters placed before a unit of measure

In the **customary** system of measurement, conversions from one unit to another are difficult because the units are so different. There are 5,280 feet in a mile, 16 ounces in a pound, 2 cups in a pint, and 36 inches in a yard. Also, the units of measure are not easily related to each other. One gallon of water weighs about 8.345 pounds.

In the **metric system,** however, the measurement units are all powers of ten. Units are easily related to each other. One liter of water weighs one kilogram.

The **meter** is used to measure length. The **liter** is used to measure capacity. The **gram** is used to measure mass or weight. Other units are named by adding these **prefixes** to meter, liter, and gram.

Prefix	Value	Symbol	Example
kilo	one thousand	k	kilometer
hecto	one hundred	h	hectometer
deka	ten	da	dekagram
deci	one-tenth	d	decimeter
centi	one-hundredth	c	centigram
milli	one-thousandth	m	milliliter

Kilo-, centi-, and milli- are the prefixes used most often in the metric system.

Sometimes deka is spelled deca.

Exercise A Give the correct name for each measurement described. Use the chart above to help you.

1. What is one-tenth of a liter called?
2. What number does the symbol *d* stand for?
3. What symbol means one thousand?
4. How many meters are in a dekameter?
5. Which prefix means one hundred?
6. What is one-thousandth of a gram called?
7. What symbol means one-hundredth?
8. How many liters are in a hectoliter?
9. How many grams are in a milligram?
10. What number does the symbol *c* stand for?

Centimeter, cm

A measure of length about equal to the width of a large paper clip

Millimeter, mm

Measure of length about equal to the width of the wire in a paper clip

The basic unit of length in the metric system is the meter. The distance from the floor to a doorknob is about one meter.

Some lengths are too short to measure in meters. We use the **centimeter** and **millimeter** for these shorter lengths. A centimeter is about the width of a large paper clip. A millimeter is about the thickness of the wire used to make the paper clip.

Look at the drawing of a metric ruler below. Each of the numbered spaces is one centimeter in length. Each of the small spaces is one millimeter in length.

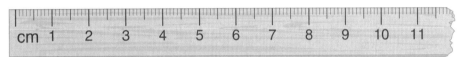

cm 1 2 3 4 5 6 7 8 9 10 11

Often, we want to give measurements as parts of a centimeter.

EXAMPLES   If a line is 8 centimeters and 4 millimeters long, then we say that it is 8.4 cm long.

8 cm + 4 mm ⟶ 8.4 cm

If an object is 9 centimeters and 6 millimeters long, then we say that it is 9.6 centimeters long.

9 cm + 6 mm ⟶ 9.6 cm

Rulers often show customary lengths on one side and metric lengths on the other.

Exercise A Use a metric ruler. Measure each line segment to the nearest centimeter and to the nearest millimeter.

1. ————————————————————————————

2. ————————————————

3. ——————————————————————

4. ——

5. ——————————————

Exercise B Measure the lengths of these bars to the nearest tenth of a centimeter.

1. [ ]

2. [ ]

3. [ ]

4. [ ]

5. [ ]

Exercise C How far is it from the beginning of the ruler to each arrow? Give your measurements to the nearest tenth of a centimeter. For example, the distance to the arrow marked with the letter A is 6.3 cm.

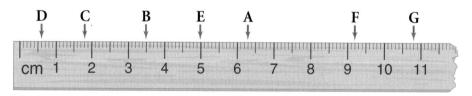

Kilometer, km
A distance of 1,000 meters, or a little more than a half mile

A centimeter is about the width of your little finger.

Use meters to measure things like the length of material for a dress, the length and width of your yard, and the height of a building.

Centimeters are used to measure shorter lengths like desktops and picture frames.

Millimeters are used for measuring very small things and when accurate measurements are needed. Wire sizes, nuts, bolts, and film are all measured in millimeters.

Long distances are measured with the **kilometer.** A kilometer is about five city blocks long. It takes about ten minutes to walk one kilometer.

Exercise A Choose the best measurement for each of these distances.

1. Height of a building
   396 mm   396 cm   396 m   396 km

2. Length of your classroom
   6 mm   6 cm   6 m   6 km

3. Length of a grasshopper
   63 mm   63 cm   63 m   63 km

4. Length of a piece of chalk
   6 mm   6 cm   6 m   6 km

5. Distance between two cities
   72 mm   72 cm   72 m   72 km

6. Length of your foot
   23 mm   23 cm   23 m   23 km

Conversion factor

Number you multiply by to change to another unit of measure

To change from one metric unit to another, multiply or divide by 10, 100, or 1,000. Since these **conversion factors** are all powers of 10, you can think of moving the decimal point to the right or left instead of actually multiplying or dividing.

$$1 \text{ kilometer} = 1,000 \text{ meters}$$
$$1 \text{ meter} = 100 \text{ centimeters}$$
$$1 \text{ centimeter} = 10 \text{ millimeters}$$
$$1 \text{ meter} = 1,000 \text{ millimeters}$$

Notice that kilometer is the largest unit. The next largest is meter, followed by centimeter, and then millimeter.

EXAMPLES   To change meters to centimeters, multiply by 100 or move the decimal point 2 places to the right.

m ___2___ cm

6.3 m = 630. cm

To change centimeters to meters, divide by 100 or move the decimal point 2 places to the left.

m ___2___ cm

84 cm = 0.84 m

Exercise A Use the chart to help you fill in the missing numbers.

1. 348 cm = ____ m

2. 784 m = ____ km

3. 56 cm = ____ mm

4. 82 m = ____ cm

5. 57 cm = ____ m

6. 43 mm = ____ cm

7. 6 m = ____ mm

8. 5 km = ____ m

9. 4.8 cm = ____ mm

10. 43.6 cm = ____ m

11. 5.23 km = ____ m

12. 586 mm = ____ m

13. 16.5 m = ____ km

14. 9.6 cm = ____ mm

15. 1,870 mm = ____ m

16. 4,280 cm = ____ m

17. 0.036 km = ____ cm

18. 5.2 m = ____ cm

When working with measurements of length, it is important to express all of the measurements in the same units. If they are not in the same units, you must change them to the same units before you can work with them.

EXAMPLE

km __3__ m __2__ cm __1__ mm

0.38 km + 12 m + 335 cm = _____ m

380 m + 12 m + 3.35 m

380
12
+   3.35
395.35 m

Exercise B Find the answers to these addition problems.

1. 42 cm + 6.5 cm + 95 cm = ___ cm

2. 58 mm + 8 cm + 37 mm = ___ mm

3. 64 m + 168 cm + 12 m = ___ m

4. 43 cm + 92 mm + 87 cm = ___ cm

5. 18 km + 7 km + 4380 m = ___ km

Exercise C Find the distance around the sides of these polygons in centimeters.

1.

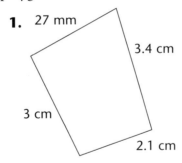

27 mm
3.4 cm
3 cm
2.1 cm

2.

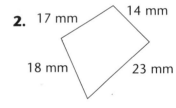

17 mm
14 mm
18 mm
23 mm

3.

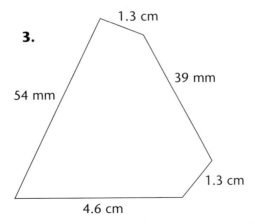

1.3 cm
39 mm
54 mm
1.3 cm
4.6 cm

The **area** of a shape is the amount of space inside the shape. Area is measured in **square units** such as square millimeters (**mm²**), square centimeters (**cm²**), square meters (**m²**), and square kilometers (**km²**). Here are the actual sizes of two of these square units.

1 square millimeter
1 mm²

1 square centimeter
1 cm²

The area of this rectangle is 10 cm².

You can find the area of a rectangle by multiplying the **length** by the **width.**

$$\text{Area} = \text{length} \times \text{width}$$

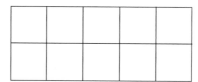

EXAMPLE

32 m

20 m

A = l × w
A = 32 × 20
A = 640

The area is 640 m².

Area, A

The amount of space inside a shape

Square unit

A measure of area

mm²

Square millimeter

cm²

Square centimeter

m²

Square meter

km²

Square kilometer

Length, l

Distance from end to end

Width, w

The distance across

Exercise A Find the area of each rectangle. Remember to include the proper units in each answer.

1.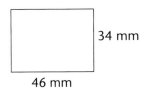
34 mm
46 mm

2.
15 cm
3 cm

3. 18 cm
24 cm

4. 2 cm
0.9 cm

5. 15 m
12 m

6. 8 km
7 km

7. 5.6 m
4 m

8.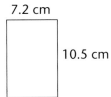
7.2 cm
10.5 cm

9.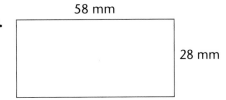
58 mm
28 mm

10.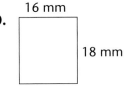
16 mm
18 mm

11.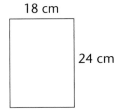
43 cm
37 cm

12.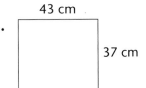
20 km
15 km

13.
14 km
6.5 km

14.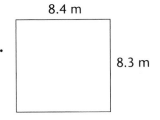
8.4 m
8.3 m

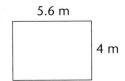

Exercise B Solve these word problems. In some of them, you must change the units so that they are all the same before you work the problem.

1. Yumi wants to fence in her yard. She measured her property and found that its sides were 27 m, 35 m, 28 m, and 39 m. How many meters of fence will she need?

2. Kaleena is buying some carpeting that costs $12.50 per m². How much will a 4 m by 5 m carpet cost?

3. Michelle measured a picture that she wants to frame. She found that the two long sides were each 82 cm. The other two sides were each 75 cm long. How many meters of framing should she buy?

4. Jesse is fencing in his pasture. It measures 180 m long and 173 m wide. How many meters of fence should Jesse buy?

5. Alonzo is carpeting three rooms. They measure 8 m by 7 m, 4 m by 5 m, and 3.5 m by 4.5 m. How many square meters of carpet does he need?

6. Juanita is training for the swimming meet. The last five days she swam 4.2 km, 520 m, 3 km, 1,280 m, and 2.8 km. How many meters did she swim altogether?

7. Enuma planned to hike 85 km in 6 days. On Monday she hiked 15 km. Tuesday she hiked 14.8 km. On Wednesday she had sore feet, so she walked only 2,400 m. Thursday and Friday Enuma hiked 16.4 km each day. How many kilometers must she hike on Saturday if she is to finish the 85 km?

8. Lucas and his team rowed 2.4 km on Tuesday and 4,800 m on Thursday. These were the only two days they rowed this week. What is the total number of meters Lucas and his team rowed?

Volume

Number of cubic units that fill a container

Cubic units

Units used to measure volume

mm^3

Cubic millimeter

cm^3

Cubic centimeter

m^3

Cubic meter

Volume is measured with **cubic units.** The most commonly used units are the cubic millimeter (**mm^3**), the cubic centimeter (**cm^3**), and the cubic meter (**m^3**).

1 cubic millimeter

1 cubic centimeter

You can think of finding the volume of a rectangular prism as filling the inside of the box. You might wish to sketch a rectangular prism to see what you are trying to calculate. To find the volume, you would multiply the length times the width times the height. The result is measured in cubic units.

$$\text{Volume} = \text{length} \times \text{width} \times \text{height}$$

EXAMPLE   Find the volume of a rectangular prism having a length of 2 cm, a width of 2 cm, and a height of 3 cm.

Volume = length × width × height
V = 2 cm × 2 cm × 3 cm

The volume is 2 × 2 × 3, or 12 cm^3.

Try This

Estimate the number of marbles that would fit into a box that is 10 cm by 10 cm by 10 cm. Estimate the number of these boxes that could be placed next to each other along the front and side of your classroom and stacked up to the ceiling. Use these estimates to guess how many marbles it would take to fill your classroom.

Exercise A Find the volume of each rectangular prism.

1.

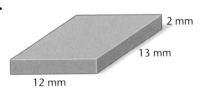

2 cm
3 cm
6 cm

7.

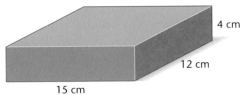

4 cm
12 cm
15 cm

2.

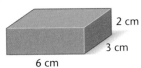

2 mm
13 mm
12 mm

8.

9 cm
8 cm
1 cm

3.

7 m
12 m
3 m

9.

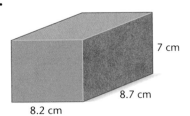

7 cm
8.7 cm
8.2 cm

4.

10 cm
11 cm
9 cm

10.

0.7 m
5.2 m
4 m

5.

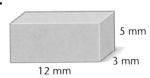

5 mm
3 mm
12 mm

11.

11 mm
11 mm
11 mm

6.

11 m
5 m
5 m

12.

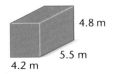

4.8 m
5.5 m
4.2 m

Exercise B Answer these questions about volume. Be sure to include the units in your answers.

1. A rectangular cake pan measures 20 cm by 15 cm by 8 cm. What is its volume?

2. An aquarium measures 60 cm by 40 cm and is 30 cm high. How many cubic centimeters of water does it hold?

3. Two guppies can live in 1,000 cm^3 of water. How many guppies can live in the aquarium in problem 2?

4. A swimming pool has an average depth of 1.7 m. It is 50 m long and 30 m wide. What is its volume?

5. How many cubic meters of air are in a room that measures 4 meters by 3 meters and is 2.5 meters high?

6. How much dirt is needed to fill in a hole that measures 4 meters by 3.2 meters by 3 meters?

7. A banquet hall measures 15 meters by 12 meters and is 2.7 meters high. How many cubic meters of air does it hold?

8. Two cubic meters of air space per person are required. How many people will the hall in problem 7 hold?

9. Another banquet hall measures 18 meters by 9 meters. It is also 2.7 meters high. How many cubic meters of air does it hold?

10. Two cubic meters of air are required for each person. How many people will the hall in problem 9 hold?

Calculator Practice

Use your calculator to find the volume of a rectangular prism.

EXAMPLE Find the volume of this rectangular prism.

length (l) = 3 mm
width (w) = 5.5 mm
height (h) = 7 mm

Volume = l × w × h

Press 3 ☒ 5.5 ☒ 7 =
The display reads 115.5.

Volume is measured in cubic units, so the volume is 115.5 mm³.

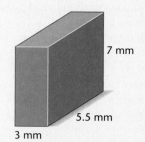

Calculator Exercise Use a calculator to find the volume of each rectangular prism. Round your answers to the nearest whole number. Express each volume in cubic units.

1. l = 23.5 m
   w = 14 m
   h = 2.3 m

2. l = 5 m
   w = 3 m
   h = 2.7 m

3. l = 5.6 m
   w = 2 m
   h = 3.2 m

4. l = 8 mm
   w = 0.3 mm
   h = 0.5 mm

5. l = 9.6 cm
   w = 1.3 cm
   h = 0.5 cm

6. l = 26.2 m
   w = 4.5 m
   h = 7.23 m

7. l = 2.3 mm
   w = 0.5 mm
   h = 10 mm

8. l = 1.3 mm
   w = 1 mm
   h = 5 mm

9. l = 4 cm
   w = 1.1 cm
   h = 3 cm

10. l = 8.2 cm
    w = 4.6 cm
    h = 5.8 cm

Capacity

The amount a container will hold when full

Milliliter, mL

Measure of capacity about equal to that of an eye dropper

Kiloliter, kL

Measure of capacity about equal to that of a small wading pool

Volume, or **capacity,** is also measured in liters (L). Both liquid and dry measurements are given in liters. Smaller amounts are measured in **milliliters** (mL). Large amounts are measured in **kiloliters** (kL).

A milliliter is equal to one cubic centimeter (cm^3). Two aspirin tablets take up about 1 mL of space. Perfume, flavor extracts, and medicine are all measured in milliliters.

A liter is equal to 1,000 cubic centimeters, or 1,000 mL. Two large juice boxes hold about 1 liter of liquid. A one-pound coffee can holds 1 liter of coffee. Liters are used to measure such things as paint, soda, and gasoline.

A kiloliter is equal to 1 cubic meter, or 1,000 liters. A king-size water bed holds about 1 kiloliter of water. Kiloliters are used to measure large amounts. The capacity of a tank truck might be measured in kiloliters.

PROBLEM SOLVING

Exercise A Tell whether you would use milliliters, liters, or kiloliters to measure each item.

1. A large bottle of soda
2. Oil in a delivery truck
3. A dose of medicine
4. A carton of ice cream
5. A carton of milk served with a school lunch
6. Punch in a bowl
7. Water in a tank at the National Aquarium
8. Amount of paint in a can
9. Water in a car's cooling system
10. A glass of lemonade
11. Water in an Olympic-sized pool

12. A bottle of perfume
13. Gas for a car
14. Annual orange juice production in Florida
15. Baking powder in a recipe for biscuits
16. Oil in a recipe for salad dressing
17. Milk drunk by a family in a week
18. Water in a town's reservoir
19. Vanilla extract used in making a cake
20. Amount of soda in a six-pack

Convert

Change to an equivalent measure

Two large glasses of milk would be about one liter.

The units of capacity that are most often used are milliliters, liters, and kiloliters. To **convert** between units of capacity, we can use a similar chart to the one we used to convert between meters, centimeters, millimeters, and kilometers.

$$1 \text{ kiloliter} = 1{,}000 \text{ liters}$$
$$1 \text{ liter} = 100 \text{ centiliters}$$
$$1 \text{ centiliter} = 10 \text{ milliliters}$$
$$1 \text{ liter} = 1{,}000 \text{ milliliters}$$

EXAMPLES   To change L to kL, divide by 1,000 or move the decimal point 3 places to the left.

kL __3__ L __2__ cL __1__ mL

786 L = 0.786 kL

To change L to mL, multiply by 1,000 or move the decimal point 3 places to the right.

kL __3__ L __2__ cL __1__ mL

7.6 L = 7,600 mL

Exercise A Use the chart above to help you fill in the missing numbers.

1. 4,700 mL = ____ L

2. 8.2 kL = ____ L

3. 480 L = ____ kL

4. 3.2 cL = ____ mL

5. 17,000 mL = ____ kL

6. 0.005 kL = ____ cL

7. 0.0042 L = ____ mL

8. 1.36 cL = ____ L

9. 5.36 L = ____ mL

10. 6 mL = ____ L

Technology Connection

We use metric measurements many places in our lives. Metric measurements are used with film for our cameras, prescription drugs, and groceries. Make a list of as many examples of metric measurements as you can think of. Notice how many of them are related to technology.

EXAMPLE Find the capacity of this rectangular prism in liters.

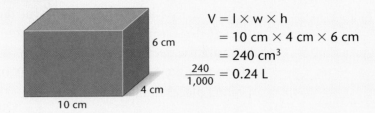

$$V = l \times w \times h$$
$$= 10 \text{ cm} \times 4 \text{ cm} \times 6 \text{ cm}$$
$$= 240 \text{ cm}^3$$
$$\frac{240}{1,000} = 0.24 \text{ L}$$

Divide 240 cm³ by 1,000 to find the capacity.
The capacity is 0.24 liters.

Exercise B Find the capacity of these rectangular prisms in liters. Remember that 1 liter (L) = 1,000 cubic centimeters (cm³). To find the volume you must multiply length by width by height. Then divide by 1,000 to find the capacity.

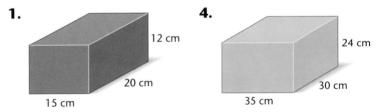

1. 12 cm, 20 cm, 15 cm

4. 24 cm, 30 cm, 35 cm

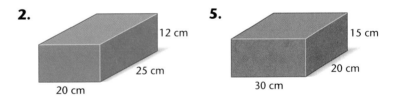

2. 12 cm, 25 cm, 20 cm

5. 15 cm, 20 cm, 30 cm

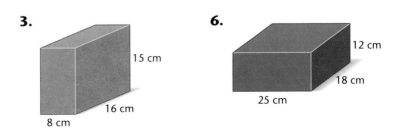

3. 15 cm, 16 cm, 8 cm

6. 12 cm, 18 cm, 25 cm

To change liters (L) to deciliters (dL), multiply by 10, or move the decimal point 1 place to the right. To change deciliters (dL) to liters (L), divide by 10, or move the decimal point 1 place to the left. To change milliliters (mL) to liters (L), divide by 1,000, or move the decimal point 3 places to the left. To change liters (L) to milliliters (mL), multiply by 1,000, or move the decimal point 3 places to the right.

$$1 \text{ kiloliter} = 1,000 \text{ liters}$$
$$1 \text{ liter} = 100 \text{ centiliters}$$
$$1 \text{ centiliter} = 10 \text{ milliliters}$$
$$1 \text{ liter} = 1,000 \text{ milliliters}$$

EXAMPLE How much does 2.5 L of oil cost if 2,000 mL costs $3.85?

Step 1 Convert 2.5 L to mL. (In this case, you're going from a larger to smaller unit, so you multiply. You know from the chart that there are 1,000 mL in 1 liter.)

1,000	Number of mL in 1 L
× 2.5	Number of L
2,500	Number of mL in 2.5 L

Step 2 Set up a proportion.
$$\$\frac{3.85}{2,000} = \frac{n}{2,500}$$

Step 3 Cross-multiply to find n.
$$\frac{\$3.85 \times 2,500}{2,000} = n \qquad \frac{9,625}{2,000} = n \qquad \$4.81 = n$$

PROBLEM SOLVING

Exercise C Solve these word problems.

1. Bob wants to buy 150 dL of soda. If 7.65 L costs $9.40, then how much will he pay for 150 dL?

2. If 3.78 liters of cranberry juice costs $6.95, then how much will Niki pay for 7.56 liters?

3. If 20 mL of medicine costs $2.00 to produce, then how much does 1 L cost?

4. Siri buys 180 milliliters of lotion for $5.00. She divides the lotion evenly among 10 smaller bottles. How many milliliters are in each bottle? How many deciliters?

5. If Tony purchases 10 mL of oil at $3.00 for 100 milliliters, then how much will Tony pay?

Mass
Measure of matter
Weight
A measure of the heaviness of an object
Milligram, mg
Measure of mass about equal to $\frac{1}{10}$ of a grain of rice
Kilogram, kg
Measure of mass about equal to the weight of four rolls of quarters

Mass is measured in grams.

The **mass** of an object is the quantity of matter in the object. The **weight** of an object is the force of Earth's gravitational pull on the mass of the object. Because the mass and the weight of an object are nearly the same when you are at Earth's surface, people use the term weight when they are talking about mass.

Milligrams, grams, and **kilograms** are used to measure weight. Milligrams are used to measure small amounts of medicine and the amount of nutrients in food. An uncooked grain of rice is about 10 milligrams.

A gram is the weight of 1 cubic centimeter of water. A large paper clip weighs about 1 gram. Grams are used to measure the weight of things like the boxes of food that you buy in a grocery store. A dollar bill is about 1 gram.

A kilogram is the weight of 1 liter of water. Two dozen medium eggs weigh about 1 kilogram. Kilograms are used to measure heavier things, like a person's weight, cuts of meat, and the weight of a bag of sugar or flour. Four rolls of quarters are about 1 kilogram.

Exercise A Choose the best measurement for each of these weights.

1. An egg
  50 mg   50 g   50 kg

2. A watermelon
  14 mg   14 g   14 kg

3. Amount of sodium in a bowl of cereal
  180 mg   180 g   180 kg

4. A box of breakfast flakes
  480 mg   480 g   480 kg

5. A plastic straw
  500 mg   500 g   500 kg

6. A high school student
  42 mg   42 g   42 kg

7. An aspirin
  235 mg   235 g   235 kg

8. A nickel
  5 mg   5 g   5 kg

9. A sack of onions
  2.3 mg   2.3 g   2.3 kg

10. A postage stamp
  14 mg   14 g   14 kg

The units of mass that are most often used are the milligram, the gram, and the kilogram. The centigram is almost never used.

$$1 \text{ kilogram} = 1,000 \text{ grams}$$
$$1 \text{ gram} = 100 \text{ centigrams}$$
$$1 \text{ centigram} = 10 \text{ milligrams}$$
$$1 \text{ gram} = 1,000 \text{ milligrams}$$

EXAMPLES   To change from mg to g, divide by 1,000 or move the decimal point 3 places to the left.

kg __3__ g __2__ cg __1__ mg

78,000 mg = 78 g

To change from kg to cg, multiply by 100,000 or move the decimal point 5 places to the right.

kg __3__ g __2__ cg __1__ mg

0.007 kg = 700 cg

Exercise A   Fill in the missing numbers.

1. 3,000 g = ___ kg

2. 0.005 g = ___ mg

3. 42 mg = ___ g

4. 0.36 kg = ___ g

5. 12 g = ___ cg

6. 0.24 cg = ___ mg

7. 82 mg = ___ g

8. 1,200 g = ___ kg

9. 0.00007 kg = ___ mg

10. 1.08 g = ___ cg

We know that 1 liter of water weighs 1 kilogram and that 1 liter is the same as 1,000 cubic centimeters. This means that 1,000 cm³ of water weighs 1 kilogram.

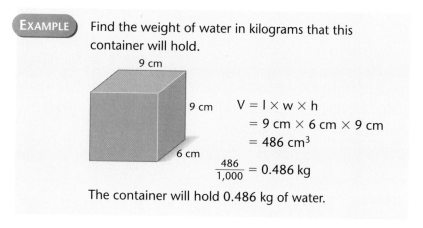

EXAMPLE Find the weight of water in kilograms that this container will hold.

9 cm

9 cm

6 cm

$V = l \times w \times h$
$= 9 \text{ cm} \times 6 \text{ cm} \times 9 \text{ cm}$
$= 486 \text{ cm}^3$

$\frac{486}{1,000} = 0.486 \text{ kg}$

The container will hold 0.486 kg of water.

Exercise B Find the weight of water in kilograms that each container will hold.

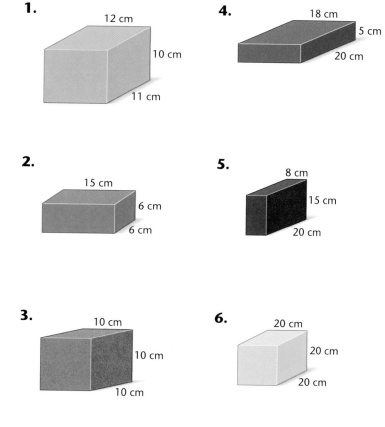

1.
12 cm
10 cm
11 cm

4.
18 cm
5 cm
20 cm

2.
15 cm
6 cm
6 cm

5.
8 cm
15 cm
20 cm

3.
10 cm
10 cm
10 cm

6.
20 cm
20 cm
20 cm

On the Fast Track

Track and field is one of the most popular sports in the world. Track events are races. Field events include jumping and throwing. The International Amateur Athletic Federation (IAAF) is the governing body of international track-and-field events. The IAAF only recognizes world records in metric distances, except for the mile run.

 EXAMPLE According to IAAF rules, an indoor running track should be 200 meters per lap. Races on an indoor track may measure from 50 to 5,000 meters. How many laps around the track are there in a 5,000-meter race?

Step 1 Find facts to solve the problem. 5,000-meter race, 200-meter track

Step 2 Write and solve an equation. 5,000 ÷ 200 = 25

Step 3 Write the answer. There are 25 laps in a 5,000-meter race.

Exercise Solve each problem.

1. Most modern outdoor tracks are 400 meters per lap. If a runner went around a 400-meter track 25 times, how long was the race?

2. Outdoor tracks are divided into 6 or 8 lanes. How wide is a track with 8 lanes if each lane is 1.25 meters wide?

3. Walking races are long-distance. How many kilometers long is a 30,000-meter walking race?

4. Hurdle races are events in which athletes run and jump over obstacles. Men's high hurdles are 107 cm high. The women's high hurdles are 84 cm high. How much higher are the men's hurdles than the women's hurdles?

5. If an athlete can walk a 5,000-meter race in 20 minutes, how many meters are walked per minute? Per second?

Chapter 8 R E V I E W

Write the letter of the best answer to each question.

1. Which unit would be best for measuring the length of a bus?
   A millimeter
   B centimeter
   C meter
   D kilometer

2. How many centimeters are there in 600 meters?
   A 6
   B 600
   C 6,000
   D 60,000

3. Find the area of the rectangle below:
   A 8,772 mm²
   B 394 mm²
   C 197 mm²
   D 61 mm²

   68 mm

   129 mm

4. A box measures 33 cm by 25 cm by 16 cm. What is its volume?
   A 39,600 cm³
   B 13,200 cm³
   C 222 cm³
   D 74 cm³

5. What is the volume in liters of a container measuring 6 cm by 8 cm by 16 cm?
   A 0.0768 L
   B 0.768 L
   C 7.68 L
   D 76.8 L

Measure these line segments to the nearest tenth of a centimeter:

6. ───────────────

7. ─────────

How far is it from the beginning of the ruler to each arrow? Give the answer to the nearest millimeter.

8.   **9.**   **10.**

Tell which is the best measurement for these distances:

11. The width of a kitchen

    4 mm   4 cm   4 m   4 km

12. The length of an adult's arm

    65 mm   65 cm   65 m   65 km

Fill in the missing numbers:

13. 37 cm = ___ mm

14. 1,200 g = ___ kg

15. 820 mL = ___ L

16. 500 mg = ___ g

17. 8.1 kL = ___ L

Find the answers to these problems:

18.   48 cm
       37 mm
    + 39 cm

19.   54 mm
       4.6 cm
       2.9 cm
    + 38 mm

Find the answers to the following questions:

20. What is the area of Yvette's yard if it measures 50 meters by 37 meters?

21. What is the volume of this rectangular prism in liters?

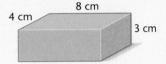

22. A swimming pool has an average depth of 1.6 m. It is 50 m long and 30 m wide. What is its volume?

23. What is the area of this rectangle?

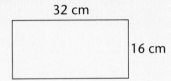

Tell whether you should use milliliters, liters, or kiloliters to measure each.

24. The amount of vanilla extract in a recipe

25. The amount of punch in a punch bowl

Tell whether you should use milligrams, grams, or kilograms to measure these weights:

26. A tenth-grade student

27. A postage stamp

28. A vitamin tablet

29. An apple

30. A truck

Test-Taking Tip

Once you have finished reviewing the chapter, try writing your own test problems with a partner. Then complete each other's tests and double-check your answers.

Customary Measurement

Measuring things is a necessary everyday activity. We measure ingredients to cook, material to sew, and courts and fields to play games. Because things are measured in many ways, we use many units of measurement. Whether we find how many gallons of gas are needed to make a trip or how much lumber is needed to build a house, knowing how to measure is a valuable skill.

In Chapter 9, you will learn about customary American units for measuring capacity, weight, length, width, area, and volume.

Goals for Learning

◆ To convert units of liquid capacity

◆ To convert units of weight

◆ To use a ruler to help you measure line segments

◆ To convert units of length and distance

◆ To find the perimeter of a given shape

◆ To calculate the area within a shape

◆ To compute the volume within a prism

Pint	The most frequently used units of liquid capacity are listed below.

Pint

Measure of liquid capacity

Fluid ounce

Unit of liquid capacity equal to $\frac{1}{16}$ of a pint

Quart

Measure of liquid capacity

Gallon

Unit of liquid capacity

The most frequently used units of liquid capacity are listed below.

1 **pint** = 16 **fluid ounces**
1 **quart** = 2 pints
1 **quart** = 32 fluid ounces
1 **gallon** = 4 quarts

When you convert a large unit to smaller units, you multiply. When you convert small units to a larger unit, you divide.

EXAMPLES

2 pints = ____ ounces
2 pints = _32_ ounces

$$\begin{array}{r} 16 \\ \times\ 2 \\ \hline 32 \end{array}$$

28 quarts = ____ gallons
28 quarts = _7_ gallons

$$4\overline{)28}\ \ ^{7}$$

Exercise A Make these conversions.

Multiply:

1. 3 quarts = ___ pints

2. 6 gallons = ___ quarts

3. 2 gallons = ___ pints

4. 5 pints = ___ ounces

5. 9 pints = ___ ounces

Divide:

6. 8 pints = ___ gallons

7. 12 pints = ___ quarts

8. 16 quarts = ___ gallons

9. 144 ounces = ___ pints

10. 20 quarts = ___ gallons

Exercise B Make these conversions. Decide whether to multiply or divide for each one.

1. 80 ounces = ___ pints

2. 8 gallons = ___ quarts

3. 3 quarts = ___ ounces

4. 6 pints = ___ quarts

5. 13 pints = ___ ounces

6. 7 quarts = ___ pints

7. 44 quarts = ___ gallons

8. 64 ounces = ___ quarts

9. 128 ounces = ___ pints

10. 6 gallons = ___ pints

Ounce
Unit of weight equal to $\frac{1}{16}$ of a pound

The weight of various objects is measured in **ounces,** pounds, or tons.

$$1 \text{ pound} = 16 \text{ ounces}$$
$$1 \text{ ton} = 2{,}000 \text{ pounds}$$

To convert a large unit to smaller units, you multiply.
To convert a small unit to larger units, you divide.

EXAMPLES

7 tons = _____ pounds
7 tons = 14,000 pounds

$$\begin{array}{r} 2{,}000 \\ \times \quad 7 \\ \hline 14{,}000 \end{array}$$

32 ounces = _____ pounds
32 ounces = __2__ pounds

$$16 \overline{)\,32}^{\,2}$$

Exercise A Make these conversions.

Multiply:

1. 5 tons = ____ pounds
2. 8 pounds = ____ ounces
3. 8 tons = ____ ounces
4. 12 pounds = ____ ounces
5. 18 tons = ____ pounds

Divide:

6. 144 ounces = ____ pounds
7. 18,000 pounds = ____ tons
8. 80 ounces = ____ pounds
9. 5,000 pounds = ____ tons
10. 192 ounces = ____ pounds

Exercise B Make these conversions. Decide whether to multiply or divide for each one.

1. 32 ounces = ____ pounds
2. 3 pounds = ____ ounces
3. 5 tons = ____ pounds
4. 176 ounces = ____ pounds
5. 50,000 pounds = ____ tons
6. 20 ounces = ____ pounds

To measure with a standard ruler, you need to know what each division on the ruler means. One inch may be divided into different parts.

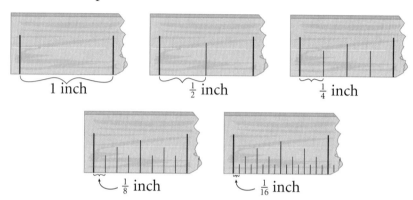

Notice that the denominator of the fraction is always equal to the number of parts that the inch is divided into.

Exercise A Number your paper from 1 to 10. Use a ruler to help you measure the length of each line segment shown below.

1. ———————————————

2. ——————————————————

3. ———————

4. ————————————————————————

5. ——————————————————

6. ————————————————

7. ——————————————————————

8. —————————

9. ———————————

10. ——————————

Exercise B Use a ruler to help you draw line segments of these lengths on another sheet of paper.

1. 4 inches

2. $2\frac{3}{4}$ inches

3. $7\frac{7}{8}$ inches

4. $2\frac{5}{8}$ inches

5. $6\frac{1}{4}$ inches

6. $3\frac{1}{2}$ inches

7. $2\frac{3}{16}$ inches

8. $5\frac{2}{4}$ inches

9. $4\frac{1}{4}$ inches

10. $1\frac{3}{8}$ inches

11. $5\frac{6}{16}$ inches

12. $\frac{3}{4}$ inch

13. $\frac{6}{8}$ inch

14. $\frac{1}{4}$ inch

15. $1\frac{3}{4}$ inches

16. $6\frac{5}{8}$ inches

Carpenters and other building professionals make careful measurements to make sure a project is done correctly.

Linear measurement

The length of a line between fixed points

Measurement of length and distance is often called **linear measurement.** Linear measurement is "straight line" measurement. The most commonly used units of linear measurement are shown below. When you convert a large unit to smaller units, you multiply. When you convert a small unit to a larger unit, you divide.

1 foot = 12 inches
1 yard = 36 inches
1 yard = 3 feet
1 mile = 5,280 feet

EXAMPLES

4 yards = ____ inches
4 yards = _144_ inches

$$\begin{array}{r} 36 \\ \times\ \ 4 \\ \hline 144 \end{array}$$

60 inches = ____ feet
60 inches = _5_ feet

$$12\overline{)60}\ \ ^5$$

Exercise A Convert these units of length and distance.

Divide:

1. 60 inches = ____ feet

2. 120 inches = ____ feet

3. 31,680 feet = ____ miles

4. 48 feet = ____ yards

5. 384 inches = ____ feet

6. 15,840 feet = ____ yards

7. 600 inches = ____ feet

8. 135 feet = ____ yards

Multiply:

9. 7 feet = ____ inches

10. 8 yards = ____ feet

11. 2 miles = ____ feet

12. 33 miles = ____ feet

13. 5 feet = ____ inches

14. 27 feet = ____ inches

15. 3 yards = ____ feet

16. 4 miles = ____ feet

When you add or subtract units of measure, you line up the like units. You may need to simplify your answer. Before you can subtract, you may need to rename or borrow.

Rewrite the problem in vertical form.

EXAMPLE   3 yards 7 inches + 2 yards 1 foot 8 inches

>   3 yards   7 inches
>   + 2 yards 1 foot   8 inches
>   ─────────────────────────────
>   5 yards 1 foot 15 inches = 5 yards 2 feet 3 inches

Exercise A Rewrite in vertical form and add. Simplify your answers.

1. 3 yards 2 feet + 5 yards 3 feet
2. 6 yards 2 feet + 7 yards 1 foot
3. 8 feet 6 inches + 2 feet 5 inches
4. 12 feet 7 inches + 5 feet 6 inches
5. 13 yards 2 feet + 4 feet 3 inches

EXAMPLE   7 feet 4 inches − 3 feet 7 inches

We cannot subtract the 7 from the 4, so we borrow 1 foot, or 12 inches, and add it to the 4 inches.

>   6   16
>   7̸ feet 4̸ inches
>   − 3 feet 7 inches
>   ──────────────────
>   3 feet 9 inches

Exercise B Rewrite in vertical form and subtract.

1. 8 feet 5 inches − 2 feet 6 inches
2. 12 feet 6 inches − 5 feet 8 inches
3. 13 yards 2 feet − 4 yards 1 foot
4. 8 yards 1 foot − 6 yards 2 feet
5. 12 feet 4 inches − 6 feet 8 inches

Exercise C Rewrite in vertical form and add or subtract. Remember to write your answers in simplest form.

1. 6 yards 3 feet 7 inches − 3 yards 2 feet 9 inches

2. 3 yards 5 feet 5 inches + 2 yards 5 feet 4 inches

3. 5 feet 3 inches − 2 feet 8 inches

4. 7 yards 2 feet 9 inches + 4 feet 7 inches

5. 8 yards 5 feet 3 inches + 3 yards 2 feet 8 inches

6. 7 feet 4 inches − 13 inches

7. 13 yards − 2 yards 5 feet 5 inches

8. 6 feet 7 inches + 5 feet 9 inches

9. 16 yards 1 foot 5 inches + 11 yards 2 feet 4 inches

10. 10 yards 6 inches − 2 feet 8 inches

11. 3 yards 4 feet 7 inches + 1 yard 4 feet 11 inches

12. 13 feet 9 inches − 2 yards 5 feet 4 inches

13. 4 yards 3 feet 4 inches + 5 yards 2 feet 9 inches

14. 14 yards − 3 yards 2 feet 7 inches

15. 7 yards 4 inches + 4 feet 7 inches

16. 11 yards 4 inches − 3 yards 2 feet 10 inches

17. 10 yards 1 foot 3 inches + 3 yards 2 feet 5 inches

When you multiply a measurement by a number, remember to multiply each part of the measurement by the number. You may need to simplify the answer.

EXAMPLES   3 times (4 feet 2 inches) = ■

```
      4 feet  2 inches
  ×          3
  ────────────────────
     12 feet  6 inches = 4 yards 6 inches
```

8 times (2 yards 3 feet 4 inches) = ■

```
      2 yards   3 feet    4 inches
  ×                          8
  ───────────────────────────────
    16 yards  24 feet  32 inches = 24 yards
                                    2 feet
                                    8 inches
```

Exercise D Rewrite each problem in vertical form and multiply. Simplify your answers.

1. 7 × (7 yards 3 feet 1 inch)
2. 3 × (2 feet 5 inches)
3. 5 × (1 foot 5 inches)
4. 6 × (5 yards 2 feet)
5. 4 × (9 yards 2 feet 2 inches)
6. 2 × (4 yards 13 feet 4 inches)
7. 8 × (7 feet 2 inches)
8. 5 × (3 yards 2 feet 6 inches)
9. 4 × (6 yards 5 feet 8 inches)
10. 12 × (9 yards 4 feet 3 inches)
11. 2 × (85 inches)
12. 3 × (9 feet 17 inches)

When you divide a measurement by a number, remember to divide each part of the measurement by the number. You may need to simplify the answer.

EXAMPLES (18 yards 10 feet) ÷ 2 = ■

$$\frac{18 \text{ yards } 10 \text{ feet}}{2} = 9 \text{ yards } 5 \text{ feet}$$

(20 yards 8 feet 8 inches) ÷ 4 = ■

$$\frac{20 \text{ yards } 8 \text{ feet } 8 \text{ inches}}{4} = 5 \text{ yards } 2 \text{ feet } 2 \text{ inches}$$

Exercise E Divide. Remember to simplify your answers.

1. (15 yards 10 feet) ÷ 5
2. (16 feet 8 inches) ÷ 2
3. (18 yards 9 inches) ÷ 9
4. (21 yards 18 feet 6 inches) ÷ 3
5. (33 feet 18 inches) ÷ 3
6. (12 yards 6 feet 9 inches) ÷ 3
7. (8 feet 10 inches) ÷ 2
8. (48 yards 24 feet 12 inches) ÷ 6
9. (45 yards 27 feet 9 inches) ÷ 3
10. (15 yards 25 feet 20 inches) ÷ 5

Perimeter

Distance around

The **perimeter** of a shape is the distance around the outside. The perimeter of a shape can be found by adding the lengths of all of the sides of the shape. Often when the opposite sides are equal, only one measurement is given for those two sides.

EXAMPLES

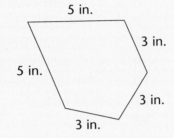

5 in.

3 in.

5 in.

3 in.

3 in.

$5 + 5 + 3 + 3 + 3 = 19$ inches

Perimeter = 19 inches

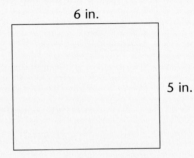

6 in.

5 in.

$6 + 5 + 6 + 5 = 22$ inches

Perimeter = 22 inches

Try This

Use graph paper to draw out the following activity. You can use triangles to estimate distances that you cannot measure directly. If you wanted to know the width of a river, you could pick a landmark directly across the river from you. Turn and take 20 steps along the riverbank. Place a stick at this spot. Walk 10 more steps in the same direction. Then walk away from the river until you get to the place where the stick is directly in line with your landmark. Count the steps back to the riverbank. The width of the river is twice this number of steps. Can you explain how this works?

Exercise A Find the perimeters.

1.

6 in.

7 in.

2.

5 in.

5 in.

8 in.

3.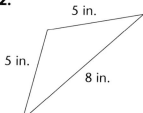

2 in.

2 in.

2 in.

2 in.

2 in.

2 in.

2 in.

2 in.

4.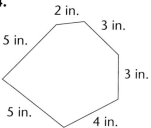

2 in.

3 in.

5 in.

3 in.

5 in.

4 in.

5.

10 in.

10 in.

10 in.

6.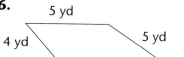

5 yd

4 yd

5 yd

4 yd

9 yd

7.

15 ft

14 ft

14 ft

8.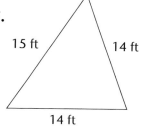

12 in.

8 in.

12 in.

9.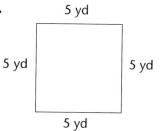

5 yd

5 yd

5 yd

5 yd

10.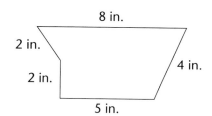

8 in.

2 in.

4 in.

2 in.

5 in.

Exercise B Find the perimeters.

1.

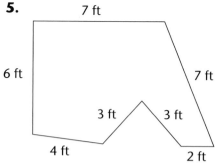

7 in.

3 in.

5.

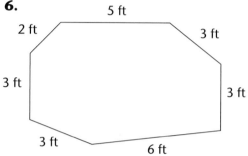

7 ft

6 ft   7 ft

3 ft   3 ft

4 ft   2 ft

2.

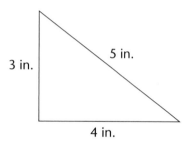

3 in.   5 in.

4 in.

6.

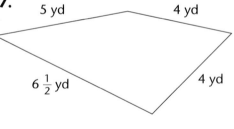

5 ft

2 ft   3 ft

3 ft   3 ft

3 ft   6 ft

3.

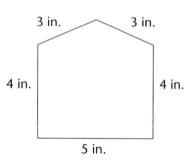

3 in.   3 in.

4 in.   4 in.

5 in.

7.

5 yd   4 yd

$6\frac{1}{2}$ yd   4 yd

4.

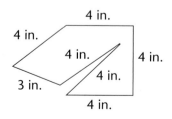

4 in.

4 in.

4 in.   4 in.

4 in.

3 in.   4 in.

8.

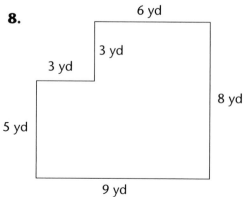

6 yd

3 yd

3 yd

5 yd   8 yd

9 yd

The area of a shape is the amount of space inside the shape. Area is measured in square units. The area of a rectangle can be found by multiplying the length times the width.

$$\text{Area} = \text{length} \times \text{width}$$

> Remember, area is the amount of space inside.

EXAMPLE   A rectangle is 8 units long and 4 units wide. What is the area of the rectangle?

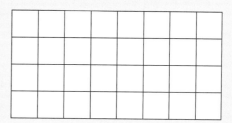

$$
\begin{aligned}
\text{Area} &= \text{length} \times \text{width} \\
&= 8 \text{ units} \times 4 \text{ units} \\
&= 32 \text{ square units}
\end{aligned}
$$

The length and the width of the rectangle must be given in the same units. If the units in the example had been inches, then the area would have been 32 square inches.

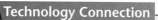

Technology Connection

Use the Internet to find the perimeter and area of the United States, Brazil, Mexico, China, and Spain. Record these measurements. Try to find the area and perimeter of these five countries at three other sites. Make a chart on a computer to record these measurements. Are the four perimeters the same for each country? Are the four areas the same for each country? Explain why the measurements could differ. Explain why they might be the same.

Exercise A Find the area of each rectangle. Include the proper units in each answer.

1.

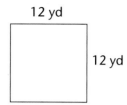

12 yd

12 yd

5.

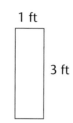

1 ft

3 ft

2.

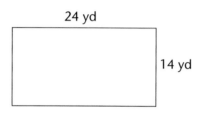

24 yd

14 yd

6.

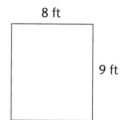

5 miles

4 miles

3.

55 ft

20 ft

7.

8 ft

9 ft

4.

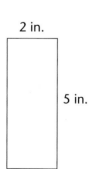

2 in.

5 in.

8.

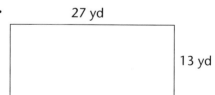

27 yd

13 yd

Computing Perimeter and Area These problems give you practice in finding the perimeter and area of different objects. Follow these steps in solving them:

Step 1 Read the problem and decide whether you are asked to find the perimeter or the area.

Step 2 Look at all the measurements to see if they are given in the same units. If not, make the necessary conversions.

Step 3 Perform the correct operation to find the answer.

Step 4 Include the correct unit of measurement in your answer.

PROBLEM SOLVING

Exercise B Solve these word problems.

1. Find the area of a rectangle that has a width of 6 inches and a length of 1 foot.

2. Yumi plans to carpet her bedroom which measures 16 feet by 11 feet. How many square feet of carpeting will she need?

3. Rita decided to put a fence around her garden. The garden is rectangular in shape, measuring 25 feet by 50 feet. How many feet of fencing will she need?

4. Kenda and her husband are building a garage with a length of 40 feet and a width of 8 yards. How many square feet of floor space will they have?

5. What is the distance around the garage?

6. The roof of the garage will be two rectangles, each measuring 40 feet by 15 feet. How many square feet of shingles will Kenda and her husband need to cover the entire roof?

Base, b

One side of a polygon
used to find area

Height, h

Distance from bottom
to top

The area of a triangle is found by multiplying $\frac{1}{2}$ times the **base** times the **height**. The answer is expressed in square units.

$$\text{Area} = \frac{1}{2} \text{ base} \times \text{height}$$

EXAMPLE

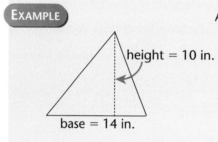

height = 10 in.

base = 14 in.

$$\text{Area} = \frac{1}{2} \text{ bh}$$
$$= \frac{1}{2} \times 14 \times 10$$
$$= 7 \times 10$$
$$= 70 \text{ square inches}$$

Exercise A Find the area of each of these triangles.

1.
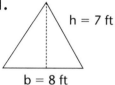
h = 7 ft
b = 8 ft

2.
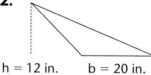
h = 12 in.   b = 20 in.

3.
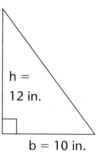
h = 12 in.
b = 10 in.

Exercise B Find the area of each triangle described below.

1. base = 25 feet
height = 10 feet

2. base = 12 yards
height = 30 yards

3. base = 11 inches
height = 50 inches

4. base = 15 inches
height = 6 inches

5. base = 15 inches
height = 4 inches

6. base = 3 inches
height = $\frac{1}{3}$ inch

7. base = 3 feet
height = 12 inches

8. base = 12 feet
height = $\frac{2}{3}$ foot

When you use a calculator with customary measurement, sometimes you will need to rename fractions as decimals.

Remember: Area = $\frac{1}{2}$ base × height.

EXAMPLE Find the area of this triangle.

base (b) = $2\frac{1}{2}$ feet
height (h) = 3 feet

h = 3 ft

b = $2\frac{1}{2}$ ft

Area = $\frac{1}{2}$ × b × h or b × h ÷ 2

Step 1 Rename the base and height measurements as decimals.

b = $2\frac{1}{2}$ feet = 2.5 feet
h = 3 feet = 3 feet

Step 2 Press 2.5 × 3 ÷ 2 =

The display reads 3.75.

Step 3 Since the measurements were given as fractions, rename 3.75 as a fraction.

$3.75 = 3\frac{3}{4}$

Area is measured in square units, so the area is $3\frac{3}{4}$ square feet.

Calculator Exercise Use a calculator to find the area of each triangle described below. Rename decimal answers to fractions. Express each area in square units.

1. b = 2 feet
    h = $1\frac{1}{2}$ feet

2. b = 3 yards
    h = $5\frac{1}{2}$ yards

3. b = $5\frac{3}{4}$ inches
    h = 2 inches

4. b = $18\frac{1}{2}$ feet
    h = $13\frac{1}{2}$ feet

5. b = $2\frac{1}{2}$ inches
    h = 90 inches

6. b = $2\frac{1}{4}$ yards
    h = 5 yards

The area of a parallelogram is found by multiplying the base times the height. The answer is expressed in square units.

$$\text{Area} = \text{base} \times \text{height}$$

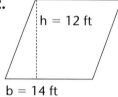

EXAMPLE

h = 5 in.
b = 18 in.

Area = bh
= 18 inches × 5 inches
= 90 square inches

Exercise A Find the area of each of these parallelograms.

1.

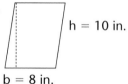

h = 10 in.
b = 8 in.

2.

h = 12 ft
b = 14 ft

3.

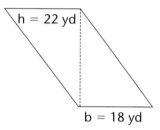

h = 22 yd
b = 18 yd

Exercise B Find the area of each parallelogram described below. You may need to convert some units.

1. base = 18 feet
height = 6 feet

2. base = 13 inches
height = 5 inches

3. base = 36 inches
height = 18 inches

4. base = 9 yards
height = 5 yards

5. base = 2 feet
height = 12 inches

6. base = 6 feet
height = 3 yards

7. base = $\frac{2}{3}$ inch
height = $\frac{3}{4}$ inch

8. base = 12 feet
height = 3 yards

The volume of a prism is the measure of the space inside the prism. A prism is a solid figure with two parallel faces of the same shape. Volume is measured in cubic units. You can find the volume of a prism by multiplying the area of its base by the height of the prism.

$$\text{Volume} = \underbrace{\text{area of base}}_{\text{length} \times \text{width}} \times \text{height}$$

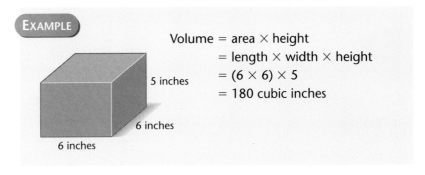

EXAMPLE

Volume = area × height
= length × width × height
= (6 × 6) × 5
= 180 cubic inches

5 inches

6 inches

6 inches

Exercise A Find the volume of each rectangular prism.

1.

6 ft
4 ft
3 ft

4.
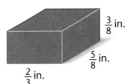
$\frac{3}{8}$ in.
$\frac{5}{8}$ in.
$\frac{2}{3}$ in.

2.
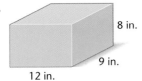
8 in.
9 in.
12 in.

5.

1 ft
9 in.
6 in.

3.
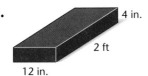
4 in.
2 ft
12 in.

6.
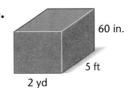
60 in.
5 ft
2 yd

Exercise B Find the volume of each rectangular prism.
Include the correct units in your answer.

1.

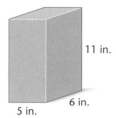

11 in.

6 in.

5 in.

2.

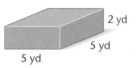

2 yd

5 yd

5 yd

3.

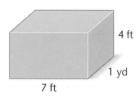

4 ft

1 yd

7 ft

4.

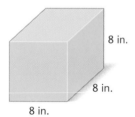

8 in.

8 in.

8 in.

5.

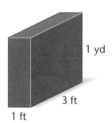

1 yd

3 ft

1 ft

6.

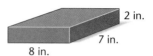

2 in.

7 in.

8 in.

7.

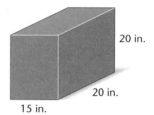

20 in.

20 in.

15 in.

8.

1 ft

1 yd

8 ft

9.

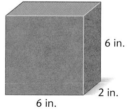

6 in.

2 in.

6 in.

10.

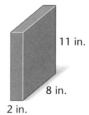

11 in.

8 in.

2 in.

The volume of a prism is found by multiplying the area of its base by the height of the prism. The volume of a triangular prism, therefore, is found by multiplying the area of the base triangle by the height of the prism. The triangle is the prism's base.

$$\text{Volume} = (\tfrac{1}{2}\,\text{base} \times \text{height})\,\text{Height}$$

The symbol for feet is '. Six feet is shown as 6'. The symbol for inches is ". Six inches is shown as 6".

EXAMPLE

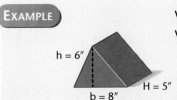

h = 6"   b = 8"   H = 5"

Volume = area of base × Height
Volume = ($\tfrac{1}{2}$ × 8 × 6) × 5
= 24 × 5
= 120 cubic inches

Exercise A Find the volume of each triangular prism. Include the correct units in your answer.

1.

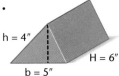

h = 4"   b = 5"   H = 6"

4.

H = 1'   b = 3"   h = 3"

7.

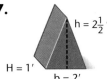

h = $2\tfrac{1}{2}$'   H = 1'   b = 2'

2.

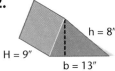

h = 8"   H = 9"   b = 13"

5.

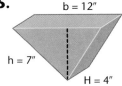

b = 12"   h = 7"   H = 4"

8.

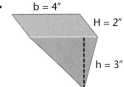

b = 4"   H = 2"   h = 3"

3.

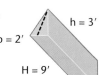

h = 3'   b = 2'   H = 9'

6.

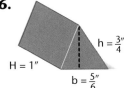

h = $\tfrac{3}{4}$"   H = 1"   b = $\tfrac{5}{6}$"

9.

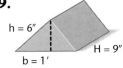

h = 6"   b = 1'   H = 9"

I've Got You Covered!

The two most common forms of wall coverings are paint and wallpaper. To find out how much paint or wallpaper to buy, first find the perimeter of the walls to the nearest foot. Then multiply the perimeter by the ceiling height to find the number of square feet to be covered. Subtract for areas such as doors, windows, and fireplaces.

When buying paint, read the label for the spreading rate. This is the amount of surface area a can of paint will cover. When buying wallpaper, find the number of square feet contained in a single roll. These figures are needed to calculate how much paint or wallpaper you will need.

EXAMPLE How much paint should you buy to paint the walls of the room shown to the right if the spreading rate of a gallon of paint is 400 square feet?

Step 1 Find the perimeter of the walls. 2(12 + 15) = 54 ft

Step 2 Calculate the area of the walls. 54 × 8 = 432 sq ft

Step 3 Find the area of the windows. 2(3 × 4) = 24 sq ft

Step 4 Find the area of the door. 3 × 7 = 21 sq ft

Step 5 Add the area of the door and windows. 24 + 21 = 45 sq ft

Step 6 Subtract from the wall area. 432 − 45 = 387 sq ft

Step 7 Divide the wall area by the spreading rate of the paint.
387 ÷ 400 = about 1

You should buy 1 gallon of paint.

Exercise Solve each problem.

1. Look at the room above. How much paint should you buy if you plan to paint the ceiling and the walls the same color?

2. Look at the room above. How many rolls of wallpaper are needed if a roll contains 36 square feet? (Figure about 30 square feet per roll to allow for cutting and trimming.)

Chapter 9 R E V I E W

Write the letter of the best answer to each question.

1. How many ounces are there in 5 pounds?

   A 16

   B 80

   C 125

   D 2,000

2. How many yards are there in 8 miles?

   A 288

   B 660

   C 14,080

   D 42,240

3. What is the perimeter of this rectangle?

   A 6 inches

   B 52 inches

   C 80 inches

   D 160 inches

4. What is the area of the figure shown below?

   A 36 square feet

   B 100 square feet

   C 1,088 square feet

   D 2,176 square feet

5. What is the volume of a rectangular prism with these measurements:

Length = 12 ft   Width = 6 ft   Height = 4 ft

   A 288 cubic feet

   B 144 cubic feet

   C 44 cubic feet

   D 16 cubic feet

Convert these units:

6. 6 gallons = ___ pints

7. 4 quarts = ___ pints

8. 48 ounces = ___ pounds

9. 3 tons = ___ pounds

10. 72 inches = ___ feet

11. 4 yards = ___ feet

12. 9 feet = ___ yards

Find these answers. Simplify if possible.

13.   15 yards 5 feet 2 inches
  −   2 feet 5 inches

14. 8 times (9 yards 5 feet 2 inches)

15. (16 feet 8 inches) ÷ 2

16.   13 feet 6 inches
  − 5 feet 8 inches

17.   5 yards 2 feet 6 inches
  +   2 feet 7 inches

Measure these line segments to the nearest $\frac{1}{8}$ inch.

18. ─────────────────

19. ──────────────

Use a ruler to draw line segments that measure:

20. $2\frac{5}{8}$ inches

21. $3\frac{3}{4}$ inches

Solve the problems below these figures:

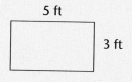

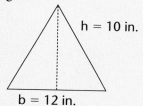

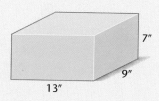

22. What is the area of the rectangle?

23. What is the perimeter of the rectangle?

24. What is the area of the triangle?

25. What is the volume of the rectangular prism?

10 Measuring Circles, Cylinders, and Time

The first part of this chapter will introduce you to two shapes: circles and cylinders. These shapes are closely related. Look for them all around you: soup cans, barrels, a glass of water. Even some buildings have parts that are cylinders or circles. An architect uses a tool called a compass to draw circles when designing a building, as shown to the left.

The concept of time is discussed in the second part of this chapter. Did you know that computing units of time is a math skill? Knowing how to do this will help you on the job, at school, in your personal life—everywhere.

In Chapter 10, you will learn all about measuring these three things: circles, cylinders, and time.

Goals for Learning

- ◆ To find the circumference of a circle
- ◆ To determine the diameter of a circle
- ◆ To calculate the area of a circle
- ◆ To compute the volume of a cylinder
- ◆ To add and subtract units of time
- ◆ To determine the elapsed time from one given time to another given time

Diameter

Distance across a circle through the center

Radius

Distance from the center of a circle to the edge of a circle

Circumference

Distance around a circle

A *circle* is a closed curved line with all points equally distant from the center.

The **diameter** of a circle is the length of a line segment through the center of the circle with its ends on the circle. A diameter divides the circle into two equal halves.

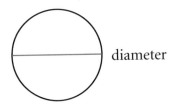

diameter

The **radius** is the length of a line segment from the center of the circle to a point on the circle. Two radii equal the diameter.

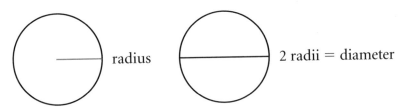

radius   2 radii = diameter

The **circumference** is the distance around the circle. The circumference of a circle is about 3.14 times as long as its diameter.

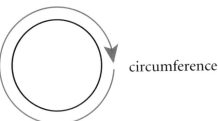

circumference

Pi, π
Ratio of the circumference to the diameter

The ratio of the circumference of a circle to its diameter is about 3.14, or $\frac{22}{7}$. We call this ratio **pi** and write it with a Greek letter, π. To compute with π, use 3.14 when it is easier to use decimals. Use $\frac{22}{7}$ when it is easier to use fractions.

$$\frac{\text{Circumference}}{\text{Diameter}} = 3.14 = \pi$$

The formulas are:

$$\text{Circumference} = \pi \times \text{diameter}$$

$$\text{Circumference} = 2 \times \pi \times \text{radius}$$

Remember that the diameter is two times the radius.

Pi is a number that cannot be represented exactly with a fraction or a decimal. Numbers like pi are called irrational numbers.

EXAMPLES Find the circumference (C) of a circle with a diameter (d) of 9 inches.

d = 9″

$C = \pi d$
$C = 3.14 \times 9$
$C = 28.26$ inches

Find the circumference (C) of a circle with a radius (r) of 14 inches.

r = 14″

$C = 2 \pi r$
$C = 2 \times \frac{22}{7} \times 14$
$C = 88$ inches

Exercise A Find the circumference of a circle for each diameter or radius given. Use $\frac{22}{7}$ for π in problems 3, 6, 7, 10, and 11.

1. d = 5 in.

2. d = 10 in.

3. d = 7 in.

4. d = 2 ft

5. r = 6 ft

6. d = $8\frac{5}{8}$ in.

7. d = 21 yd

8. r = 3 ft

9. d = 23 yd

10. r = $13\frac{1}{2}$ in.

11. d = 28 ft

12. d = 100 yd

The formula for finding the diameter (d) of a circle is:

$$\text{Diameter} = \frac{\text{Circumference}}{\pi}$$

EXAMPLE Find the diameter of a circle with a circumference of 34.54 inches.

C = 34.54"

$$d = \frac{C}{\pi}$$

$$d = \frac{34.54}{3.14}$$

d = 11 inches

Exercise B Find the diameter of a circle for each circumference.

1. C = 21.98 in.

2. C = 15.7 in.

3. C = 9.42 yd

4. C = 40.82 mi

5. C = 31.4 ft

6. C = 12.56 yd

7. C = 29.83 ft

8. C = 41.134 mi

9. C = 47.1 ft

10. C = 53.38 mi

11. C = 97.34 mi

12. C = 97.34 yd

PROBLEM SOLVING

Exercise C Answer these questions about circumference.

1. The circumference of a can of soup is 9.42 inches. What is the diameter of the can?

2. The distance around a circular pond is 78.5 yards. What is the distance across the pond at its widest point?

3. What is the diameter of a circular sports arena with a circumference of 47.1 yards?

4. The diameter of the expressway surrounding Northwood is 50.24 miles. What is the distance around (circumference of) the expressway?

5. What is the diameter of a round table with a circumference of 301.44 inches?

The area of a circle can be found by multiplying π times the radius times the radius. If you are given the diameter of the circle instead of the radius, divide the diameter by 2 to get the radius.

$$\text{Area of a Circle} = \pi \times (\text{radius})^2$$

EXAMPLES   Find the area of a circle whose radius is 7 inches.

r = 7″

$A = \pi\, r^2$
$A = 3.14 \times 7 \times 7$
$A = 153.86$ square inches

Find the area of a circle whose diameter is 8 inches.

d = 8″

$A = \pi\, r^2$
$A = 3.14 \times 4 \times 4$
$A = 50.24$ square inches

Exercise A Use the formula $A = \pi\, r^2$ to find the area of each of these circles.

1. r = 4 in.
2. r = 1.5 yd
3. r = 3.5 ft
4. r = 7 ft
5. r = 10 yd
6. r = 8 in.
7. r = 20 ft
8. r = 15 in.
9. d = 10 yd
10. r = 2.5 ft
11. r = 9 in.
12. d = 22 in.

13. r = 2.3 mi
14. r = 2 yd
15. r = 1 yd
16. r = 8.6 yd
17. d = 2 ft
18. d = 5 in.
19. r = 12 yd
20. r = 1.7 yd
21. d = 3 ft
22. r = 5.1 ft
23. r = 14 in.
24. d = 24 in.

Exercise B Find the area of each circle.

1. r = 13 ft
2. r = 5 in.
3. r = 7 yd
4. r = 3.3 in.
5. d = 8 in.

6. r = 6 ft
7. r = 11.6 ft
8. d = 6 in.
9. d = 4 in.
10. d = 12 ft

Use your calculator to find the area of a circle.

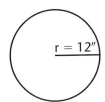

r = 12"

> **EXAMPLE** Find the area of a circle with a radius of 12 in.
> Area = π r² or π × (r × r)
>
> Press *3.14* M+
>
> Since π = 3.14 in the formula, store 3.14 as a constant in the calculator's memory.
>
> Press C to clear the display.
>
> Press MR × *12* × *12* =
>
> The display reads *452.16*
>
> Area is measured in square units, so the area is 452.16 sq in.

Calculator Exercise Use a calculator to help you find the area for each of these circles.

1. r = 6 in.

2. r = 10 ft

3. r = 4 yd

4. r = 3 mi

5. r = 7 in.

6. r = 8 ft

7. r = 5 yd

8. r = 2 mi

9. r = 9 ft

10. r = 12 ft

11. r = 11 in.

12. r = 16 yd

13. r = 19 ft

14. r = 14 in.

15. r = 10.5 in.

16. r = 16.5 ft

The volume of a cylinder is found by multiplying the area of the base times the height of the cylinder. The volume is always measured in cubic units.

$$\text{Volume of a Cylinder} = \text{area of base} \times \text{height}$$
$$= \pi\, r^2\, H$$

Volume = Area of the base times the height.

EXAMPLE   Find the volume of this cylinder.

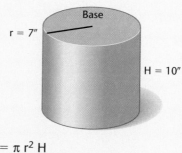

$V = \pi\, r^2\, H$
$V = 3.14 \times 7 \times 7 \times 10$
$V = 1{,}538.6$ cubic inches

Exercise A Find the volume of each cylinder.

1. r = 2 in.
   H = 3 in.

2. r = 5 ft
   H = 11 ft

3. r = 5 ft
   H = 2 ft

4. r = 8 in.
   H = 2 in.

5. d = 8 in.
   H = 4 in.

6. d = 16 ft
   H = 5 ft

Cylinders are all around us. Containers such as paint cans are cylinders.

Exercise B Find the volume of the cylinders described below.

1. r = 2 in.
   H = 3 in.

2. r = 3 ft
   H = 5 ft

3. r = 7 yd
   H = 2 yd

4. r = 3 ft
   H = 2 ft

5. r = 6 in.
   H = 2 in.

6. r = 5 in.
   H = 1 in.

7. r = 3 ft
   H = 6 ft

8. r = 4 yd
   H = 6 yd

9. r = 7 in.
   H = 3 in.

10. r = 8 in.
   H = 2 in.

11. r = 6 ft
   H = 5 ft

12. r = 4 yd
   H = 3 yd

13. r = 1 ft
   H = 3 ft

14. r = 10 in.
   H = 12 in.

15. r = 1 ft
   H = 10 ft

16. d = 10 yd
   H = 2 yd

17. d = 20 ft
   H = 5 ft

18. d = 30 in.
   H = 1 in.

19. r = 2.1 ft
   H = 2 ft

20. r = 4 in.
   H = 3.1 in.

21. r = 1.1 ft
   H = 2 ft

22. r = 4 yd
   H = 2.2 yd

23. r = 6 ft
   H = 5 ft

24. r = $\frac{1}{4}$ in.
   H = 2 in.

 PROBLEM SOLVING

Exercise C Solve these area and volume word problems. Be sure that you include the units in your answers.

1. Find the volume of a can with a radius of 2 inches and a height of 5 inches.

2. Iwu's father asked him to compute the area of their patio. The patio was circular with a diameter of 18 feet. What was the area?

3. A can of Alpine soup has a radius of 2 inches and a height of 6 inches. A can of Family Brand soup has a radius of 2$\frac{1}{2}$ inches and a height of 5 inches. Which can holds more soup? How much more?

4. Astronauts found a cylindrical spaceship with a diameter of 50 yards and a height of 200 yards. What is the volume of the spaceship?

5. There is a circular park in Chicago with a diameter of 119 yards. What is the area of the park?

Time is measured the same all over the world. The same units—minutes, hours, days—are standard to time measurement.

$$1 \text{ minute} = 60 \text{ seconds}$$
$$1 \text{ hour} = 60 \text{ minutes}$$
$$1 \text{ day} = 24 \text{ hours}$$
$$1 \text{ week} = 7 \text{ days}$$
$$1 \text{ year} = 52 \text{ weeks}$$

When you add or subtract units of time, you often need to rename the units.

EXAMPLES   Subtract 10 minutes from 5 hours, 6 minutes.

$$
\begin{array}{ll}
\overset{4}{\cancel{5}} \text{ hours} & \overset{66}{\cancel{6}} \text{ minutes} \\
- & 10 \text{ minutes} \\
\hline
4 \text{ hours} & 56 \text{ minutes}
\end{array}
$$

1 hour = 60 minutes
60 minutes + 6 minutes = 66 minutes

Add 5 days, 16 hours to 4 days, 14 hours.

$$
\begin{array}{ll}
5 \text{ days} & 16 \text{ hours} \\
+4 \text{ days} & 14 \text{ hours} \\
\hline
9 \text{ days} & 30 \text{ hours} = 10 \text{ days } 6 \text{ hours}
\end{array}
$$

30 hours = 24 hours + 6 hours
= 1 day + 6 hours

Exercise A Add or subtract as shown. Write your answers in simplest form.

1. 28 minutes   7 seconds
  − 2 minutes 10 seconds

2. 6 hours   5 minutes
  +3 hours   8 minutes

3. 15 minutes 45 seconds
  + 8 minutes 30 seconds

4. 13 hours   3 minutes
  −2 hours   9 minutes

Exercise B Add or subtract as shown. Write your answers in simplest form.

1.   7 weeks   5 days
      − 2 weeks   8 days

2.   3 days   18 hours
      + 2 days   21 hours

3.   15 weeks   5 days
      +   8 days

4.   7 years   24 weeks
      +   38 weeks

5.   9 years   5 weeks
      + 2 years   9 weeks

6.   7 years   2 weeks
      − 2 years   3 weeks

7.   5 years   5 weeks   2 days
      −   5 weeks   5 days

8.   4 years   2 days
      −   3 days

9.   2 days   8 hours
      + 3 days   20 hours

10.   4 years   8 weeks   1 day
       − 1 year   4 weeks   5 days

11.   6 weeks   6 days
       + 2 weeks   2 days

12.   8 years   30 weeks
       − 5 years   42 weeks

13.   6 years   2 weeks
       − 5 years   4 weeks

14.   10 weeks   5 days
       + 3 weeks   3 days

15.   2 days   12 hours
       + 1 day   16 hours

16.   12 years   3 weeks
       − 9 years   4 weeks

Try This

Use a calendar to figure out how long it is until your birthday. Write down the number of weeks (if longer than a week away) and the number of days. Work with a partner to find out whose birthday is closer and by how long. To do this, set up a subtraction problem using the two lengths of time.

Elapsed time
How long an event lasts

Elapsed time is the amount of time that has passed from one given time to another given time.

EXAMPLES

How much time has elapsed from the time shown on Clock A to the time shown on Clock B?

In these examples, Clock A and Clock B are in the same period of day: before noon or after noon. Remember, these periods of the day are known as A.M. and P.M. The A.M. times are before noon. The P.M. times are after noon.

Clock A	Clock B
Clock A shows 5:15.	Clock B shows 7:25.

Always write the later time first.

```
  7:25
− 5:15
  2:10   or 2 hours 10 minutes
```

How much time has elapsed from the time shown on Clock A to the time shown on Clock B?

Clock A	Clock B
Clock A shows 1:35.	Clock B shows 9:20.

Rename 1 hour to 60 minutes and add to the 20 minutes.

```
  8 80
  9:20
− 1:35
  7:45   7 hours and 45 minutes have elapsed.
```

Technology Connection

Daylight Savings Time sets our clocks back one hour in the fall and forward one hour in the spring. It has been estimated that setting clocks forward reduces energy use in the U.S. by about 1% each year.

EXAMPLE How much time has elapsed from the time shown on Clock A to the time shown on Clock B?

Clock A   Clock B

Clock A shows 11:15 A.M.   Clock B shows 1:28 P.M.

Add 12 hours to the 1 to work the problem.

```
  13
  1:28
-11:15
  2:13    2 hours and 13 minutes have elapsed.
```

Exercise A Subtract to find how much time has elapsed from the time shown on Clock A to the time shown on Clock B.

1. A    B

4. A    B

2. A    B

5. A    B

3. A    B

6. A    B

Exercise B Subtract to find the amount of time that has elapsed.

1. From 3:50 to 6:40
2. From 1:55 to 4:30
3. From 2:45 to 9:30
4. From 10:45 to 1:38
5. From 8:15 to 11:30
6. From 9:30 to 12:15
7. From 11:36 to 2:12
8. From 2:02 to 1:05

9. From 3:05 to 7:20
10. From 6:10 to 9:20
11. From 1:00 to 9:35
12. From 4:55 to 8:40
13. From 9:16 to 2:48
14. From 10:35 to 10:48
15. From 8:48 to 1:00
16. From 8:12 to 10:05

 PROBLEM SOLVING

Exercise C Solve these problems about time. You will need to use the clock above each problem.

1. Lapeta put a turkey in the oven at the time shown. The turkey needs to roast for 5 hours 30 minutes. At what time should she take the turkey out of the oven?

3. Sophonie determines that it will take her 2 hours and 15 minutes to drive to Toronto. What time will it be when she arrives at Toronto?

2. Yunang's bus should arrive at 10:55. He looks to see what time it is now. How long will he have to wait?

4. Samuel went to sleep at 10:36 last night. When he woke up, he looked at the clock by his bed. How long did Samuel sleep?

Time Zones

The system used to tell time around the world is called Standard Time. In Standard Time, the world is divided into 24 time zones. Each one runs north and south, from the North Pole to the South Pole. Each time zone has a one hour difference from its neighboring zones. The time is earlier in the west and later in the east. When you travel to the west, set your watch back one hour for each zone. When you travel to the east, set your watch forward one hour for each zone. The time at any particular place is called local time.

The United States has six time zones, as shown on the map.

EXAMPLE	A flight from New York to Los Angeles takes about 5 hours. If you leave New York at 9:00 A.M., what will be the local time in Los Angeles when you arrive?

Step 1   Add the flight time to New York time.
9:00 A.M. + 5 hours = 2:00 P.M.

Step 2   Determine the time zone difference. 3 hours

Step 3   Going west, subtract the number of hours.
2:00 P.M. − 3 hours = 11:00 A.M.

The time in Los Angeles will be 11:00 A.M.

Exercise Use the time zone map above to help you solve each problem.

1. In which time zone is each of these cities? Salt Lake City, Dallas, Sacramento, Boston.

2. If it is 1:00 P.M. in Chicago, what time is it in these cities? Denver, New York, Seattle.

3. If you make a call in Miami at 8:15 P.M. to a friend in Reno, what time is it in Reno?

4. A flight from Seattle to Chicago is about 4 hours. If you leave Seattle at 2:00 P.M., what will be the local time in Chicago when you arrive?

Chapter 10 REVIEW

Write the letter of the best answer to each question.

1. What is the circumference of the circle below?

    A 2.5 in.

    B 12.56 in.

    C 25.12 in.

    D 50.24 in.

d = 8 in.

2. What is the diameter of the circle below?

    A 24 in.

    B 48 in.

    C 75.36 in.

    D 452.16 in.

r = 24 in.

3. What is the area of the circle below?

    A 6 sq ft

    B 12 sq ft

    C 18.84 sq ft

    D 113.04 sq ft

d = 12 ft

4. What is the volume of a cylinder with a radius of 4 feet and a height of 8 feet?

    A 12.56 cu ft

    B 50.24 cu ft

    C 100.48 cu ft

    D 401.92 cu ft

5. How much elapsed time is there from 1:30 P.M. to 6:58 P.M?

    A 5 hr 28 min

    B 5 hr 18 min

    C 4 hr 28 min

    D 4 hr 18 min

Answer the questions about circles A, B, and C:

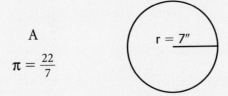

A

$\pi = \frac{22}{7}$

r = 7"

B

$\pi = 3.14$

d = 16"

C

$\pi = 3.14$

r = 10"

6. What is the radius of A?

7. What is the diameter of A?

8. What is the circumference of A?

9. What is the diameter of B?

10. What is the radius of B?

11. What is the circumference of B?

12. What is the radius of C?

13. What is the diameter of C?

14. What is the area of C?

Find the volume for each:

15.

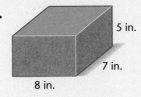

5 in.

7 in.

8 in.

16.

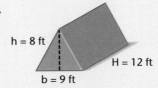

h = 8 ft

H = 12 ft

b = 9 ft

17. r = 9 in.

H = 16 in.

Solve these problems:

18. Elisha's alarm clock woke him up at 7:30 A.M. He has to be at his bus stop at 1:15 P.M. How much time does he have before he needs to be at his bus stop?

19. 9 hr   6 min   40 sec
     +   55 min   22 sec

20. 13 hr   6 min
     − 5 hr   8 min

Test-Taking Tip

Try making study flashcards for the formulas you have learned. On the front of the card identify the formula (area of a circle, for example). On the back of the card write the formula with two or three examples.

Graphs

Pick up any newspaper or magazine. Study the weather or look at car sales trends. The information is often presented in a graph. Many of these graphs are created by computers. To succeed in school and at work, you must be able to understand graphs. Creating graphs for yourself can help give you a clearer picture of how you are spending your money or how you are spending your time.

In Chapter 11, you will learn how to read and create many types of graphs. You will also learn how graphs are used to report information, and sometimes how they are used to mislead us.

Goals for Learning

◆ To read and construct pictographs from data in chart form

◆ To read and construct bar graphs and double bar graphs

◆ To read and construct divided bar graphs from data in chart form

◆ To read and construct line graphs and circle graphs

◆ To redraw and correct a misleading graph

Graph

A visual way to show information

Scale

A ratio of the original size to the size on a map or model

Pictograph

A graph that uses pictures or symbols

Graphs are used to present information that can be read quickly. All graphs must have a title and a **scale** so that people will know what information is being presented. A **pictograph** is a graph that uses pictures to make it more attractive and interesting.

EXAMPLE

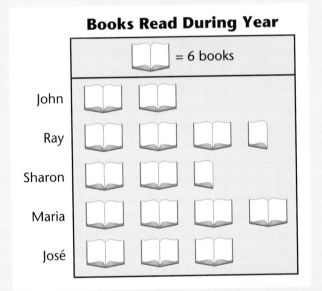

Often the pictures in pictographs represent more than one item. In this pictograph, each picture of one book represents 6 books. John read 2 × 6, or 12, books.

Try This

Look for examples of pictographs in newspapers or magazines. Find at least three. For each one, write down the title and scale. Share the pictographs you found with your class.

Exercise A Use this pictograph to answer the questions below.

Vehicles in the Teachers' Parking Lot

= 4 vehicles

Minivans	
Pickup Trucks	
Station Wagons	
Hatchbacks	
Sports Cars	
4-door Sedans	

1. What is the title of this graph?

2. Where is the graph's scale?

3. What type of car do most of the teachers drive?

4. What type of car is driven least?

5. Why is part of a car drawn next to 4-door Sedans?

6. How many Pickup Trucks are in the parking lot?

7. About how many vehicles are in the parking lot?

Constructing Pictographs When you construct a pictograph, follow these steps:

Step 1 Decide how you are going to present the information.

Step 2 Choose a scale and a **symbol**.

Step 3 Graph the **data**.

Step 4 Write the title.

Step 5 Write the scale.

Exercise B Make a pictograph to show this information. Be sure that you include a title and a scale. You might use a picture of a cat as a symbol for 5 cats.

Cat Population of Five Streets	
Street	**Number of Cats**
Stricker	25
Fleet	5
Mount	20
Saratoga	10
Water	13

Exercise C Make a pictograph to show this information. Round the numbers to the nearest 100.

Dog Population of Five Towns		
Town	**Number of Dogs**	**Rounded Number**
Sludge Creek	782	_____
Furnace Flats	415	_____
Rosetowne	1,276	_____
Millersville	804	_____
Magnolia	892	_____

Bar graph

A graph that compares amounts by using bars

Pictographs take a long time to construct. Each figure must be drawn accurately and put into the correct place. **Bar graphs,** however, are easier to construct. They are often used instead of pictographs to present information. To tell how many objects are being represented in a bar graph, you compare the length of the bar to the scale.

EXAMPLE

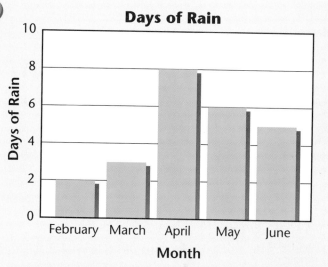

Days of Rain

In this bar graph, April had eight days of rain. If the bar does not extend to the next line on the scale, estimate the value. In this bar graph, March had three days of rain. Use a straightedge to help you.

A bar graph is a popular tool for business presentations.

Exercise A Use this bar graph to answer the questions below.

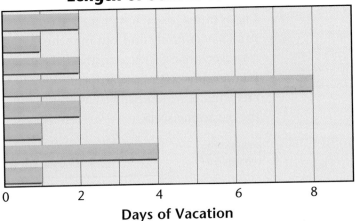

Length of School Vacations

1. What is the graph's title?

2. Where is the scale of the graph?

3. What is the longest vacation?

4. How long is the midterm break?

5. How long is the spring vacation?

6. How many days of vacation come before the midterm break?

7. How many days of vacation are there in all?

8. How does the length of the midterm break compare to the length of the spring vacation?

Using Vertical Bar Graphs Often, the bars are drawn up and down instead of across. This type of bar graph is called a vertical bar graph. You can tell the amount that each bar represents by comparing the height of the bar to the scale on the left.

Exercise B Use this bar graph to answer the questions below.

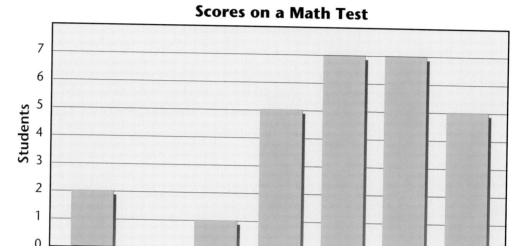

Scores on a Math Test

1. What is the title of this graph?

2. Where is the scale?

3. How many students scored a 90 on this test?

4. How many students got a 30?

5. Why is there no bar above the 40 on this graph?

6. How many students scored a 70 or an 80?

7. If 60 is the passing grade, how many students failed this test?

8. If 70 is the passing grade, how many students passed this test?

9. How many students took this test?

Calculator Practice

You know how to use a calculator to find the average of a set of numbers. You also know how to use your calculator's memory key. You can use both of these skills to calculate an average number or score from data you might find on a bar graph.

EXAMPLE The results of a midterm test show the following scores: 2 students scored 100, 6 students scored 90, 8 students scored 80, 5 students scored 70, and 3 students scored 60. What is the average score?

Step 1 Add the scores for all the students. You will need to multiply the number of students by each score and add the products. Use the memory key to store and add each product.

Press 2 $\times$ 100 $=$ M+

Press 6 $\times$ 90 $=$ M+

Press 8 $\times$ 80 $=$ M+

Press 5 $\times$ 70 $=$ M+

Press 3 $\times$ 60 $=$ M+

Press MR . The display reads 1910.

Step 2 Find the total number of student scores.
Press 2 $+$ 6 $+$ 8 $+$ 5 $+$ 3 $=$
The display reads 24.

Step 3 Divide the sum of the products by the total number of student scores.

Press MR $\div$ 24 $=$
The display reads 79.583333. Round to the nearest whole number. The average score is 80.

Step 4 Press MC before starting the next problem.

Calculator Exercise Use a calculator to find the average for each set of data. Round your answer to the nearest whole number.

1.

Score	Number of Students
88	3
82	4
79	6
75	7
68	9

2.

Age	Number of People
17 years	6
18 years	8
20 years	3
27 years	2
43 years	1

3.

Kilometers	Number of Runners
2	3
5	8
6	4
24	2

4.

High Temp.	Number of Days
70°	6
72°	1
76°	3
78°	6
92°	7
93°	4
95°	3

Constructing a Bar Graph When you make a bar graph, follow these steps:

Step 1 Decide if you want to make a vertical or horizontal bar graph.

Step 2 Choose a scale.

Step 3 Label the vertical **axis** and horizontal axis.

Step 4 Draw the bars.

Step 5 Give the graph a title.

Exercise C Make a horizontal bar graph to show this information.

Softball Distance Throw	
Contestant	**Distance**
Mario	100 ft
Jennifer	140 ft
Brian	110 ft
Heather	150 ft
Rawkeem	170 ft
Kim	125 ft

Exercise D Make a vertical bar graph to show this information.

High Jump	
Contestant	**Height Jumped**
Joe	54 in.
Luke	56 in.
Rita	48 in.
Anita	59 in.
Josh	63 in.
Yumi	52 in.

Divided bar graph

A graph that uses parallel bars to compare information

Key

An explanation of the symbols used

Sometimes more than one kind of information is presented in the same bar graph. One way this is done is with a **divided bar graph.** We use a divided bar graph when the total of the two parts is important. Use the **key** to determine what the bars in the graph represent. A divided bar graph shows the information with a divided bar like this:

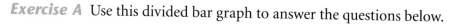

Exercise A Use this divided bar graph to answer the questions below.

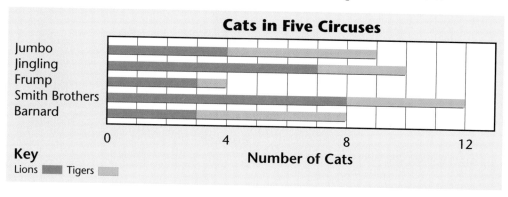

1. What is the title of this graph?

2. Where is the scale?

3. How many cats are in the Jingling Circus?

4. How many lions are in the Jumbo Circus?

5. How many tigers are in the Frump Circus?

6. What two circuses have the same number of lions?

7. Which circus has the most lions?

8. What two circuses have the same number of tigers?

9. What two circuses have more tigers than lions?

10. How many more tigers does Barnard Circus have than Frump Circus?

Using Multiple Bar Graphs Another way to present more than one kind of information at a time is to use a **multiple bar graph.** We use a multiple bar graph when the comparison of the parts is important. A multiple bar graph shows the information with two or more bars side by side like this:

Exercise B Use this multiple bar graph to answer the questions.

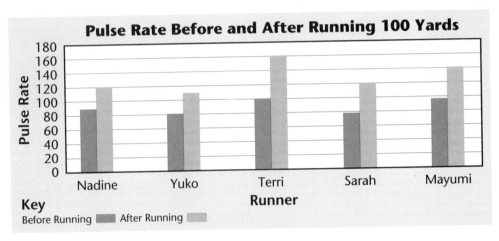

1. What is the title of this graph?

2. Where is the scale?

3. Whose pulse rate was the lowest before running?

4. Whose pulse rate was the lowest after running?

5. Whose pulse rate was highest before running?

6. Whose pulse rate was 110 beats after running?

7. Whose pulse rate was 90 beats before running?

8. Whose pulse rate increased the least?

9. Whose pulse rate increased the most?

10. Which two runners had the same rate as each other after running?

When making a bar graph, be sure to follow these steps:

Step 1 Decide if you want to make a vertical or a horizontal bar graph.

Step 2 Choose a scale.

Step 3 Label the vertical and horizontal axes.

Step 4 Draw the bars.

Step 5 Give the graph a title.

Exercise A Make a divided bar graph to show this information.

Housing in the Jamala Islands		
Year	Owned	Rented
1975	7 million	9 million
1985	11 million	13 million
1995	15 million	20 million
2005	35 million	15 million

Exercise B Make a multiple bar graph to show this information.

Scores on the Midterm and the Final		
Student	Midterm	Final
Sheila	80	85
Andy	70	80
Kim	65	90
Tony	60	75
Raj	70	75
Desi	75	80

A **line graph** is used to show change over a period of time. Instead of drawing bars, a dot is placed at the correct height. Then the dots are connected in order from left to right.

You can tell the number represented at a particular time. First find the time on a **horizontal axis.** Then go up the graph, and finally go over to the **vertical axis.** You can read the amount from this scale.

Line graph

A graph composed of connected line segments that shows change in amounts

Horizontal axis

The line of reference that is parallel to the horizon

Vertical axis

The line of reference that is up and down

Time is usually shown on the horizontal axis.

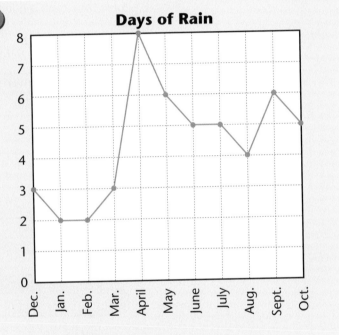

EXAMPLE

Days of Rain

In this line graph, April had eight days of rain. June and July both had five days of rain.

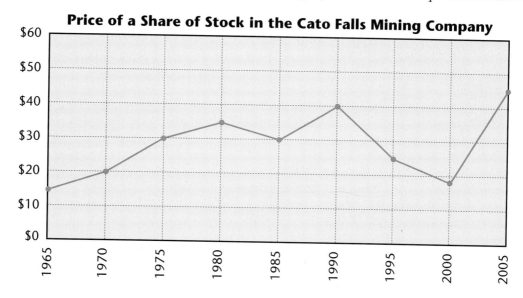

Price of a Share of Stock in the Cato Falls Mining Company

1. What is the title of this graph?

2. Where is the scale?

3. What was the price of a share of stock in 1975?

4. What was the price of a share of stock in 1995?

5. What was the approximate price of a share in 1972?

6. During what five-year period was the greatest increase in the price of a share of stock?

Try This

Use a line graph to graph the distance covered and the elapsed time for a car trip. Make the vertical axis the distance covered. Make the horizontal axis the elapsed time. Record the distance from your starting point every few minutes. What does the line graph look like? What does the line look like?

Constructing a Line Graph When you make a line graph, follow these steps:

Step 1   Draw the horizontal and vertical axes.

Step 2   Choose a convenient scale for the numbers. You may need to round off large numbers.

Step 3   Enter these numbers on the vertical axis and the time units on the horizontal axis. Label the scales.

Step 4   Above each time, make a dot at the appropriate height.

Step 5   Connect the dots in order.

Step 6   Give the graph a title.

Exercise B Make a line graph to show the following data.

1.

Yuri's Weight Loss	
Week of Diet	**Yuri's Weight**
0	205 lbs
1	204 lbs
2	201 lbs
3	197 lbs
4	195 lbs
5	191 lbs

2.

Average Monthly Temperature in Cincinnati	
January	29°
February	32°
March	42°
April	52°
May	64°
June	72°
July	76°
August	78°
September	69°
October	57°
November	41°
December	32°

Circle graph

A graphic way to compare amounts using segments of a circle

Allotted

Assigned

Sector

A part of a circle bounded by two radii

A **circle graph** is used to show how the whole of something is divided into parts. You can guess how much is **allotted** to the different parts by comparing the sizes of the **sectors.** The exact allotment is usually shown in the graph by percent or a fraction.

The Wang Family Budget

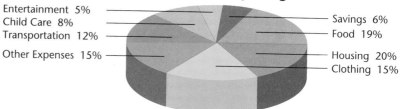

Entertainment 5%
Child Care 8%
Transportation 12%
Other Expenses 15%

Savings 6%
Food 19%
Housing 20%
Clothing 15%

Exercise A Use this circle graph to answer the questions.

1. What is the title of this graph?

2. What do the Wangs spend most of their money on?

3. How much do they spend for housing if their yearly income is $36,800.00?

4. What do they spend for food?

5. What do they spend for clothing?

6. How much do they save each year?

7. Make a chart to show how much the Wangs spend for each item in their budget if their yearly income is $36,800.00.

Exercise B Use this circle graph to answer these questions.

**Student Government
Election Results**

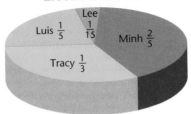

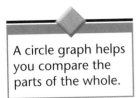

A circle graph helps you compare the parts of the whole.

1. What is the graph's title?

2. Who won the election?

3. Who got the fewest votes?

4. Who came in second?

5. If 1,095 votes were cast, how many votes did each person get?

Exercise C Copy this chart. Complete the missing information by multiplying the percent or the fraction by 360°. Round to the nearest degree.

	Fractions				Percents				
Part of the Circle	$\frac{1}{3}$	$\frac{1}{2}$	$\frac{1}{6}$	$\frac{1}{12}$	10%	35%	5%	12%	32%
Number of Degrees									

Constructing Circle Graphs When you make a circle graph, follow these steps:

Step 1 Draw a conveniently sized circle. Mark the center with a dot.

Step 2 Find out how many degrees are in each sector. To do this, multiply the percent or the fraction by the 360° in a circle.

Step 3 Draw a radius.

Step 4 Use a protractor to measure and draw each sector. Use the center of the circle as the vertex of each angle.

Step 5 Label each sector and mark the appropriate percent or fraction.

Step 6 Give the graph a title.

Exercise D Make a circle graph to show this information.

The Soler Family Budget	
Budget Item	**Percent Allotted**
Food	30%
Housing	25%
Clothing	20%
Car	10%
Savings	8%
Other	7%

Technology Connection

Computers have become the most popular tool for making graphs. They allow the user to create accurate graphs quickly. Imagine if you always had to draw a graph by hand? What problems might this cause? Choose a topic that interests you, such as a sport, a breed of dog, or a movie. Then research your topic. Create a graph on a computer using data you have collected. Present your graph to a partner or to the class.

Mislead

*Cause a person to reach
unrealistic conclusions*

Sometimes graphs are drawn so that they **mislead** the person
who is reading them for information.

EXAMPLES

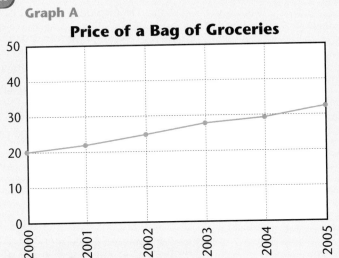

Graph A

Price of a Bag of Groceries

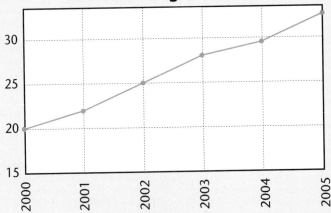

Graph B

Price of a Bag of Groceries

Graph A makes it appear that there was a slight
increase in price. Graph B makes it appear there
was a large increase in price. The vertical scales
differ. These differences can mislead the person
reading the graphs.

Graph A

Cato Falls Mining Co.

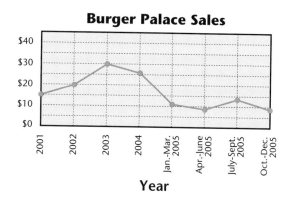

Graph B

Cato Falls Mining Co.

1. Which graph makes it appear that the price of a share of stock is going up?

2. Which graph makes the value of a share of stock appear to be decreasing?

3. How do the two graphs differ?

Burger Palace Sales

4. Does it appear that sales at Burger Palace for 2005 were more or less than sales for 2004?

5. What were the total sales during all of 2005?

6. Were the total sales for 2005 more or less than the total sales for 2004?

7. What is wrong with this graph?

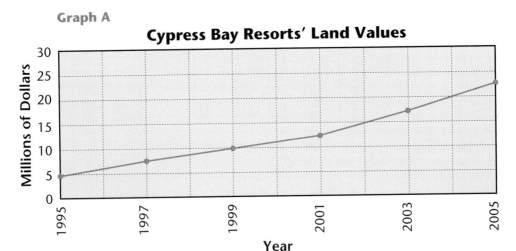

Exercise B Answer the questions about the graphs.

Graph A

Cypress Bay Resorts' Land Values

Graph B

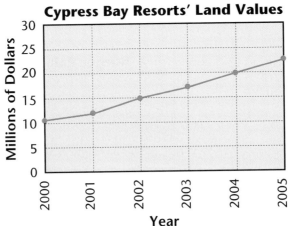

Cypress Bay Resorts' Land Values

1. Which graph makes it appear that there has been a gradual increase in land values at Cypress Bay Resorts?

2. Which graph makes it appear that there has been a large increase in land values at Cypress Bay Resorts?

3. Which graph do you think a salesperson for Cypress Bay Resorts would use?

4. How do the two graphs differ?

Exercise C Answer the questions below this graph.

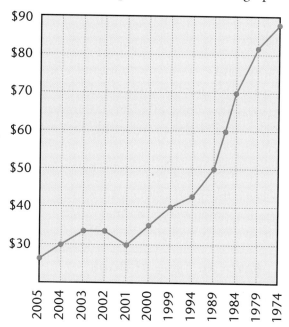

1. What is the title of this graph?

2. What is wrong with the vertical axis?

3. Name two things that are wrong with the horizontal axis.

4. How is the spacing on the horizontal and vertical axes different?

5. Redraw this graph so that it accurately shows the data. Make up a title for your graph.

Graphic Choices

The old saying "a picture is worth a thousand words" takes on a special meaning when a graph shows statistical data. A graph can replace several sentences, or even paragraphs, of numerical information in a written report. It can allow the reader to see lots of data easily and quickly.

EXAMPLE Justin wanted to make the table below into a graph.

Below is the graph Justin made. Is this graph appropriate for the data? Could he have made a different graph?

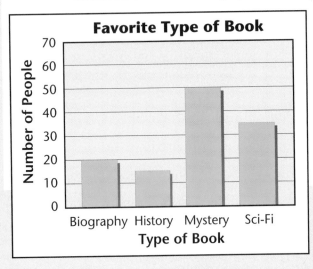

Favorite Type of Book

Type	Number of People
Biography	20
History	15
Mystery	50
Sci-Fi	35

Justin made a bar graph. He could have made a pictograph or a circle graph to show the information in a slightly different way.

Exercise For each table, construct the most appropriate graph from the graphs you learned about in this chapter. Explain your choice.

1.

Temperatures for One Week

Day	High	Low
Mon.	45°	25°
Tues.	50°	25°
Wed.	55°	35°
Thur.	53°	32°
Fri.	60°	35°

2.

Aluminum Cans Collected

Grade	Boys	Girls
Grade 7	200	225
Grade 8	250	175
Grade 9	275	200

Chapter 11 REVIEW

Write the letter of the best answer to each question.

1. A pictograph's scale uses a computer for a symbol. The scale says that one computer symbol equals 12 computers. How many computers are there if 8 computer symbols are shown in the pictograph?

   A 8   **C** 20

   B 12   **D** 96

2. Look at the bar graph to the right. How many more movies did Van watch than John?

   A 15   **C** 30

   B 23   **D** 45

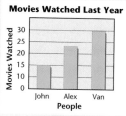

3. Look at the bar graph to the right. How many college graduates are there in Kelso?

   A 50   **C** 550

   B 500   **D** 1,050

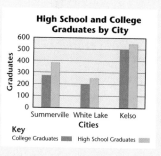

Use this circle graph for questions 4–5.

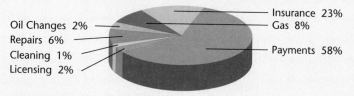

4. What is the second highest car expense for the Lopez family?

   A Insurance   **C** Gas

   B Payments   **D** Repairs

5. If the Lopez family spent $6,210.00 on car expenses last year, how much of it was spent on repairs?

   A $3.73   **C** $372.60

   B $37.26   **D** $3,726.00

Answer the following questions about pictographs:

6. If 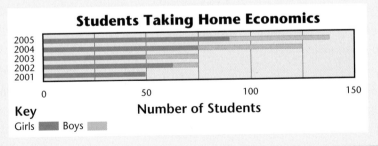 represents 4 cars, how many cars would be represented by ?

7. If ▯ represents 100 cans of soup, how many symbols would you draw to represent 875 cans of soup?

Make a vertical bar graph to show the information in this chart:

8.

Evan's Test Scores	
Test 1	85
Test 2	72
Test 3	90
Test 4	86
Test 5	92

Make a multiple bar graph to show the information in this chart:

9.

Scores on the Midterm and Final		
Student	Midterm	Final
Lance	65	85
Wanda	90	90
Maria	70	95
Emiko	80	70

Use this divided bar graph to find answers for the questions on page 287.

Students Taking Home Economics

Year	Number of Students
2005	
2004	
2003	
2002	
2001	

0   50   100   150

Number of Students

Key

Girls ▮   Boys ▯

10. In what year did boys first take home economics?

11. How many girls took home economics in 2004?

12. How many students took home economics in 2003?

13. How many boys took home economics in 2004?

Make a line graph to show the information in this table:

14.

| Pherooz's Weight | |
Week	Weight
1	185
2	183
3	180
4	175
5	178
6	170

Look at this incorrect graph. Make one that is correct.

15.

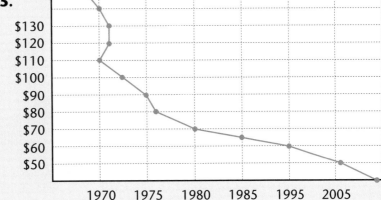

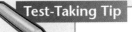

Test-Taking Tip

When you create a graph from a chart of data, check the number of facts you are supposed to record from the chart. Count to be sure you have the same number of facts on the graph.

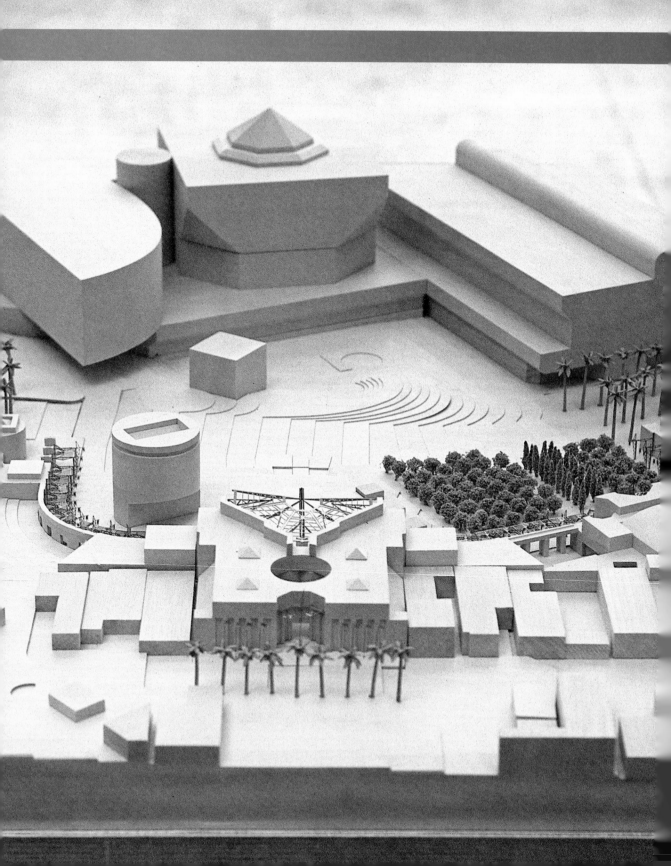

12 Scale Drawing

Have you ever wanted to plan an addition to your home, or design a deck, a building, or a landscape? Would you enjoy making model buildings, planes, trains, or automobiles? Does the idea of finding the best route for your next vacation sound like a smart idea? Whether you are creating plans or reading maps, being able to use a scale is helpful.

In Chapter 12, you will learn how to use floor plans, maps, scale models, and scale drawings. You will solve problems involving proportions and see how plans help designers, homeowners, and architects.

Goals for Learning

◆ To solve problems involving actual objects and models, using scale drawings and ratios

◆ To measure a drawing to the nearest eighth of an inch, and then solve a proportion to find the size of the actual object

◆ To use floor plans and ratios to determine the amount of carpet or tile needed to cover actual rooms

◆ To measure distances between two points on a map or drawing to the nearest eighth of an inch, and then use the scale to find the real distance

Gauge

Scale of model trains

The scale of a model is a description of the size of the model in relation to the full-size object. This is a picture of a model steam engine made to a 1:288 scale. The scale 1:288 means that if a part of the model is 1 mm, the same part on the actual steam engine is really 288 mm.

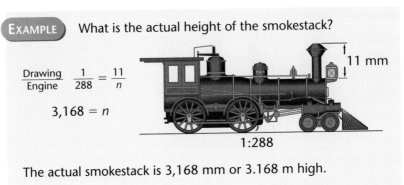

EXAMPLE   What is the actual height of the smokestack?

$$\frac{\text{Drawing}}{\text{Engine}} \quad \frac{1}{288} = \frac{11}{n}$$

$$3{,}168 = n$$

1:288

The actual smokestack is 3,168 mm or 3.168 m high.

Exercise A Use your metric ruler to measure the parts described on the drawing above. Then use a proportion to find the real-life sizes. Give your answers in meters.

1. Width of a window
2. Height of a window
3. Width of the cab
4. Width of the smokestack
5. Rear wheel diameter
6. Overall height
7. Length of the cab roof
8. Distance between the centers of the big wheels

The chart below shows that Z gauge is the smallest and O gauge is the largest.

Gauge	Ratio
O	1:43.5
OO	1:76
HO	1:87
N	1:148
Z	1:220

Model railroaders use letters to describe their scales. Each scale is called a **gauge.** The chart to the left tells what the scales mean. Use the ratios to find the model size or the actual size of a railroad car. The ratio in the chart tells how many model units to real units. If an O-gauge model is 1 inch long, the real one is 43.5 inches.

EXAMPLES An O-gauge railroad car measures 12 inches long. How many inches long is the real car?

$$\frac{\text{Model}}{\text{Real}} \quad \frac{1}{43.5} = \frac{12}{n}$$

$$n = 522 \text{ inches}$$

The real car is 522 inches long.

A railroad car is 43.5 feet long. How many inches long is an HO-gauge model?

$$\frac{\text{Model}}{\text{Real}} \quad \frac{1}{87} = \frac{n}{43.5 \text{ ft}}$$

$$\frac{1}{87} = \frac{n}{522 \text{ in.}}$$

$$\frac{522}{87} = n$$

$$6 = n$$

The model is 6 inches long.

Exercise B Use the ratios in the chart on page 290 to answer these questions. Round to the nearest whole number if needed.

1. A switching engine is 49 feet long. About how many inches will the N-gauge model be?

2. An OO-gauge boxcar is 6 inches long. How many feet long is the real boxcar?

3. A caboose is 12 feet high. About how many inches high would the O-gauge model be?

4. A tank car is 37 feet long. About how many inches long would a Z-gauge model be?

5. About how many inches tall should the model people be in an OO-gauge layout if real people are about 6 feet tall?

6. About how many inches tall should the people be in an O-gauge layout?

7. An HO-gauge train car is 8 inches long. How many feet long is the real car?

8. About how many inches tall should a house be to fit into an HO-gauge train layout? The real house is 30 feet high.

9. A water tower in an OO-gauge layout is 3 inches tall. How many feet tall is the real water tower?

10. An O-gauge bridge is 24 inches long. How many feet long would the real bridge be?

The scale of some model trains is 1 foot to $\frac{1}{4}$ inch. This means that each foot on the real car is represented by $\frac{1}{4}$ inch on the model car.

This is a sketch of the side view of a caboose. You can use the measurements of the real car to find the measurements of the model car.

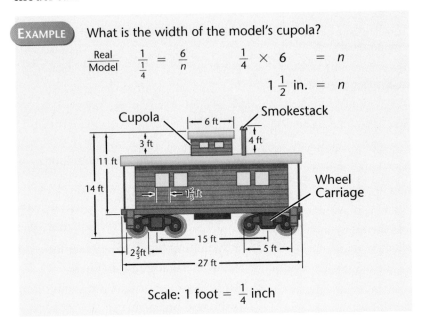

EXAMPLE   What is the width of the model's cupola?

$\frac{\text{Real}}{\text{Model}}$ $\frac{1}{\frac{1}{4}} = \frac{6}{n}$ $\frac{1}{4} \times 6 = n$

$1\frac{1}{2}$ in. $= n$

Scale: 1 foot $= \frac{1}{4}$ inch

Exercise C Use the real measurements from the sketch and a proportion to find the sizes of these parts on the model.

1. Overall length of the caboose

2. Height of the smokestack

3. Diameter of a wheel

4. Overall height of the caboose

5. Height of the cupola

6. Width of a lower window

7. Distance between the centers of the wheel carriages

8. Width of the wheel carriages

9. Height of the car without the wheel carriages

10. Height of the wheel carriages

Use your calculator to solve a proportion with an unknown term.

EXAMPLES Solve for *n*.

$$\frac{4}{5} = \frac{n}{20}$$

Multiply on the diagonal and divide by the third number.

Press 4 ⊠ 20 ÷ 5 =
The display reads *16*.
n = 16

$$\frac{n}{30} = \frac{5}{6}$$

Press *30* ⊠ 5 ÷ *6* =
The display reads *25*.
n = 25

Calculator Exercise Use a calculator to solve for the unknown term in each proportion.

1. $\dfrac{n}{6} = \dfrac{15}{30}$

2. $\dfrac{5}{7} = \dfrac{n}{35}$

3. $\dfrac{8}{9} = \dfrac{n}{72}$

4. $\dfrac{6}{11} = \dfrac{n}{77}$

5. $\dfrac{9}{20} = \dfrac{n}{60}$

6. $\dfrac{18}{20} = \dfrac{n}{100}$

7. $\dfrac{35}{62} = \dfrac{n}{124}$

8. $\dfrac{12}{30} = \dfrac{96}{n}$

Try This

A person who is 6 feet tall is 72 inches tall. About how tall would an OO model of that person be? The scale is 1:76. Estimate the number of these model people that could be placed end to end across your math textbook cover. Use a ruler to find how many would fit end to end.

Scale drawing

A picture in which the relative sizes have been kept

In a book, you might see a **scale drawing** like the one below of a bird. A drawing that is the same size as the real-life object may be too large or too small to fit well into the book. Then the artist draws the object to scale and includes a scale with the drawing.

The scale of this drawing is 1:2. This means that each inch on the drawing represents two inches on the real-life object. The first number refers to the drawing. The second number refers to the real object.

If the first number in the scale is smaller than the second number, the real object is larger than the drawing. If the first number is larger, then the real object is smaller than the drawing. A scale of 1:1 means that the drawing is life-size.

You can find the actual size of the object drawn by measuring the drawing with a ruler and then using the scale to write a proportion.

Measure from arrow point to arrow point in the drawing of the bird on this page.

EXAMPLE How long is the bird above?
The length of the drawing is $2\frac{5}{8}$ inches.

$$\frac{\text{Drawing}}{\text{Real}} \quad \frac{1}{2} = \frac{2\frac{5}{8}}{n}$$

$$2 \times 2\frac{5}{8} = n$$

$$5\frac{1}{4} = n$$

The bird is $5\frac{1}{4}$ inches long.

Exercise A Measure the distance between the points of the arrows to the nearest $\frac{1}{8}$ inch. Use the scale to write a proportion. Solve the proportions to find the length of the real-life object in inches.

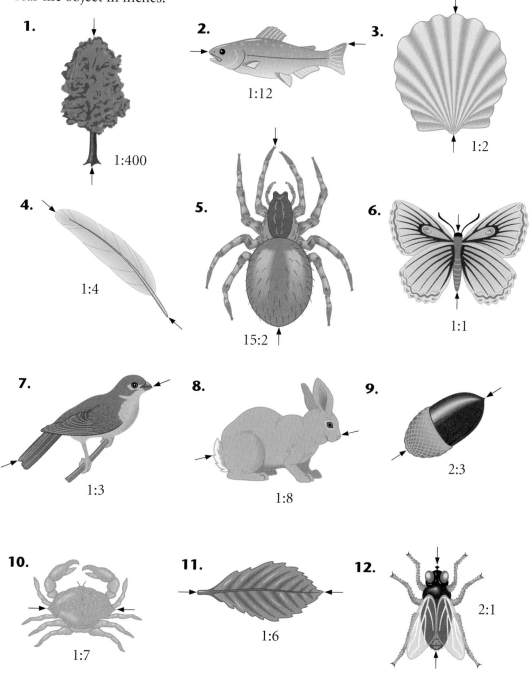

1.

1:400

2.

1:12

3.

1:2

4.

1:4

5.

15:2

6.

1:1

7.

1:3

8.

1:8

9.

2:3

10.

1:7

11.

1:6

12.

2:1

Dimensions

Measure, such as length, width, or height, of the size of an object

Floor plans of houses and apartments are drawn to scale. They are used by construction workers, tenants, and interior decorators. These drawings can be used to plan improvements or arrange furniture. You can find the real **dimensions** of the rooms by measuring the drawing with a ruler and then solving a proportion.

EXAMPLE What is the actual length and width of this living room?

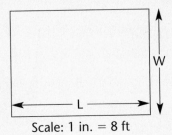

Scale: 1 in. = 8 ft

Length of drawing = $1\frac{1}{2}''$ Width of drawing = $1\frac{1}{8}''$

$\dfrac{\text{Drawing}}{\text{Real}} \quad \dfrac{1}{8} = \dfrac{1\frac{1}{2}}{n}$

$8 \times 1\frac{1}{2} = 1 \times n$

$8 \times \dfrac{3}{2} = n$

$12 = n$

The living room is 12 feet long.

$\dfrac{\text{Drawing}}{\text{Real}} \quad \dfrac{1}{8} = \dfrac{1\frac{1}{8}}{n}$

$8 \times 1\frac{1}{8} = 1 \times n$

$8 \times \dfrac{9}{8} = n$

$9 = n$

The living room is 9 feet wide.

Try This

How much would it cost to carpet the living room in the example above if carpeting costs $15.00 per square yard? (Hint: You must find the area in square feet, then divide by 9 to find the area in square yards.)

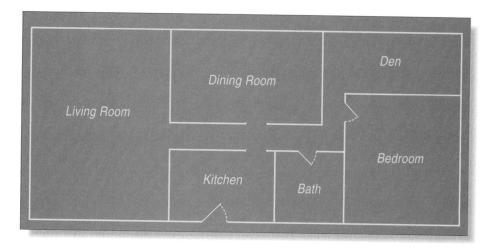

Exercise A Measure the length and width of each room to the nearest $\frac{1}{8}$ inch. Then use a proportion to find the real dimensions of each room using the scale 1 in. = 8 ft.

1. Living room

2. Dining room

3. Kitchen

4. Bath

5. Den

6. Bedroom

Architects use blueprints and floor plans to design and build houses and apartments.

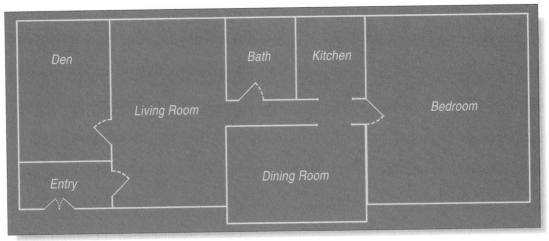

Scale: 1 inch = 8 feet

PROBLEM SOLVING

Exercise B Use a ruler and the floor plan above to answer the questions.

1. What are the real-life dimensions of the den?

2. If you wanted to tile the entry with 1-foot by 1-foot tiles, how many tiles would you need?

3. How many square feet of carpet would be needed to install wall-to-wall carpeting in the dining room?

4. What would this be in square yards?

5. How much would it cost to install wall-to-wall carpeting in the living room and the den? The carpet costs $18.00 per square yard.

6. Tile costs 79¢ per square foot. How much would it cost to put tile in the kitchen?

7. What is the length and the width of the bedroom?

8. What is the length and width of the bath?

9. How much will it cost to carpet the dining room if the carpeting costs $14.75 per square yard?

10. How many square yards of carpeting would be needed to carpet the living room, the dining room, and the den?

Lesson 4 Map Distances

Map distance

Space between two points as measured on a map

Real distance

Actual space between two locations

You can find the shortest distance between two cities. First, measure the distance on the map. This is the **map distance.** Then multiply the map distance by the number of miles represented by one inch. This is the **real distance.** Make all your measurements to the nearest eighth of an inch.

Scale: 1 inch = 880 miles

EXAMPLE   Distance between Washington, D.C. and Seattle

Map Distance: $2\frac{5}{8}''$

$2\frac{5}{8} \times 880 = \frac{21}{8} \times \frac{880}{1} = 2{,}310$ miles

Exercise A Copy and complete this chart.

	Trip	Map Distance (inches)	Real Distance (miles)
1.	Chicago to Washington, D.C.	___	___
2.	Miami to Omaha	___	___
3.	Seattle to Los Angeles	___	___
4.	San Francisco to Montreal	___	___
5.	Boston to Quebec	___	___

Road distance

Space between two locations along a road indicated by a number on a map

You can use a ruler to find the distance between two cities on a map. Then you multiply to find the actual distance.

The roads do not usually follow this straight line. To find the distance along the roads, you would add the **road distances** between each pair of arrows along your route.

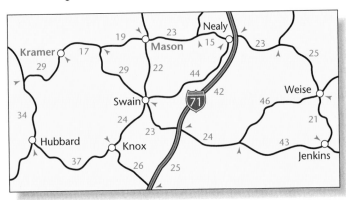

Scale: 1 inch = 32 miles

Road distance is greater than the straight line distance.

EXAMPLE The distance from Kramer to Mason = ■

Map distance: measurement $= \frac{7}{8}''$

$\frac{7}{8} \times 32 = 28$ miles

Road distance: 17 miles + 19 miles = 36 miles

Technology Connection

Did you know that some cars can now tell drivers which route to take? Computers use satellites in space to plot the best course from one place to another. Drivers may never be lost again once this technology becomes more common.

Exercise B Copy and complete this chart. Use the map on page 300. Make all measurements to the nearest eighth of an inch.

	Trip	Map Distance (inches)	Real Distance (miles)	Shortest Road Distance (miles)
1.	Kramer to Swain	_____	_____	_____
2.	Knox to Hubbard	_____	_____	_____
3.	Nealy to Weise	_____	_____	_____
4.	Jenkins to Swain	_____	_____	_____
5.	Swain to Weise	_____	_____	_____
6.	Nealy to Hubbard	_____	_____	_____
7.	Hubbard to Jenkins	_____	_____	_____
8.	Kramer to Nealy	_____	_____	_____
9.	Knox to Jenkins	_____	_____	_____
10.	Knox to Nealy	_____	_____	_____

Architecture and Mathematics

Architecture is the planning and designing of buildings, bridges, and towers. It is also one of the oldest art forms. Architecture often reflects the ideals and lifestyle of a society. For example, the ancient Greeks had a style that was balanced and orderly. During the Middle Ages—a deeply religious time—tall cathedrals were built.

As a guide for building a structure, architects use mechanical drawings that are drawn to scale. A copy of a mechanical drawing is called a blueprint. Creating mechanical drawings on a computer is known as computer-aided design (CAD). High school students interested in becoming an architect should study art, history, social studies, mechanical drawing, and mathematics. Geometry, measurement skills, and algebra are needed to design and read blueprints.

EXAMPLE The drawing length of the bedroom to the right is $1\frac{3}{4}$ inches. What is the actual length of the bedroom?

Scale: 1 in. = 8 ft

Step 1 Look at the scale. Scale: 1 inch = 8 feet

Step 2 Write a proportion.

$$\frac{\text{Drawing}}{\text{Real}} \quad \frac{1 \text{ in.}}{8 \text{ ft}} = \frac{1\frac{3}{4} \text{ in.}}{n \text{ ft}}$$

Step 3 Solve the proportion.

$$1 \times n = 8 \times 1\frac{3}{4}$$

$$n = 14$$

The actual bedroom is 14 feet long.

Exercise Solve problems 1–3. You may want to use graph paper to complete problem 4.

1. Scale: 1 in. = $2\frac{1}{4}$ ft; drawing length: 8 in.; actual length: ?

2. Scale: 1 cm = 12 m; actual length: 30 m; drawing length: ?

3. Drawing length: 5.5 m; actual length: 44 m; scale: 1 cm = ?

4. Make a scale drawing of your classroom. Measure the length and width to the nearest inch. Choose a scale for your drawing. Show where the windows, doors, tables, and desks are located.

Chapter 12 REVIEW

Write the letter of the best answer to each question.

1. A real railroad car is 48 feet long. OO-gauge models are built at the scale of 1:76. About how many inches is the OO model of the car?

   A 1 inch

   B 2 inches

   C 8 inches

   D 76 inches

2. An N-gauge bridge is 6 inches long. N-gauge models are built to the scale of 1:148. How long is the real bridge?

   A 2 inches

   B 25 inches

   C 74 inches

   D 888 inches

3. The scale of a drawing is 1 inch = 4 feet. The drawing shows a bedroom measuring 4 inches by 5 inches. What is the actual size of the bedroom?

   A 4 feet by 5 feet

   B 16 feet by 20 feet

   C 20 feet by 20 feet

   D 20 feet by 25 feet

4. The scale on a map is 1 inch = 16 miles. The distance between Luthertown and Birch Park on the map is $1\frac{3}{4}$ inches. How many miles apart are the two towns?

   A 16 miles

   B 20 miles

   C 28 miles

   D 48 miles

Answer these questions about scale models:

5. A real switching engine is 52 feet long. HO-gauge models are built to the scale of 1:87. About how many inches long would an HO model switching engine be?

6. The length of a real caboose is 27 feet. How long would the model be if the scale is 1 foot to $\frac{1}{4}$ inch?

7. An O-gauge car is $13\frac{1}{2}$ inches long. O-gauge models are built to the scale of 1:43.5. How long is the real car to the nearest $\frac{1}{4}$ inch?

8. A model tank is built to a 1:48 scale. How long would the real tank be if the model is $3\frac{1}{2}$ inches long? Give the answer in feet.

Use your ruler to measure the sizes of the rooms in the diagram below to the nearest eighth of an inch. Then answer these questions.

9. What is the actual length and width of the bathroom?

10. Tile costs 89¢ per square foot. How much would it cost to tile the kitchen?

11. What is the actual length and width of the dining room?

12. How many square yards of carpet are needed to cover the living room and dining room?

13. Ceramic tile costs $1.29 per square foot. How much will it cost to tile the bath?

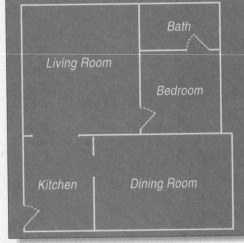

Scale: 1 inch = 8 feet

Find the map line distance and the shortest road distance between each pair of cities. Give answers in miles.

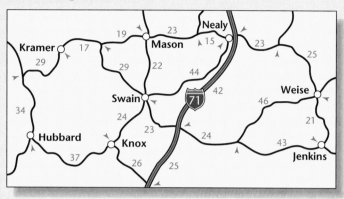

Scale: 1 inch = 32 miles

	map line distance	shortest road distance
14. Hubbard and Knox	_____	_____
15. Weise and Nealy	_____	_____
16. Mason and Hubbard	_____	_____
17. Jenkins and Knox	_____	_____
18. Kramer and Hubbard	_____	_____

Measure the distance between the arrows to the nearest $\frac{1}{8}$ inch. Then find the lengths of the real-life creatures.

19.

1:2

20.

2:3

Test-Taking Tip

When answering questions about a drawing, the information you gather in one problem may be useful in others.

Introduction to Algebra

People who work with money on the job often have to figure out gains and losses. If a company earned $3,000.00 less than its expenses for one month, that amount is called a negative number. If that same company earned $4,500.00 more than expenses the next month, the amount is called a positive number. You will learn all about positive and negative numbers—or integers—in this chapter. This is just one part of a kind of mathematics called algebra.

In Chapter 13, you will get a basic understanding of algebra. You will learn about integers and solve problems that have unknown quantities.

Goals for Learning

◆ To use number lines to help calculate and represent mathematical steps

◆ To compare integers, using symbols < and >

◆ To state the absolute value of any positive or negative integer

◆ To solve operations sentences with positive and negative integers

◆ To solve for a variable in an open sentence involving addition, subtraction, multiplication, and division

Integers

All whole numbers and their opposites
$(\ldots -2, -1, 0, 1, 2, \ldots)$

Positive integer

A whole number greater than zero

Negative integer

A whole number less than zero

Sometimes we need to use a direction as well as an amount when we use numbers. Walking three steps to the right is the *opposite* of walking three steps to the left. A score of 35 points is the *opposite* of a score of 35 points in the hole.

Exercise A Give the opposite of each phrase.

1. 3,000 feet above sea level
2. Twelve degrees below zero
3. Losing 5 yards on a down
4. Rewinding the tape to the beginning
5. Moving the clocks up 1 hour

Going to the right is usually thought of as going in a positive direction. Going up is also thought of as a positive move. Going left or going down is going in a negative direction. We use **integers** when we want to talk about amounts with a direction. A number line can be used to show **positive integers** and **negative integers.**

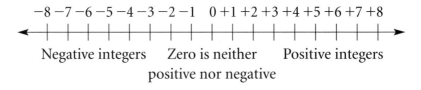

$-8\ -7\ -6\ -5\ -4\ -3\ -2\ -1\quad 0\ +1\ +2\ +3\ +4\ +5\ +6\ +7\ +8$

Negative integers   Zero is neither   Positive integers
positive nor negative

EXAMPLES   Each number below is listed with its opposite.

$$+17, -17 \qquad\qquad -35, +35$$
$$-9, \ +9 \qquad\qquad +73, -73$$

Exercise B Name the opposite of each of these integers.

1. -8	**5.** $+8$	**9.** -24
2. $+1$	**6.** -12	**10.** -238
3. $+17$	**7.** -5	**11.** $+14$
4. -6	**8.** $+108$	**12.** 0

Any number added to its opposite is equal to zero. Any number added to zero is equal to that number.

EXAMPLES

$$6 + (-6) = 0 \qquad 3 + 0 = 3$$
$$-9 + 9 = 0 \qquad 0 + 7 = 7$$
$$10 + (-10) = 0 \qquad 9 + 0 = 9$$

Exercise C Find the sum of these integers.

1. $6 + (-6)$ **5.** $23 + 0$ **9.** $16 + (-16)$
2. $-12 + 12$ **6.** $8 + (-8)$ **10.** $0 + 3$
3. $0 + 76$ **7.** $-12 + 12$ **11.** $5 + (-5)$
4. $-7 + 0$ **8.** $0 + (-11)$ **12.** $-12 + 0$

On a number line, the larger of two numbers is the one that is to the right of the other number. Since the positive numbers are to the right of the negative numbers, we can say that any positive number is greater than any negative number.

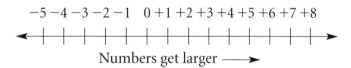

$$-5 \ -4 \ -3 \ -2 \ -1 \quad 0 \ +1 \ +2 \ +3 \ +4 \ +5 \ +6 \ +7 \ +8$$

Numbers get larger ⟶

EXAMPLES

+18 and +12
+18 is farther to the right, so $+18 > +12$

−11 and 0
0 is farther to the right, so $0 > -11$

−6 and −7
−6 is farther to the right, so $-6 > -7$

Exercise D Use a number line to help you compare each pair of integers, using $>$ or $<$.

1. -3 $+2$ **6.** -7 -2 **11.** -6 0
2. $+8$ $+1$ **7.** $+3$ -1 **12.** -2 -8
3. -9 -4 **8.** $+6$ -9 **13.** -36 $+4$
4. -5 $+5$ **9.** $+5$ -9 **14.** -58 -72
5. $+6$ $+8$ **10.** $+6$ 0 **15.** $+23$ -468

Use a number line to help you think through these problems.

Positive means
move to the right.
Negative means
move to the left.

EXAMPLES   If you begin at +5 and move four spaces to the right,
you will end at +9.

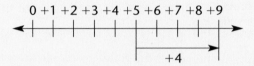

Write an addition sentence: +5 + (+4) = +9

If you begin at +5 and move three spaces to the left,
you will end at +2.

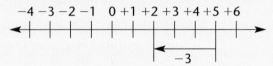

Write an addition sentence: +5 + (−3) = +2

Exercise A Write an addition sentence to describe each move.
Be sure to include the answer in your sentence.

$$-12\ -11\ -10\ -9\ -8\ -7\ -6\ -5\ -4\ -3\ -2\ -1\quad 0\ +1\ +2\ +3\ +4\ +5\ +6\ +7\ +8\ +9\ +10$$

1. Begin at +5. Move +3.

2. Begin at +7. Move −7.

3. Begin at −7. Move +4.

4. Begin at +1. Move −8.

5. Begin at −8. Move +5.

6. Begin at −4. Move +5.

7. Begin at +2. Move −8.

8. Begin at −6. Move −3.

9. Begin at −4. Move −5.

10. Begin at −6. Move 0.

A number line can be used to understand adding integers. The first addend tells us where to begin. The second addend tells us which direction and how far to move. The place we stop is the sum of the integers.

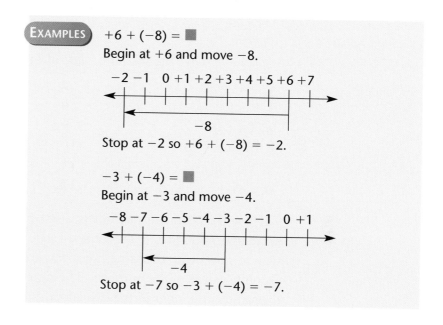

EXAMPLES

$+6 + (-8) = \blacksquare$

Begin at +6 and move −8.

Stop at −2 so $+6 + (-8) = -2$.

$-3 + (-4) = \blacksquare$

Begin at −3 and move −4.

Stop at −7 so $-3 + (-4) = -7$.

Exercise B Use the number line to help you find the sums.

1. $+5 + (-7)$
2. $-4 + (-4)$
3. $+6 + (+3)$
4. $-7 + (+3)$
5. $+3 + (+3)$
6. $-6 + (-1)$
7. $-4 + (-6)$
8. $-8 + (+9)$
9. $+7 + (-7)$
10. $+9 + (-9)$
11. $-7 + (-2)$
12. $+4 + (-8)$

13. $+3 + (+2)$
14. $-7 + (-2)$
15. $+8 + (-6)$
16. $+4 + (-9)$
17. $-5 + (-5)$
18. $+1 + (-9)$
19. $-10 + (+7)$
20. $-2 + (-5)$
21. $-3 + (-2) + (+6)$
22. $+4 + (-8) + (+7)$
23. $-5 + (-3) + (+6)$
24. $-8 + (+5) + (+7)$

The **absolute value** of a number is the distance that the number is from zero. The absolute value of a number is always positive.

EXAMPLES $|+6| = 6$ $|-3| = 3$ $|0| = 0$

The absolute value symbol is a pair of vertical lines.

Exercise C Give the absolute value of each number.

1. $|-4|$

2. $|+8|$

3. $|+108|$

4. $|+6|$

5. $|-108|$

6. $|+11|$

7. $|0|$

8. $|-3|$

9. $|-273|$

10. $|+3|$

11. $|+23|$

12. $|-19|$

When you use the number line to add two integers with the same sign, you move in the same direction. When you add two numbers with the same signs, you are also adding the absolute values of the numbers. The sign of the answer is the same as the signs of the two addends.

EXAMPLES $+3 + (+2) = \blacksquare$

$-2\ -1\quad 0\ +1\ +2\ +3\ +4\ +5\ +6$

$+3$ $+2$

$+3 + (+2) = +5$
Both move to the right. The sum is positive.

$-4 + (-2) = \blacksquare$

$-8\ -7\ -6\ -5\ -4\ -3\ -2\ -1\quad 0$

-2 -4

$-4 + (-2) = -6$
Both move to the left. The sum is negative.

When you add two numbers with unlike signs on the number line, you first go one direction and then the other. When you add two numbers with unlike signs you subtract the absolute values of the numbers. The sign of the answer is the same as the sign of the number with the larger absolute value.

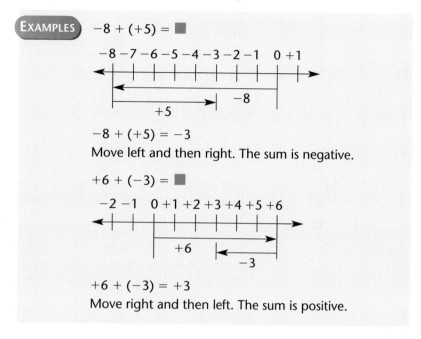

EXAMPLES

$-8 + (+5) = $ ▪

$-8 + (+5) = -3$
Move left and then right. The sum is negative.

$+6 + (-3) = $ ▪

$+6 + (-3) = +3$
Move right and then left. The sum is positive.

You can position a negative or a positive sign in two places: $^-8$ or -8 and $^+3$ or $+3$. For example, you could write $^-8 + {}^-8 = {}^-16$ or $^+3 + {}^+3 = {}^+6$. The problems may be less confusing if you write the numbers in parentheses like $-4 + (+6)$ instead of $-4 + {}^+6$.

Exercise D Find the sums.

1. $-3 + (+8)$
2. $-28 + (-36)$
3. $+52 + (+38)$
4. $-1 + (-2)$
5. $-92 + (+203)$
6. $-7 + (-9)$
7. $-2 + (-5)$
8. $+27 + (-45)$

9. $-38 + (+19)$
10. $+6 + (-203)$
11. $+4 + (+23)$
12. $-24 + (+6)$
13. $-206 + (+27)$
14. $+16 + (-33)$
15. $0 + (-6)$
16. $-16 + (-31)$

Subtraction is the opposite operation of addition. Subtraction of integers can best be accomplished by expressing as addition.

> **EXAMPLE** $-2 - (+4)$
>
> **Step 1** Change the operation.
>
> $-2 - (+4) \longrightarrow -2 + (+4)$
>
> **Step 2** Change the integer sign.
>
> $-2 + (+4) \longrightarrow -2 + (-4)$
>
> Therefore:
> $-2 - (+4)$ as a subtraction problem changes to
> $-2 + (-4)$ as an addition problem.
>
> Study these examples below. Notice that the first operational sign is changed to addition. The sign of the subtrahend is changed to the opposite.
>
> This sign always changes to the opposite.
>
> $+3 - (+4)$ $+5 - (+2)$ $6 - (+19)$ $+11 - (-1)$
> $+3 + (-4)$ $+5 + (-2)$ $6 + (-19)$ $+11 + (+1)$
>
> The operation changes to addition.

Try This

The example above shows 5 subtraction problems and 5 addition problems. Try solving each subtraction problem first. Then try solving the addition problems. Your set of subtraction answers should match the set of addition answers. Were the addition problems easier to solve? Why or why not?

Exercise A Copy and express these subtraction problems as addition. You do not need to solve the problems.

1. $-2 - (+5)$

2. $-5 - (-5)$

3. $+6 - (+2)$

4. $+2 - (+7)$

5. $-7 - (+3)$

6. $+6 - (+8)$

7. $+8 - (+9)$

8. $-1 - (+8)$

9. $+4 - (-6)$

10. $-8 - (-6)$

11. $-3 - (-5)$

12. $+4 - (-4)$

13. $-5 - (-1)$

14. $-1 - (+7)$

15. $+4 - (+1)$

16. $-9 - (+3)$

EXAMPLE   Addition of integers requires using two simple rules:

Rule 1   If the integer signs are the same, then keep the sign and add the integer.

$$-7 + (-4) = -11$$

Rule 2   If the integer signs are different, then subtract and use the sign next to the larger numeral.

$$-5 + (+9) = +4$$

Exercise B Express these subtraction problems as addition problems and compute the answers using the two rules above.

1. $-23 - (-16)$

2. $+17 - (-46)$

3. $-26 - (+51)$

4. $+42 - (+38)$

5. $-35 - (-23)$

6. $+18 - (+35)$

7. $-45 - (+26)$

8. $-73 - (-43)$

9. $+82 - (-37)$

10. $-52 - (+36)$

11. $+35 - (+28)$

12. $-23 - (-44)$

13. $+16 - (+39)$

14. $+92 - (-54)$

15. $-64 - (+31)$

16. $+43 - (-12)$

We can use positive and negative integers to help us solve word problems.

EXAMPLE   A football team gained 3 yards on the first down, lost 5 yards on the second down, and gained 7 yards on the third down. How many yards did they gain?
+3 + (−5) + (+7) = 5
They gained 5 yards.

PROBLEM SOLVING

Exercise A Write an addition sentence and solve each problem.

1. On Monday the temperature goes up 7°, by Thursday the temperature goes up another 4°, and by Sunday the temperature goes down 2°. How much has the temperature changed over the course of the week?

2. On Friday your checking account balance is $122.00. On Saturday you shop at the mall and write two checks for $17.00 and $31.00. What is your checking account balance now?

3. During the course of the game, the team scores 56 points, then they lose 18 points, and finally they score 32 more points. What is their final score?

4. Marta takes a three-part physical endurance test. In part 1 she loses 18 points. In part 2 she gains 22 points, and in part 3 she gains 4 points. What is Marta's score on the endurance test?

5. The Giants lose 12 yards on the first down in the football game. They gain 7 yards on the second down. On the third down they gain 8 yards. What is the total yardage gained by the Giants?

6. Hector works on the 4th floor of a high rise building. He needs to go up 9 floors to get to the cafeteria for lunch, and then go down 5 floors to attend a meeting. On what floor does the meeting take place?

7. Kwon has 82 books in his collection. He donates 26 paperbacks to the library book drive, and recycles 4 that are too worn out to keep. Kwon then goes to the bookstore and buys 3 books. How many books are now in his collection?

The multiplication of positive and negative integers is just like the multiplication of whole numbers.

EXAMPLES

Rule The product of two numbers with like signs will be positive.

$+9 \times (+2) = +18$
$-3 \times (-7) = +21$

Both signs are the same so the product is positive.

EXAMPLES

Rule The product of two numbers with unlike signs will be negative.

$-6 \times (+3) = -18$
$+2 \times (-7) = -14$

Both signs are different so the product is negative.

Exercise A Find the products.

1. $-2 \times (-6)$
2. $+3 \times (-3)$
3. $+3 \times (+7)$
4. $-5 \times (-3)$
5. $-6 \times (-4)$
6. $-3 \times (-1)$
7. $+10 \times (-2)$
8. $-4 \times (-5)$
9. $-4 \times (+6)$
10. $+6 \times (+12)$
11. $-1 \times (-1)$
12. $-4 \times (-13)$

13. $-7 \times (-7)$
14. $-7 \times (+6)$
15. $+5 \times (+8)$
16. $+9 \times (-8)$
17. $+4 \times (-18)$
18. $+45 \times (-2)$
19. $-6 \times (-9)$
20. $-11 \times (-11)$
21. $+11 \times (-11)$
22. $-7 \times (+10)$
23. $+22 \times (-2)$
24. $+3 \times (-35)$

Sometimes it may be necessary to multiply with more than two numbers. Simply multiply the first two numbers and replace them with their product.

EXAMPLE $-3 \times (-5) \times (-2)$

$+15 \times (-2) = -30$

Exercise B Find the products.

1. $-4 \times (-3) \times (+3)$
2. $+5 \times (-2) \times (-5)$
3. $+5 \times (-1) \times (-1)$
4. $-2 \times (-3) \times (-1)$
5. $+6 \times (-4) \times (-3)$
6. $-6 \times (+6) \times (-9)$
7. $-4 \times (-4) \times (-4)$
8. $+8 \times (+1) \times (-10)$
9. $-2 \times (+4) \times (-1)$
10. $-12 \times (-12) \times (-1)$
11. $-3 \times (-1) \times (-12)$
12. $+11 \times (-11) \times (-1)$

13. $+13 \times (-2) \times (-1)$
14. $-16 \times (+11) \times (+2)$
15. $-3 \times (-4) \times (-9)$
16. $-7 \times (-5) \times (-1)$
17. $-5 \times (+5) \times (-1)$
18. $+6 \times (+2) \times (-1)$
19. $-4 \times (-1) \times (-5)$
20. $+11 \times (-1) \times (+4)$
21. $-30 \times (-10) \times (-3)$
22. $+12 \times (+4) \times (-20)$
23. $-22 \times (-10) \times (-1)$
24. $-3 \times (-2) \times (-14)$

Try This

Study your answers in Exercise B. Can you find any patterns? Then study this list:

- The product of two negative numbers and a positive number is a positive number.

- The product of two positive numbers and a negative number is a negative number.

- The product of three negative numbers is a negative number.

Use this list to check all of your answers in Exercise B. If an answer does not follow the rules of this list, try reworking the problem.

The addition and multiplication operations have special properties. The **commutative property** states that two numbers may be added in either order.

Commutative property

States that two numbers may be added or multiplied in either order

EXAMPLES   Commutative Property of Addition

$$3 + 4 = 4 + 3$$

7   7   Both sums equal 7.

$$+4 + (-7) = -7 + (+4)$$

−3   −3   Both sums equal −3.

$$-6 + (-2) = -2 + (-6)$$

−8   −8   Both sums equal −8.

Commutative
Property of
Addition:
$a + b$ is the
same as $b + a$.

The commutative property also states that two numbers may be multiplied in either order.

Commutative
Property of
Multiplication:
$a \times b$ is the same
as $b \times a$.

EXAMPLES   Commutative Property of Multiplication

$$2 \times 7 = 7 \times 2$$

14   14   Both products equal 14.

$$-5 \times (-3) = -3 \times (-5)$$

15   15   Both products equal 15.

$$-6 \times (+7) = +7 \times (-6)$$

−42   −42   Both products equal −42.

Associative
property

*Allows you to add or
multiply with different
groupings; the final
answer does not change*

The **associative property** allows you to add with different
groupings. Sometimes this property is called the grouping
property.

EXAMPLE Associative Property of Addition

$$(3 + 4) + 8 = 3 + (4 + 8)$$
$$7 + 8 = 3 + 12$$
$$15 = 15$$

Both sums equal 15. Adding the 3 and 4 first or adding
the 4 and 8 first does not change the final answer.

The associative property also allows you to multiply with
different groupings.

EXAMPLE Associative Property of Multiplication

$$(2 \times 3) \times 5 = 2 \times (3 \times 5)$$
$$6 \times 5 = 2 \times 15$$
$$30 = 30$$

Both products equal 30. Multiplying the 2 and 3 first
or multiplying the 3 and 5 first does not change the
final answer.

Exercise A Write the name of the property demonstrated
(commutative or associative). Refer to the examples if necessary.

1. $2 + 6 = 6 + 2$

2. $5 + (6 + 2) = (5 + 6) + 2$

3. $8 + 1 = 1 + 8$

4. $8 \times 4 = 4 \times 8$

5. $12 + 5 + 2 = 12 + 2 + 5$

6. $10 \times 9 = 9 \times 10$

7. $(9 + 2) + 3 = 9 + (2 + 3)$

8. $(8 + 2) + 5 = 8 + (2 + 5)$

9. $(3 \times 4) = (4 \times 3)$

The **distributive property** applies to problems that contain multiplication and addition or multiplication and subtraction. The distributive property allows you to multiply each term in parentheses by a single factor.

EXAMPLES Distributive Property of Multiplication

$$3 \times (5 + 6) = 3 \times 5 + 3 \times 6$$
$$3 \quad \times \quad 11 \quad = \quad 15 \quad + \quad 18$$
$$33 \qquad = \qquad 33$$

Recall the Order of Operations from Chapter 1. Multiply 3×5 and 3×6 before adding. Then add the products $15 + 18$.

Both solutions equal 33. Instead of adding the 5 and 6 in parentheses first, you can multiply each by the 3 and then add. The final answer does not change.

$$4 \times (6 + 2) = 4 \times 6 + 4 \times 2$$
$$= \quad 24 \quad + \quad 8$$
$$= \qquad 32$$

$$5 \times (9 - 2) = 5 \times 9 - 5 \times 2$$
$$= \quad 45 \quad - \quad 10$$
$$= \qquad 35$$

Exercise B Use the distributive property of multiplication to simplify these expressions. Show your steps as shown in the examples above.

1. $5 \times (7 + 5)$

2. $6 \times (8 + 10)$

3. $3 \times (12 - 10)$

4. $5 \times (6 - 2)$

5. $4 \times (7 + 2)$

6. $7 \times (6 + 2)$

7. $8 \times (11 - 4)$

8. $4 \times (11 + 3)$

9. $7 \times (10 - 2)$

10. $5 \times (12 - 4)$

11. $8 \times (5 - 2)$

12. $18 \times (2 + 3)$

13. $5 \times (20 - 5)$

14. $15 \times (3 - 1)$

15. $9 \times (8 + 3)$

16. $3 \times (4 + 9)$

Division of positive and negative integers requires the use of the same rules used in multiplication.

EXAMPLES

Rule The quotient of two numbers with like signs will be positive.

$$-14 \div (-2) = +7$$
$$+16 \div (+8) = +2$$

Both signs are the same so the quotient is positive.

EXAMPLES

Rule The quotient of two numbers with unlike signs will be negative.

$$-18 \div (+2) = -9$$
$$+20 \div (-4) = -5$$

The signs are unlike so the quotient is negative.

Division problems can be expressed as fractions.

EXAMPLES $+15 \div (-3)$ is the same as $\frac{15}{-3}$ and $-\frac{15}{3} = -5$

$$\frac{-12}{-4} = +3 \qquad \frac{-17}{18} = -\frac{17}{18}$$

Exercise A Solve for the quotients.

1. $-16 \div (-8)$
2. $-9 \div (+3)$
3. $-9 \div (-9)$
4. $+36 \div (+2)$
5. $+30 \div (+3)$
6. $+35 \div (-7)$
7. $+52 \div (-2)$
8. $-32 \div (+32)$

9. $+24 \div (-6)$
10. $-7 \div (-7)$
11. $-1 \div (-1)$
12. $-6 \div (+3)$
13. $+88 \div (-11)$
14. $+34 \div (-17)$
15. $+82 \div (-2)$
16. $-77 \div (-11)$

17. $-39 \div (-3)$
18. $-28 \div (-4)$
19. $+30 \div (-15)$
20. $+21 \div (-7)$
21. $-10 \div (-1)$
22. $-61 \div (+1)$
23. $+85 \div (-5)$
24. $-90 \div (-2)$

Exercise B Simplify these fractions by dividing.

1. $\dfrac{-28}{+4}$

2. $\dfrac{+35}{-7}$

3. $\dfrac{-60}{-1}$

4. $\dfrac{-14}{-7}$

5. $\dfrac{-32}{-2}$

6. $\dfrac{-56}{+2}$

7. $\dfrac{+78}{-2}$

8. $\dfrac{-21}{+3}$

9. $\dfrac{-25}{-5}$

10. $\dfrac{+52}{-26}$

11. $\dfrac{-44}{+11}$

12. $\dfrac{-17}{-1}$

13. $\dfrac{-24}{-12}$

14. $\dfrac{-88}{+44}$

15. $\dfrac{+46}{-23}$

16. $\dfrac{+52}{+26}$

Exercise C Simplify these fractions.

1. $\dfrac{-14}{+5}$

2. $\dfrac{+33}{-10}$

3. $\dfrac{-19}{-12}$

4. $\dfrac{+22}{-10}$

5. $\dfrac{-78}{-11}$

6. $\dfrac{+22}{+12}$

7. $\dfrac{-10}{+4}$

8. $\dfrac{-11}{+10}$

9. $\dfrac{-10}{-10}$

10. $\dfrac{+18}{-12}$

11. $\dfrac{+55}{-11}$

12. $\dfrac{+57}{-23}$

13. $\dfrac{-200}{+20}$

14. $\dfrac{+140}{+70}$

15. $\dfrac{-80}{-12}$

16. $\dfrac{+34}{-16}$

17. $\dfrac{-26}{-19}$

18. $\dfrac{+57}{-27}$

19. $\dfrac{-70}{+30}$

20. $\dfrac{-71}{-20}$

Variable

A symbol, usually a letter, that represents an unknown number

A **variable** is a letter such as *a, b, n, x,* or *y* that represents an unknown number. You can use any letter or symbol to stand for an unknown number. When you know the value of the variable, you can replace the letter with a number.

All numbers can be represented on the number line.

EXAMPLES Graph $x = 4$ on the number line.

Step 1 Use a number line like the one shown.

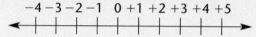

Step 2 Locate the $x = 4$ and draw a shaded circle as shown.

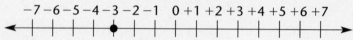

Graph $x = -3$ on the number line.

Exercise A Draw number lines to graph these values.

1. $x = 6$ **8.** $x = -1$

2. $x = 5$ **9.** $x = -3$

3. $x = -7$ **10.** $x = 3$

4. $x = 7$ **11.** $x = -4$

5. $x = 4$ **12.** $x = -5$

6. $x = -6$ **13.** $x = 0$

7. $x = -2$ **14.** $x = 1$

x-axis

The horizontal line on a grid that passes through the origin

y-axis

The vertical line on a grid that passes through the origin

Origin

The point on a grid with the coordinates (0, 0)

x-coordinate

The first number in an ordered pair describing the location of a point

y-coordinate

The second number in an ordered pair describing the location of a point

Ordered pair

Two numbers that give the location of a point on a grid

When a vertical number line is drawn so that it crosses a horizontal number line at zero, it forms a grid. The horizontal line is called the **x-axis.** The vertical line is called the **y-axis.** The point where the two lines cross at zero is the **origin.**

Any point on the grid can be named by its **x-coordinate** and its **y-coordinate.** The x-coordinate is the first number and the y-coordinate is the second number in an **ordered pair** (x, y). For x, move to the right or left on the horizontal number line. For y, move up or down on the vertical number line.

EXAMPLE Graph the ordered pairs $(-3, -2)$, $(-2, 2)$, $(0, 1)$, $(3, 4)$, and $(4, -1)$.

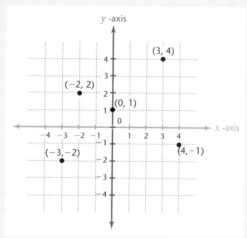

Exercise A Graph the ordered pairs.

1. $(-2, -2), (0, 2), (2, 2)$

2. $(3, 3), (3, 0), (3, -3)$

3. $(-2, 2), (0, 0), (2, -2)$

4. $(-2, 0), (0, 2), (2, 4)$

5. $(-2, -1), (-1, 1), (0, 3)$

6. $(-1, 1), (0, -2), (1, -5)$

An **equation** is a mathematical sentence that states two expressions are equal. For example, $13 + 5 = 18$. When an equation includes at least one variable, we call it an **open sentence.**

Equation

Two mathematical expressions separated by an equal sign

Open sentence

An equation with an unknown

Equations with variables are easy to solve using opposites. Remember the opposite of $+8$ is -8 because when you add them together the answer is zero. The opposite of -5 is $+5$ because $-5 + 5 = 0$ or $-5 + (+5) = 0$.

EXAMPLES   Solve the equation $n + 5 = +18$.

In the equation $n + 5 = +18$ we must remove the $+5$ from the equation by adding the opposite -5 to both sides of the equation.

$$n + 5 = +18$$
$$\underline{-5 \quad\;\; - 5}$$
$$n + 0 = +13 \quad \text{because } 18 - 5 = 13$$
$$n = +13$$

Check: $13 + 5 = +18$

Find x for $x - 7 = +10$.

Recall that subtraction problems can be solved by changing to add the opposite.
Think of $x - 7 = +10$ as $x + (-7) = +10$.

$$x - 7 = +10 \qquad\qquad\qquad \text{Think: } x + (-7) = +10$$
$$\underline{+7 \quad + 7} \qquad\qquad\qquad\qquad\qquad\quad \underline{+7 \quad\;\; + 7}$$
$$x = +17 \quad \text{because } 10 + 7 = 17 \qquad\quad x = 17$$

Check: $17 - 7 = +10$

Find a for $a + 5 = -11$.

$$a + 5 = -11$$
$$\underline{-5 \qquad -5} \quad \text{Add } -5 \text{ to both sides of the equal sign.}$$
$$a = -16 \quad \text{because } -11 - 5 = -16$$

Check: $-16 + 5 = -11$

Exercise A Solve for the variable. Refer to the examples if you need help.

Add the opposite to both sides of the equation.

1. $x + 2 = +10$

2. $a + 6 = +20$

3. $t + 2 = +18$

4. $n + 5 = +22$

5. $x + 1 = +20$

6. $y + 7 = +30$

7. $a + 8 = +38$

8. $c + 10 = +25$

9. $r + 20 = +30$

10. $s + 7 = +17$

11. $n + 3 = +28$

12. $x + 30 = +30$

13. $y + 32 = +90$

14. $b + 9 = +39$

15. $r + 34 = +54$

16. $p + 45 = +60$

17. $v + 2 = +32$

18. $w + 12 = +21$

19. $x + 10 = +10$

20. $s + 4 = +5$

Exercise B Solve for the variable. Check your answers.

1. $d - 5 = +30$

2. $a - 10 = +22$

3. $f - 1 = +2$

4. $x - 13 = +23$

5. $g - 5 = +20$

6. $t - 1 = +30$

7. $y - 28 = +40$

8. $m - 2 = +26$

9. $n - 23 = +1$

10. $x - 17 = +30$

11. $a - 7 = +7$

12. $b - 1 = +1$

13. $u - 3 = +3$

14. $w - 7 = 0$

15. $c - 9 = +11$

16. $m - 1 = 0$

17. $h - 3 = +30$

18. $k - 5 = +2$

19. $x - 12 = +3$

20. $y - 5 = +2$

Exercise C Solve for the variable. Check your answers.

1. $p - 7 = -10$
2. $q - 4 = -4$
3. $a + 5 = -11$
4. $m + 3 = -5$
5. $r - 5 = -30$
6. $d + 1 = -1$
7. $x - 6 = -50$
8. $h + 2 = -3$
9. $x + 10 = -3$

10. $j - 3 = -19$
11. $z + 11 = -12$
12. $b + 17 = -33$
13. $s - 29 = -9$
14. $n - 21 = -3$
15. $u + 1 = -1$
16. $f - 14 = -14$
17. $x - 1 = -1$
18. $k + 120 = -100$

Sometimes the open sentence may be in the form of $-5 + x = 12$.
Solving for the variable requires the same basic operation as before.

EXAMPLES   Solve for the variable.

$$-4 + a = 15$$
$$\underline{+4 \qquad\quad +4}$$
$$a = 19$$ Add +4 to both sides of the equation.

Check: $-4 + 19 = 15$

$$-7 + x = -2$$
$$\underline{+7 \qquad\quad +7}$$
$$x = +5$$ Add +7 to both sides of the equation.

Check: $-7 + 5 = -2$

$$20 = a - 7$$
$$\underline{+7 \qquad\quad +7}$$
$$+27 = a$$ Add +7 to both sides of the equation.

Check: $20 = 27 - 7$

$$8 + x = -12$$
$$\underline{-8 \qquad\quad -8}$$
$$x = -20$$ Add −8 to both sides of the equation.

Check: $8 + (-20) = -12$

$$-14 = c + 6$$
$$\underline{-6 \qquad\quad -6}$$
$$-20 = c$$ Add −6 to both sides of the equation.

Check: $-14 = -20 + 6$

So far in this chapter, positive numbers have a positive (+) sign. Sometimes a number does not have a positive or a negative sign next to it. These numbers are always positive.

Exercise D Solve for the variable. Check your answers.

1. $8 + x = 20$
2. $-5 + y = -15$
3. $20 = a + 4$
4. $8 = x - 15$
5. $-30 = c - 31$
6. $-5 + x = 0$
7. $-8 = x - 21$
8. $-10 + y = 10$

9. $-9 + c = 21$
10. $-16 = c + 5$
11. $-7 = x - 5$
12. $-10 = y - 10$
13. $9 = a - 20$
14. $-6 = x + 1$
15. $-25 + c = 50$
16. $-1 = c - 1$

PROBLEM SOLVING

Exercise E Write an open sentence for each word problem and solve the equation.

1. Sumi has $243.00 in her checking account. She needs to write a check for $324.00. How much money does she need to deposit to prevent her check from bouncing?

2. Antonio listens to the evening weather report and hears that the temperature has dropped 18 degrees since the day's high. The current temperature is -16 degrees. What was the high temperature for the day?

3. After selling 24 calendars for the community center fund-raiser, Amy has 14 left. How many calendars did she have before she sold any?

4. Wally lost 25 pounds but he gained a few pounds on vacation. Now his net weight loss is 17 pounds. How many pounds did he gain on vacation?

Some open sentences require the use of multiplication or division to solve for the variable. Write expressions like $2 \times n = 12$ without the multiplication symbol. Numbers are understood to be positive if the sign is omitted.

EXAMPLES $+2 \times n$ is the same as $2n$.   Rewrite without the multiplication symbol. The number is positive.

$-3 \times p$ is the same as $-3p$.

Use division to solve for the variable.

EXAMPLES   Find y for $6y = 18$.

$$\frac{6y}{6} = \frac{18}{6}$$ Divide both sides by $+6$.

$$y = 3$$ because $18 \div 6 = 3$

Check: $6 \times 3 = 18$

Find a for $4a = 36$.

$$\frac{4a}{4} = \frac{36}{4}$$ Divide both sides by $+4$.

$$a = 9$$ because $36 \div 4 = 9$

Check: $4 \times 9 = 36$

Find x for $-7x = 20$.

$$\frac{-7x}{-7} = \frac{20}{-7}$$

$$x = \frac{20}{-7} \quad \text{or} \quad -\frac{20}{7}$$

Check: $-7 \times \frac{-20}{7} = 20$

In algebra, improper fractions are preferred rather than mixed numbers. Therefore, answers like $-\frac{20}{7}$ are in an acceptable form.

You can also use multiplication to solve for the variables.

EXAMPLES Find n for $n \div 4 = 10$.

$$\frac{n}{4} = 10 \qquad \text{Rewrite in vertical form.}$$

$$4 \times \frac{n}{4} = 10 \times 4 \qquad \text{Multiply both sides by } +4.$$

$$n = 40 \qquad \text{because } 10 \times 4 = 40$$

Check: $\frac{40}{4} = 10$

Find x for $\frac{x}{-5} = -12$.

$$\frac{x}{-5} = -12$$

$$-5 \times \frac{x}{-5} = -12 \times -5 \quad \text{Multiply both sides by } -5.$$

$$x = +60 \qquad \text{because } -12 \times -5 = +60$$

Check: $\frac{+60}{-5} = -12$

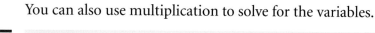

Multiple or divide both sides of the equation by the same number.

Exercise A Solve for the variable. Check your answers.

1. $5x = 40$

2. $6a = 54$

3. $5s = 20$

4. $6r = 30$

5. $12t = 24$

6. $6x = 42$

7. $2a = 56$

8. $3b = 96$

9. $19z = 38$

10. $8x = 72$

11. $4w = 16$

12. $13a = 130$

13. $\frac{b}{10} = 5$

14. $\frac{x}{22} = 2$

15. $\frac{r}{12} = 4$

16. $\frac{n}{11} = 8$

17. $\frac{n}{10} = 6$

18. $\frac{x}{4} = 23$

19. $\frac{a}{21} = 3$

20. $\frac{b}{48} = 2$

21. $\frac{t}{7} = 9$

22. $\frac{r}{2} = 23$

23. $\frac{n}{5} = 9$

24. $\frac{x}{10} = 10$

Exercise B Solve for the variable. Check your answers.

1. $12x = -36$

2. $-3a = -24$

3. $\dfrac{r}{-10} = 4$

4. $\dfrac{x}{4} = -3$

5. $\dfrac{y}{20} = 4$

6. $7b = 63$

7. $-5f = -20$

8. $\dfrac{s}{3} = -8$

9. $25p = -100$

10. $\dfrac{n}{-2} = -24$

11. $13u = -42$

12. $-16w = -64$

13. $\dfrac{x}{-12} = 6$

14. $\dfrac{n}{-20} = -1$

15. $-2x = -30$

16. $-5t = -55$

17. $\dfrac{n}{7} = -4$

18. $\dfrac{a}{-16} = 5$

19. $-2a = 66$

20. $8a = -96$

21. $-34d = -68$

22. $\dfrac{b}{-5} = -20$

23. $\dfrac{n}{10} = -3$

24. $8p = -64$

25. $-3r = -15$

26. $\dfrac{a}{2} = -21$

27. $-\dfrac{a}{2} = -21$

28. $\dfrac{a}{-2} = 21$

29. $-4a = -1$

30. $-2g = -7$

31. $\dfrac{s}{-6} = -5$

32. $-1a = -44$

33. $\dfrac{n}{-19} = -5$

34. $-7x = 63$

35. $\dfrac{v}{2} = -2$

36. $-5y = -25$

37. $\dfrac{b}{2} = -34$

38. $-1y = -20$

39. $\dfrac{w}{16} = -4$

40. $2x = -7$

41. $9r = -8$

42. $-4v = -9$

43. $-3b = 40$

44. $-4x = 9$

45. $-2a = 5$

Calculator Practice Use your calculator to solve for the variable.

> **EXAMPLES** $7n = 20$
>
> Press 20 ÷ 7 =
>
> The display reads 2.8571428.
> Round to the nearest tenth.
>
> $n = 2.9$
>
> $\frac{x}{14} = 3$
>
> Press 3 × 14 =
>
> The display reads 42.
>
> $x = 42$

Calculator Exercise Use a calculator to solve for the variable. Round your answer to the nearest tenth, if necessary.

1. $23x = 50$

2. $3c = 38$

3. $\frac{a}{9} = 4$

4. $31n = 85$

5. $\frac{x}{12} = 5$

6. $\frac{z}{3} = 17$

7. $18a = 52$

8. $\frac{x}{4} = 9$

9. $16c = 32$

10. $\frac{n}{8} = 48$

11. $5p = 30$

12. $\frac{k}{3} = 22$

13. $\frac{d}{5} = 36$

14. $14f = 8$

15. $28r = 103$

Technology Connection

Scientists often use variables in their work. Perhaps one of the most famous scientific equations with variables is Albert Einstein's $E = mc^2$. The equation shows that matter can be changed to energy. The variables in this formula mean:

E = energy m = matter or mass c = speed of light

Einstein's work and this equation changed science and made atomic energy possible.

Equations in the form of $2x + 5 = 25$ can best be solved using two steps as shown.

> Undo the addition or subtraction first. Then undo the multiplication or division.

EXAMPLES $3x + 4 = 19$

Solution: $3x + 4 = 19$

$$\underline{\quad -4 \quad -4 \quad}$$ **Step 1** Add -4 to both sides.

$$3x = 15$$

$$\frac{3x}{3} = \frac{15}{3}$$ **Step 2** Divide both sides by 3.

$$x = 5$$

Check: $(3 \times 5) + 4 = 15 + 4 = 19$

$5y - 6 = 20$

Solution: $5y - 6 = 20$

$$\underline{\quad +6 \quad +6 \quad}$$ **Step 1** Add $+6$ to both sides.

$$5y = 26$$

$$\frac{5y}{5} = \frac{26}{5}$$ **Step 2** Divide both sides by 5.

$$y = \frac{26}{5}$$ Leave as an improper fraction.

Check: $(5 \times \frac{26}{5}) - 6 = 26 - 6 = 20$

$-25 = 3a - 2$

Solution: $-25 = 3a - 2$

$$\underline{\quad +2 \qquad +2 \quad}$$ **Step 1** Add $+2$ to both sides.

$$-23 = 3a$$

$$-\frac{23}{3} = \frac{3a}{3}$$ **Step 2** Divide both sides by $+3$.

$$-\frac{23}{3} = a$$ Leave as an improper fraction.

Check: $-25 = (3 \times -\frac{23}{3}) - 2 = -23 - 2$

Exercise A Solve for the variable. Check your answers.

1. $2a - 6 = 30$

2. $5y + 10 = -20$

3. $2c - 1 = 9$

4. $3a + 3 = -15$

5. $3c - 1 = 11$

6. $5x + 2 = 22$

7. $6x - 1 = -19$

8. $-6 + 2x = 20$

9. $13 + 3x = -5$

10. $3a + 1 = 22$

11. $6x + 2 = 20$

12. $3c + 2 = -19$

13. $9y + 18 = 0$

14. $2y - 3 = 20$

15. $10c + 1 = 81$

16. $7a - 4 = 30$

17. $3 + 2n = 31$

18. $-8 + 11n = 25$

EXAMPLE

Check your answer by substituting your answer for the variable. Is the sentence true?

$$-5a + 2 = 32$$
$$\underline{\quad -2 \quad -2 \quad}$$ **Step 1** Add -2 to both sides.
$$-5a = 30$$

$$\frac{-5a}{-5} = \frac{30}{-5}$$ **Step 2** Divide both sides by -5.

$$a = -6$$ because $+30 \div (-5) = -6$

Check: $(-5 \times -6) + 2 = 30 + 2 = 32$

Exercise B Solve for the variable. Check your answers.

1. $-3a - 1 = 1$

2. $-2a + 2 = 18$

3. $-9a - 2 = 34$

4. $-1a - 6 = 20$

5. $-6c + 10 = 40$

6. $-6a - 1 = -17$

7. $-4a + 2 = 20$

8. $4 - 3a = 40$

9. $-1c + 2 = 30$

10. $-2x + 3 = -25$

Combining like terms is similar to adding or subtracting integers.

EXAMPLES Remember $-4 + (-5) = -9$
Then $-4a + (-5a) = -9a$
or $-4a - 5a = -9a$

Notice that the addition sign is not always shown when you add a negative integer.
$-4a + (-5a)$ is the same as $-4a - 5a$.

$-3a - 6a = -9a$ $-9x + 2x = -7x$
$-4a + 5a = 1a$ $4a - 5a = -1a$
or $-4a + 5a = a$ or $4a - 5a = -a$

We usually refer to "$1a$" or "$-1a$" as simply "a" or "$-a$."

Exercise A Simplify by combining like terms.

1. $+3a - 4a$

2. $+6x - 4x$

3. $+9y - 3y + 2y$

4. $+y + 2y$

5. $-17c + 7c$

6. $-8c - 2c + 10c$

7. $+25a + 2a + 3a$

8. $-3c - 6c + 8c$

9. $+8c - 2c$

10. $-10x - 10x$

11. $-12c + 12c$

12. $-9c - 2c$

13. $-15c + 5c - 5c$

14. $-13x + 2x - 3x$

15. $+16a - 20a$

16. $+11y - 2y + 3y$

Sometimes when you combine like terms, other variables may be present.

Always look for like terms.

EXAMPLES Simplify $+7a + 3c + 4a - 9c$ by combining like terms.

$$+7a + 4a + 3c - 9c$$

Arrange like terms together, then combine like terms.

$$+11a - 6c$$

Simplify $-8x + 3y - 2x - 10y$ by combining like terms.

$$-8x - 2x + 3y - 10y$$

Arrange like terms together, then combine like terms.

$$-10x - 7y$$

Other terms without variables may also be present. Combine as you would with variables.

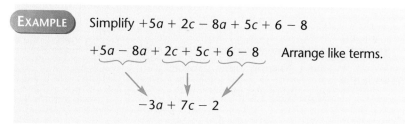

EXAMPLE Simplify $+5a + 2c - 8a + 5c + 6 - 8$

$$+5a - 8a + 2c + 5c + 6 - 8$$ Arrange like terms.

$$-3a + 7c - 2$$

Exercise B Simplify by combining like terms.

1. $-3a + 9c + 8c$

2. $+4x + 2 + 5x$

3. $-5c + 7c + 6c$

4. $+4a - 6a - 2a + 3$

5. $+4 - 5c + 2c - 6c + 2$

6. $+30c + 2c - 6c + 4c$

7. $-6x + 2y + 8y - 3x$

8. $+3y - 8y + 6 - 9$

9. $+5a + 8a - 2a + 6a$

10. $+5 - 8x - 2x + 3x + 7x + 6$

11. $-6y - 3y + 6y + 6x$

12. $+4c + 5c + 2c - 9c + 1$

Chilly Integers

Have you noticed how much colder you feel on a windy day? Wind chill is an estimate of the relationship between wind speed and temperature.

Frostbite—the freezing of a part of the body—can occur at very cold temperatures. The table to the right shows how wind chill makes the temperature feel colder. It also shows how wind chill and cold affect frostbite. The top row shows the temperature. The far left column shows the wind speed. Match these up to find the wind chill and the time it takes for frostbite to occur.

Wind Chill
Temperature (Degrees F)

Wind Speed (mph)	40	35	30	25	20	15	10	5	0	-5	-10	-15	-20	-25
5	36	31	25	19	13	7	1	-5	-11	-16	-22	-28	-34	-40
10	34	27	21	15	9	3	-4	-10	-16	-22	-28	-35	-41	-47
15	32	25	19	13	6	0	-7	-13	-19	-26	-32	-39	-45	-51
20	30	24	17	11	4	-2	-9	-15	-22	-29	-35	-42	-48	-55
25	29	23	16	9	3	-4	-11	-17	-24	-31	-37	-44	-51	-58
30	28	22	15	8	1	-5	-12	-19	-26	-33	-39	-46	-53	-60
35	28	21	14	7	0	-7	-14	-21	-27	-34	-41	-48	-55	-62
40	27	20	13	6	-1	-8	-15	-22	-29	-36	-43	-50	-57	-64
45	26	19	12	5	-2	-9	-16	-23	-30	-37	-44	-51	-58	-65
50	26	19	12	4	-3	-10	-17	-24	-31	-38	-45	-52	-60	-67

Frostbite Times

☐ 30 minutes ☐ 10 minutes ☐ 5 minutes

EXAMPLE Suppose the air temperature is 10°F. What is the wind chill temperature with a wind of 20 mph? How much colder would it feel with 30-mph winds?

Step 1 Look at the table. The wind chill temperature for 10°F with a wind of 20 mph is −9°F.

Step 2 To calculate how much colder it feels with a 30-mph wind, subtract.

$$-12 - (-9) = -3°$$

It would feel 3 degrees colder.

Exercise Use the wind chill table above to solve the problems.

1. Air temperature: 15°F; wind: 35 mph; wind chill factor: ?

2. Air temperature: −10°F; wind: 10 mph; wind chill factor: ?

3. Andy is snowboarding. The temperature is −5°F with a 20-mph wind. What is the frostbite time?

4. Which weather condition below feels colder? How much colder?

■ air temperature of 10°F with a 25-mph wind

■ air temperature of −10°F with a 5-mph wind

Chapter 13 R E V I E W

Write the letter of the best answer to each question.

1. How many spaces apart are -5 and $+5$ on the number line below?

   A 0

   B 5

   C 10

   D 15

$$-5\ -4\ -3\ -2\ -1\ \ \ 0\ +1\ +2\ +3\ +4\ +5$$

2. What is the absolute value of -9?

   A -9

   B 0

   C 1

   D 9

3. $-65 + (-22) =$

   A -87

   B -43

   C $+43$

   D $+87$

4. $-16 \times (+12) =$

   A -192

   B -4

   C $+4$

   D $+192$

5. $2n + 32 = 64$

   A 2

   B 16

   C 32

   D 48

6. Find the absolute value of $+7$.

7. Find the absolute value of -8.

8. Find the opposite of -31.

Compare the pairs of integers with $>$ or $<$.

9. $-6 \quad -4$

10. $+2 \quad -5$

Give the absolute value.

11. $|-2|$

12. $|+13|$

Perform the indicated operations.

13. $-6 + (-7)$

14. $+5 - (-7)$

15. $-3 + 5$

16. $+3 - 4$

17. $-2 \times (-5)$

18. $+10 \times (-2)$

19. $-8 \div (-4)$

20. $-9 \div (-3)$

21. $-64 \div (+4)$

Find the value for the variable.

22. $n - 12 = 20$

23. $a + 6 = -10$

24. $3 \times n = -18$

25. $-5x = 30$

26. $5 = 3a + 5$

27. $-3x + 5 = 20$

Combine like terms.

28. $-3a - 4c + 7a$

29. $-8a - 3 + 7a - 9a + 7$

30. Construct a number line with the graph of $x = -3$.

Solve each problem.

31. The team loses 38 points and then loses 16 points. They finally score 88 points, and then lose just 6 points. What is the team's final score?

32. You are in the basement of the office building gathering some old paperwork. Next you go up 9 floors to your office, and down 2 floors to drop off your mail. On what floor is the mailroom?

33. The football team loses 11 yards on the first down of the game. On the second down they gain 15 yards, and on the third down they lose 18 yards. What is the team's total gain or loss of yardage?

Graph each set of ordered pairs.

34. $(3, 3), (3, -3), (-3, -3), (-3, 3)$

35. $(0, 4), (4, 0), (0, -4), (-4, 0)$

Test-Taking Tip

Whenever you solve an open sentence and find the value of a variable, always check your answer. Substitute the value you found for the variable in the equation. Then, evaluate each side of the equation and be sure that the two sides are equal.

Whole Numbers

Exercise A Write the name of the place for each underlined digit.

   1. 50,<u>7</u>13
   2. 71,3<u>7</u>8
   3. 6,502,33<u>1</u>
   4. 1<u>1</u>2,450
   5. <u>7</u>0,300
   6. <u>4</u>00,045
   7. <u>3</u>,060,017
   8. 9,064,43<u>7</u>
   9. 8<u>8</u>,675,000
  10. 505,<u>6</u>00
  11. 600,<u>4</u>65
  12. 74,023,7<u>6</u>9
  13. 7,<u>6</u>48,493
  14. 20,2<u>3</u>6,200
  15. 4,90<u>3</u>,002

Exercise B Round each number to three different places.

		Tens	Hundreds	Thousands
1.	567	____	____	____
2.	7,098	____	____	____
3.	6,005	____	____	____
4.	765,365	____	____	____
5.	36,667	____	____	____
6.	906,380	____	____	____
7.	326,511	____	____	____
8.	65,409,811	____	____	____
9.	65,800,409	____	____	____
10.	43,000	____	____	____
11.	16	____	____	____
12.	453	____	____	____

Whole Numbers

Exercise C Add.

1. 4 +9	**2.** 0 +8	**3.** 2 +4	**4.** 9 +0	**5.** 6 +7	**6.** 6 +1	**7.** 4 +6	**8.** 5 +7
9. 1 +1	**10.** 1 +2	**11.** 1 +9	**12.** 7 +0	**13.** 1 +6	**14.** 2 +2	**15.** 7 +2	**16.** 0 +5
17. 9 +4	**18.** 0 +1	**19.** 0 +7	**20.** 3 +8	**21.** 4 +0	**22.** 9 +1	**23.** 9 +5	**24.** 7 +9
25. 5 +8	**26.** 0 +2	**27.** 7 +7	**28.** 2 +9	**29.** 3 +3	**30.** 8 +8	**31.** 6 +5	**32.** 9 +9
33. 2 +3	**34.** 8 +5	**35.** 8 +4	**36.** 5 +0	**37.** 3 +4	**38.** 7 +4	**39.** 1 +8	**40.** 0 +0
41. 4 +8	**42.** 6 +0	**43.** 9 +2	**44.** 3 +5	**45.** 9 +6	**46.** 0 +4	**47.** 8 +1	**48.** 4 +2

Exercise D Write these addends in vertical form. Then add.

1. 23 + 467 + 829
2. 5,602 + 910 + 874
3. 1,035 + 267 + 8,412
4. 3,567 + 8,103 + 103
5. 7,108 + 468 + 2,081
6. 4,017 + 3,008 + 26
7. 429 + 207 + 4,610
8. 4,191 + 468 + 462
9. 305 + 8,135 + 607
10. 981 + 628 + 6,740
11. 43 + 638 + 9,005
12. 611 + 683 + 60

13. 487 + 36 + 8,739
14. 236; 487; 7,105; 238
15. 4,083; 1,032; 6,297; 42
16. 726; 2,913; 6,213; 781
17. 468; 2,963; 2,903; 76
18. 1,711; 4,804; 1,357; 9; 1
19. 521; 26; 4,835; 6,291
20. 9,183,629; 396,298
21. 67,037; 7,038; 5,013
22. 11,038; 5,073; 643,509
23. 51,602; 40,050; 64,576
24. 102; 64; 8; 5,009; 68,308

Whole Numbers

Exercise E Write these problems vertically. Then subtract.

1. 263 − 28
2. 4,820 − 785
3. 9,163 − 562
4. 5,032 − 863
5. 9,100 − 1,629
6. 4,103 − 1,263
7. 92,063 − 4,845
8. 8,300 − 402
9. 200,342 − 198,342
10. 673,902 − 570,942
11. 105,031 − 97,025
12. 10,000 − 5,460
13. From 9,126 subtract 358

14. Subtract 923 from 8,203
15. Subtract 6,855 from 10,000
16. From 2,913 subtract 809
17. Subtract 2,098 from 4,083
18. From 7,023 subtract 298
19. From 30,356 subtract 8,735
20. From 29,803 subtract 8,135
21. Subtract 9,898 from 19,200
22. From 33,600 subtract 699
23. Subtract 3,032 from 31,011
24. From 1,200 subtract 994
25. From 293 subtract 82
26. From 70,311 subtract 3,983

Exercise F Multiply.

1. 7 × 5
2. 5 × 3
3. 2 × 0
4. 3 × 1
5. 2 × 7
6. 3 × 7
7. 5 × 5

8. 1 × 4
9. 4 × 3
10. 3 × 2
11. 4 × 8
12. 5 × 0
13. 9 × 2
14. 3 × 5

15. 9 × 6
16. 0 × 4
17. 8 × 1
18. 4 × 2
19. 6 × 6
20. 3 × 9
21. 1 × 9

22. 7 × 0
23. 1 × 6
24. 2 × 2
25. 7 × 2
26. 0 × 5
27. 9 × 4
28. 0 × 1

29. 0 × 7
30. 3 × 8
31. 3 × 6
32. 7 × 1
33. 6 × 2
34. 4 × 5
35. 7 × 8

36. 1 × 5
37. 5 × 9
38. 1 × 0
39. 2 × 5
40. 2 × 8
41. 6 × 8
42. 1 × 3

Whole Numbers

Exercise G Write these problems in vertical form. Then multiply.

1. 38×29
2. 42×35
3. 271×34
4. 715×42
5. 962×43
6. $8,910 \times 23$
7. $50,203 \times 9,015$
8. $6,044 \times 1,032$
9. $3,104 \times 1,090$
10. $4,570 \times 2,740$
11. $3,672 \times 1,010$
12. $5,401 \times 300$
13. 385 and 27
14. 761 and 39
15. 640 and 20
16. 6,035 and 52
17. 7,803 and 120
18. 1,760 and 87
19. 13,206 and 7,214
20. 3,203 and 670
21. 6,625 and 550
22. 1,030 and 2,037
23. 6,601 and 4,110
24. 309 and 7,104
25. 203 and 4,670
26. 176 and 245
27. 6,107 and 723
28. 87,161 and 409

Exercise H Copy these problems and divide.

1. $1,080 \div 8$
2. $954 \div 9$
3. $1,172 \div 4$
4. $2,877 \div 7$
5. $2,496 \div 8$
6. $18,009 \div 29$
7. $72,980 \div 178$
8. $16,426 \div 43$
9. $30,000 \div 50$
10. $6,399 \div 81$
11. $8,925 \div 85$
12. $6,820 \div 62$
13. $16,856 \div 28$
14. $5,332 \div 43$
15. $6,750 \div 54$
16. $31,356 \div 78$
17. $56,960 \div 80$
18. $398,888 \div 56$
19. $86,388 \div 276$
20. $113,764 \div 239$
21. $21,627 \div 27$
22. $32,240 \div 52$
23. $19,076 \div 38$
24. $26,659 \div 53$
25. $9,672 \div 62$
26. $42,840 \div 21$
27. $7,440 \div 62$
28. $19,872 \div 32$
29. $60,600 \div 30$
30. $220,320 \div 72$

Whole Numbers

Exercise I Write the value of each expression.

1. 5^3
2. 6^2
3. 8^3
4. 7^3
5. 9^2
6. 8^4
7. 9^3
8. 12^2
9. 11^2
10. 13^2
11. 14^2
12. 4^5
13. 20^2
14. 40^3
15. 25^2
16. 26^2
17. 11^3
18. 10^3
19. 15^4
20. 25^3
21. 7^4
22. 18^3
23. 24^5
24. 48^3
25. 72^3
26. 36^4
27. 30^5
28. 85^2
29. 125^3
30. 200^6

Exercise J Find the answers. Perform the operations in the correct order.

1. $33 - 8 \times 2 \div 4$
2. $15 + 6 \times 2 - 6$
3. $5^2 + 8^2 \div 4 - 2$
4. $12^1 - 8 \times 4 \div 2^2$
5. $2^5 \div 8 - 12 \div 12 + 2$
6. $36 \div 3 - 6 + 2 \times 2^3$
7. $35 \div 7 \times 2 + 16 \div 4^1 - 1$
8. $25 - 2^3 + 3^2 \times 2 \div 3$
9. $16 - 4^2 + 6^2 \times 2 \div 4 - 8$
10. $50 + 25 - 8^2 + 4 \times 3^3$
11. $35 - 4^2 + 6 \times 2^3 \div 6$
12. $13 \times 3 - 6 \times 2^3 \div 12$
13. $26 + 3 \times 10 \div 2 - 48 \div 16$
14. $3^2 + 2^2 + 6^2 \times 2 - 4^2$
15. $2^3 + 3^3 \div 9 - 2$
16. $32 - 2^4 + 3 \times 6$
17. $13 - 6^2 \div 6 + 8 \times 2^3$
18. $5^2 - 6^2 \div 2 + 8 \times 4 \div 2 + 3$
19. $25 - 5^3 \div 25 + 8 - 2^3$
20. $36 + 8 \times 5 \div 2^3 - 6 \times 2$
21. $5^2 - 4 \times 3^2 \div 2 + 12^2 \times 2^2 \times 2$
22. $8^2 - 2^4 \div 2 + 64 \div 4$
23. $12^2 \div 16 \times 2^2 - 10^2 \div 20$
24. $9 - 6^2 \div 4 + 12 \times 4 \div 2^4 - 3$

Fractions

Exercise A Express these fractions in higher terms.

1. $\frac{3}{4} = \frac{\blacksquare}{24}$

2. $\frac{2}{7} = \frac{\blacksquare}{56}$

3. $\frac{5}{7} = \frac{\blacksquare}{84}$

4. $\frac{8}{9} = \frac{\blacksquare}{108}$

5. $\frac{6}{7} = \frac{\blacksquare}{63}$

6. $\frac{5}{8} = \frac{\blacksquare}{96}$

7. $\frac{11}{12} = \frac{\blacksquare}{132}$

8. $\frac{5}{23} = \frac{\blacksquare}{92}$

9. $\frac{4}{9} = \frac{\blacksquare}{126}$

10. $\frac{17}{24} = \frac{\blacksquare}{120}$

11. $\frac{16}{17} = \frac{\blacksquare}{51}$

12. $\frac{31}{34} = \frac{\blacksquare}{102}$

13. $\frac{19}{20} = \frac{\blacksquare}{80}$

14. $\frac{13}{15} = \frac{\blacksquare}{45}$

15. $\frac{7}{8} = \frac{\blacksquare}{104}$

16. $\frac{8}{22} = \frac{\blacksquare}{110}$

Exercise B Rename these fractions in simplest form.

1. $\frac{24}{56}$

2. $\frac{38}{82}$

3. $\frac{45}{55}$

4. $\frac{72}{81}$

5. $\frac{46}{62}$

6. $\frac{34}{68}$

7. $\frac{77}{121}$

8. $\frac{33}{132}$

9. $\frac{18}{99}$

10. $\frac{36}{128}$

11. $\frac{98}{147}$

12. $\frac{42}{105}$

13. $\frac{26}{52}$

14. $\frac{36}{75}$

15. $\frac{13}{104}$

16. $\frac{21}{147}$

Exercise C Rename these mixed numbers as improper fractions.

1. $5\frac{4}{6}$

2. $4\frac{3}{4}$

3. $6\frac{3}{8}$

4. $8\frac{2}{7}$

5. $8\frac{5}{6}$

6. $2\frac{4}{5}$

7. $9\frac{6}{7}$

8. $16\frac{2}{3}$

9. $33\frac{5}{6}$

10. $19\frac{11}{12}$

11. $13\frac{10}{14}$

12. $34\frac{15}{16}$

13. $10\frac{5}{20}$

14. $14\frac{10}{11}$

15. $10\frac{1}{8}$

16. $14\frac{1}{2}$

Exercise D Rename these improper fractions as mixed numbers or whole numbers.

1. $\frac{16}{5}$

2. $\frac{17}{8}$

3. $\frac{19}{7}$

4. $\frac{23}{5}$

5. $\frac{29}{11}$

6. $\frac{32}{6}$

7. $\frac{49}{16}$

8. $\frac{108}{9}$

9. $\frac{92}{4}$

10. $\frac{73}{6}$

11. $\frac{205}{15}$

12. $\frac{69}{13}$

13. $\frac{67}{57}$

14. $\frac{156}{12}$

15. $\frac{36}{8}$

16. $\frac{75}{12}$

Fractions

Exercise E Express the following mixed numbers in simplest form.

1. $5\frac{4}{3}$

2. $8\frac{9}{5}$

3. $7\frac{12}{16}$

4. $12\frac{10}{9}$

5. $15\frac{14}{10}$

6. $16\frac{10}{14}$

7. $33\frac{23}{20}$

8. $27\frac{24}{12}$

9. $18\frac{44}{11}$

10. $52\frac{20}{6}$

11. $34\frac{7}{3}$

12. $10\frac{9}{27}$

13. $51\frac{48}{15}$

14. $28\frac{45}{60}$

15. $36\frac{8}{44}$

16. $64\frac{35}{7}$

17. $13\frac{26}{5}$

18. $22\frac{26}{20}$

19. $38\frac{44}{14}$

20. $15\frac{37}{15}$

21. $39\frac{45}{9}$

22. $17\frac{32}{15}$

23. $63\frac{58}{50}$

24. $28\frac{45}{10}$

25. $74\frac{80}{10}$

26. $40\frac{30}{13}$

27. $25\frac{20}{5}$

28. $54\frac{35}{6}$

29. $13\frac{54}{80}$

30. $75\frac{42}{38}$

31. $14\frac{6}{15}$

32. $63\frac{36}{34}$

Exercise F Multiply these mixed numbers. Write your answers in simplest form.

1. $\frac{2}{7} \times 2\frac{6}{7}$

2. $\frac{3}{4} \times 3\frac{1}{2}$

3. $\frac{3}{5} \times 2\frac{3}{4}$

4. $\frac{2}{3} \times 22\frac{1}{2}$

5. $1\frac{1}{3} \times \frac{1}{2}$

6. $2\frac{3}{4} \times \frac{6}{11}$

7. $2\frac{1}{5} \times \frac{10}{22}$

8. $1\frac{4}{5} \times \frac{2}{9}$

9. $2\frac{7}{8} \times \frac{16}{23}$

10. $3\frac{3}{8} \times \frac{8}{12}$

11. $5\frac{2}{5} \times 1\frac{1}{9}$

12. $4\frac{1}{5} \times 1\frac{3}{7}$

13. $2\frac{4}{5} \times 1\frac{11}{14}$

14. $5\frac{2}{8} \times 2\frac{2}{7}$

15. $6\frac{6}{7} \times 2\frac{2}{6}$

16. $1\frac{1}{2} \times 1\frac{7}{9}$

17. $3\frac{1}{5} \times 1\frac{9}{16}$

18. $4\frac{1}{2} \times 1\frac{1}{15}$

19. $7\frac{1}{5} \times 1\frac{2}{3}$

20. $5\frac{1}{4} \times 2\frac{1}{7}$

21. $3\frac{3}{7} \times 2\frac{1}{3}$

22. $5\frac{5}{8} \times 1\frac{7}{9}$

23. $3\frac{4}{9} \times \frac{27}{62}$

24. $\frac{8}{12} \times 3\frac{2}{16}$

Fractions

Exercise G Divide these mixed numbers.
Write your answers in simplest form.

1. $2\frac{1}{5} \div \frac{11}{15}$

2. $3\frac{2}{3} \div \frac{22}{24}$

3. $7\frac{1}{2} \div \frac{5}{6}$

4. $8\frac{2}{3} \div \frac{13}{15}$

5. $1\frac{1}{2} \div \frac{6}{7}$

6. $2\frac{3}{5} \div \frac{2}{15}$

7. $5\frac{2}{12} \div \frac{62}{3}$

8. $3\frac{5}{9} \div 2\frac{2}{3}$

9. $4\frac{5}{7} \div 1\frac{1}{14}$

10. $2\frac{1}{6} \div 5\frac{4}{7}$

11. $1\frac{7}{9} \div 4\frac{4}{5}$

12. $5\frac{3}{12} \div 2\frac{1}{4}$

Exercise H Change to common denominators and add.
Write your answers in simplest form.

1. $\frac{2}{3} + \frac{1}{5}$

2. $\frac{3}{9} + \frac{1}{5}$

3. $\frac{5}{9} + \frac{2}{6}$

4. $\frac{4}{12} + \frac{1}{4}$

5. $\frac{6}{7} + \frac{1}{14}$

6. $\frac{2}{11} + \frac{3}{22}$

7. $\frac{6}{13} + \frac{2}{26}$

8. $\frac{10}{24} + \frac{3}{12}$

9. $\frac{1}{8} + \frac{5}{6}$

10. $\frac{2}{12} + \frac{1}{9}$

11. $\frac{5}{72} + \frac{2}{9}$

12. $\frac{6}{7} + \frac{3}{8}$

Exercise I Change to common denominators and subtract.
Write your answers in simplest form.

1. $6\frac{1}{5} - 4\frac{2}{3}$

2. $9\frac{2}{3} - 4\frac{7}{8}$

3. $8\frac{5}{6} - 1\frac{7}{18}$

4. $5\frac{13}{15} - \frac{27}{30}$

5. $21\frac{4}{7} - 2\frac{2}{3}$

6. $14\frac{1}{6} - 3\frac{5}{8}$

7. $11\frac{3}{4} - 5\frac{16}{18}$

8. $8\frac{2}{15} - 2\frac{9}{20}$

9. $7\frac{8}{17} - 1\frac{21}{34}$

10. $36\frac{1}{7} - 2\frac{3}{8}$

11. $19\frac{2}{9} - 4\frac{1}{2}$

12. $5\frac{3}{16} - 2\frac{5}{8}$

13. $7\frac{2}{5} - 3\frac{22}{45}$

14. $40 - 16\frac{1}{3}$

15. $23\frac{2}{5} - 5\frac{1}{3}$

16. $14\frac{2}{7} - 9\frac{3}{5}$

17. $2\frac{1}{7} - 1\frac{4}{9}$

18. $12\frac{5}{16} - 2\frac{2}{3}$

19. $19 - 14\frac{11}{15}$

20. $10\frac{2}{3} - 4\frac{19}{20}$

21. $5\frac{4}{9} - 2\frac{2}{3}$

Decimals

Exercise A Write the name of the place for each underlined digit.

1. 57.4̲5392

2. 56.483̲9

3. 0.1009̲8

4. 0.008̲974

5. 0.5609̲85

6. 453.05̲67

7. 0.5608̲9

8. 0.84̲7109

9. 0.75̲7056

10. 1.101988̲

11. 564.31̲

12. 7.45078̲

13. 0.401̲015

14. 0.5̲60902

15. 14.02̲

16. 0.07575̲2

Exercise B Complete the chart by rounding each decimal to the places named.

		Tenths	Hundredths	Thousandths
1.	47.7581	_____	_____	_____
2.	5.04745	_____	_____	_____
3.	85.86086	_____	_____	_____
4.	14.06	_____	_____	_____
5.	47.5	_____	_____	_____
6.	4.00987	_____	_____	_____
7.	0.88809	_____	_____	_____
8.	5.46469	_____	_____	_____
9.	9.87431	_____	_____	_____
10.	6.9874909	_____	_____	_____

Decimals

Exercise C Write these problems in vertical form. Then add.

1. 2.3 + 4 + 5.98

2. 5 + 0.46 + 0.045

3. 0.3409 + 6.6 + 0.08

4. 43.4 + 0.048 + 3

5. 6.6 + 9.02 + 5

6. 9.4 + 0.45 + 7

7. 6 + 8.9 + 0.02

8. 0.553 + 0.09 + 3.7

9. 4 + 1.09 + 0.06

10. 6.4 + 0.3 + 0.56

11. 57.3 + 5.6 + 7

12. 9 + 0.6 + 0.32 + 0.07

13. 3.4, 2.04, 5.67

14. 364, 5.607, 3.04

15. 45.402, 6.907, 97

16. 6.4, 50, 7.2, 6.04

17. 47.02, 64, 70.2

18. 63.5, 70.3, 86.03

19. 0.004, 0.056, 3.02

20. 4.56, 8.023, 0.0304

21. 8.45, 0.0081, 0.06

22. 67.7, 60, 0.046, 85

23. 42.4, 66.78, 0.632

24. 56.4, 0.004, 0.3045

25. 0.05, 0.044, 0.1

26. 3.5, 6, 7.89, 10

Exercise D Write these problems in vertical form. Then subtract.

1. 13.5 − 2.4

2. 37.8 − 2.67

3. 4.9 − 2.34

4. 3.62 − 0.8

5. 19.4 − 0.36

6. 67.8 − 0.07

7. 46.78 − 9

8. 0.4507 − 0.23

9. 564 − 56.7

10. 5.9 − 0.67

11. 0.007 − 0.0023

12. 6.8 − 5.78

13. From 2 subtract 0.8

14. From 3.4 subtract 2.43

15. Subtract 0.34 from 3.8

16. From 0.46 subtract 0.097

17. From 0.362 subtract 0.08

18. Subtract 0.362 from 1

19. Subtract 0.464 from 8.09

20. From 23 subtract 21.8

21. Subtract 6 from 24.6

22. From 3.4 subtract 0.935

23. From 6.7 subtract 0.465

24. Subtract 5 from 46.78

25. From 87.09 subtract 9.8

26. From 46.9 subtract 9

27. Subtract 3.58 from 36

28. Subtract 0.36 from 6

29. From 3.4 subtract 0.0056

30. From 3 subtract 0.456

Decimals

Exercise E Write these problems in vertical form. Then multiply.

1. 2.3 × 6.3

2. 4.2 × 0.41

3. 0.26 × 3.4

4. 4.62 × 1.2

5. 5.8 × 0.2

6. 60.9 × 0.03

7. 0.983 × 2.8

8. 0.803 × 6.91

9. 5.03 × 0.071

10. 89.6 × 0.003

11. 28.4 × 0.34

12. 5.02 × 2.3

13. 0.68 × 7.9

14. 0.08 × 64

15. 36.5 × 8.8

16. 3.8 and 6.2

17. 9.08 and 0.3

18. 0.523 and 0.02

19. 6.21 and 0.28

20. 5.36 and 9.6

21. 9.86 and 1.2

22. 2.61 and 0.25

23. 8.2 and 93

24. 128 and 2.9

25. 4.63 and 1.9

26. 5.5 and 4.7

27. 80.3 and 0.34

28. 74.2 and 6.7

29. 2.34 and 9.04

30. 3.46 and 3.56

Exercise F Write these numbers in scientific notation.

1. 2,350

2. 46,800

3. 383,000

4. 84,100,000

5. 76,004

6. 357,000

7. 340,000,000

8. 72,300,000

9. 64,200

10. 83,020,000

11. 654,000

12. 2,100,000,000

13. 519

14. 700

15. 750,000

16. 423,000,000

Decimals

Exercise G Write these decimals in scientific notation.

1. 0.4506

2. 0.00076

3. 0.0000003

4. 0.00000452

5. 45.58

6. 0.7809

7. 0.000000457

8. 0.000917

9. 0.75053

10. 0.00004079

11. 508.04

12. 0.9407

Exercise H Copy these problems and divide.

1. 25.74 ÷ 9

2. 1.75 ÷ 5

3. 16.48 ÷ 8

4. 9.269 ÷ 23

5. 2,527.7 ÷ 92

6. 179.4 ÷ 39

7. 80.28 ÷ 36

8. 62.4 ÷ 15

9. 1.15 ÷ 50

10. 133.14 ÷ 42

11. 1.984 ÷ 16

12. 1.95 ÷ 15

Exercise I Copy these problems and divide.

1. 1.3 ÷ 0.5

2. 0.008 ÷ 0.4

3. 15.06 ÷ 0.6

4. 5.6 ÷ 0.16

5. 0.192 ÷ 2.4

6. 0.1446 ÷ 0.002

7. 0.322 ÷ 0.07

8. 0.06 ÷ 2

9. 0.134 ÷ 0.02

10. 2.9 ÷ 5.8

11. 0.004 ÷ 0.08

12. 0.2268 ÷ 0.081

Decimals

Exercise J Find the answers.

1. $0.8 - 0.3$

2. $0.3 + 0.6$

3. 4×0.02

4. $0.4 + 9$

5. $0.267 \div 3$

6. $12.37 - 0.283$

7. 0.3×0.2

8. $0.04 + 1.6$

9. $405 \div 90$

10. 0.046×0.003

11. $16 - 0.37$

12. 12.5×0.367

13. $0.0036 \div 0.2$

14. $29.06 - 9.9$

15. $0.204 + 1.35$

16. $42.81 \div 0.3$

17. $1.3 - 0.42$

18. $0.048 \div 5.4$

19. 0.48×3.7

20. $7 + 3.92$

21. $3.0612 \div 4$

22. $5.036 - 3.27$

23. 0.26×0.3

24. $29.8 + 4.73$

25. $0.004 + 36.49$

26. $46.86 \div 1.1$

27. $24 - 0.362$

28. 28.2×0.038

29. $5.7 - 0.604$

30. $6.3 \div 8.4$

31. $0.8 + 0.6$

32. 0.23×0.9

33. $0.37 - 0.04$

34. $0.47 + 0.06$

35. $91.8 \div 36$

36. $0.46 - 0.38$

37. 5×0.018

38. $1.42 + 8$

39. $5 \div 8$

40. $8 - 3.4$

41. 0.32×0.16

42. $0.205 + 4.378$

43. $0.09 \div 4.5$

44. $0.07 - 0.0634$

45. $1.82 + 138$

46. 0.003×0.08

Percents

Exercise A Rename each percent as a decimal.

1. 8%

2. 42%

3. 105%

4. 246%

5. 0.9%

6. $32\frac{5}{8}$%

7. 25.3%

8. 0.046%

9. 346%

10. $\frac{3}{4}$%

Exercise B Rename each percent as a fraction in simplest form.

1. 8%

2. 68%

3. 1.35%

4. $83\frac{1}{3}$%

5. $2\frac{1}{2}$%

6. $1\frac{7}{8}$%

7. $\frac{3}{4}$%

8. $2\frac{2}{3}$%

9. $\frac{5}{9}$%

10. $105\frac{1}{3}$%

Exercise C Rename each number as a percent.

1. 0.05

2. 0.4

3. 1.36

4. 0.1675

5. 0.056

6. 0.00036

7. 0.43

8. 3.24

9. 1.1625

10. 0.572

Percents

Exercise D Fill in the missing fractions, decimals, and percents in this chart.

	Fraction	Decimal	Percent
1.	$\frac{5}{8}$		
2.		0.4	
3.			$11\frac{2}{3}\%$
4.		0.025	
5.			$3\frac{1}{3}\%$
6.		1.6	
7.			1.32%
8.			$\frac{3}{4}\%$
9.	$\frac{3}{200}$		
10.		0.45	
11.			124%
12.	$\frac{4}{11}$		
13.		1.08	
14.	$\frac{7}{25}$		
15.			48%
16.		0.0036	
17.	$\frac{3}{20}$		
18.			4.5%

Percents

Exercise E Find the percentage.

1. 42% of 150 is ____

2. ____ is 30% of 96

3. ____ is 8% of 45

4. $22\frac{1}{2}$% of 28 is ____

5. 4.6% of 15 is ____

6. ____ is 106% of 35

7. ____ is 0.4% of 750

8. $\frac{3}{4}$% of 200 is ____

9. $2\frac{1}{2}$% of 1,600 is ____

10. 18% of 75 is ____

Exercise F Find the base.

1. 30% of ____ is 27

2. 36 is 45% of ____

3. $2\frac{1}{2}$ is 20% of ____

4. 15% of ____ is 27

5. $6\frac{2}{3}$% of ____ is 4

6. 13 is $12\frac{1}{2}$% of ____

7. 21 is 4.2% of ____

8. 35% of ____ is 56

9. 8% of ____ is 16

10. 63 is 28% of ____

Exercise G Find the rate.

1. ____% of 32 is 12

2. 34 is ____% of 40

3. 6 is ____% of 45

4. ____% of 126 is 18

5. ____% of 72 is 24

6. $2\frac{1}{2}$ is ____% of 10

7. ____% of 81 is 36

8. ____% of 63 is 42

9. 18 is ____% of 150

10. 10.40 is ____% of 52

Percents

Exercise H Find the missing numbers.

1. 8% of 95 is ____

2. ____% of 54 is 9

3. 52% of ____ is 13

4. ____ is 42% of 60

5. 35% of ____ is 483

6. 2 is ____% of 40

7. ____% of 40 is 3

8. 0.3 is 6% of ____

9. 5 is ____% of 80

10. $37\frac{1}{2}$% of 108 is ____

11. $2\frac{2}{3}$ is ____% of $13\frac{1}{3}$

12. $\frac{4}{5}$ is 16% of ____

13. 4.5% of 160 is ____

14. 20% of ____ is 6

15. ____ is 9% of 500

16. ____% of $12\frac{1}{2}$ is 3

17. 4.3 is 4.3% of ____

18. 6 is ____% of $12\frac{1}{2}$

19. ____% of 0.3 is 0.015

20. 45 is 0.9% of ____

21. ____ is 0.02% of 500

22. $16\frac{2}{3}$ is ____% of 100

23. 0.03% of ____ is 0.003

24. ____ is 120% of 35

Exercise I Fill in the missing amounts in these discount problems.

	List Price	Discount Rate	Discount	Sale Price
1.	$145.00	20%		
2.	$26.50	40%		
3.	$80.00		$16.00	
4.	$75.50	10%		
5.	$300.00	$33\frac{1}{3}$%		
6.	$45.00	$13\frac{1}{3}$%	$6.00	
7.	$18.00	$3\frac{1}{3}$%		
8.			$5.00	$45.00
9.	$38.50	24%		
10.			$5.46	$40.04

Percents

Exercise J Solve these sales tax problems. Remember that you round up when working sales tax problems.

1. Jacket costs $68.00.
   Tax rate of 5%

   Tax _____
   Cost after tax _____

2. Boots cost $125.00.
   Tax rate of 3%

   Tax _____
   Cost after tax _____

3. CD player costs $137.50.
   Tax rate of 7%

   Tax _____
   Cost after tax _____

4. CDs cost $37.89.
   Tax rate of 3%

   Tax _____
   Cost after tax _____

5. Sports car costs $28,650.00.
   Tax rate of 7%

   Tax _____
   Cost after tax _____

6. Tape costs 69 cents.
   Tax rate of 3%

   Tax _____
   Cost after tax _____

Exercise K Compute the total interest.

1. $84.00 at 7% for 4 years

2. $39.00 at 12% for 4 months

3. $38.00 at 11% for 5 years

4. $428.00 at 8% for 3 years

5. $52.00 at 5% for 1 year

6. $608.00 at 7% for 9 months

7. $300.00 at 12% for 18 months

8. $45.00 at 8% for 1 year

9. $53.00 at 14% for 4 years

10. $76.00 at 9% for 5 years

11. $730.00 at 12% for 1 year

12. $204.00 at 8% for 4 years

13. $48.00 at 10% for 3 months

14. $20.00 at $6\frac{1}{2}$% for 8 years

15. $445.00 at 9% for 6 months

16. $400.00 at 13% for 15 months

17. $638.00 at $11\frac{1}{2}$% for 4 years

18. $636.00 at 9% for $1\frac{1}{2}$ years

19. $804.00 at $4\frac{1}{2}$% for 2 years

20. $600.00 at 9% for 3 years

Percents

Exercise L Solve these problems.

1. Joe buys a TV for $300.00. He is going to pay $30.00 per month. He will pay $1\frac{1}{2}\%$ finance charge on the unpaid balance each month. Fill in this chart to show how Joe will pay for the TV.

Month	Previous Balance	Finance Charge	Before Payment	Monthly Payment	New Balance
January	$300.00	$4.50	$304.50	$30.00	$274.50
February	$274.50	_____	_____	$30.00	_____
March	_____	_____	_____	$30.00	_____
April	_____	_____	_____	$30.00	_____
May	_____	_____	_____	$30.00	_____
June	_____	_____	_____	$30.00	_____
July	_____	_____	_____	$30.00	_____
August	_____	_____	_____	$30.00	_____
September	_____	_____	_____	$30.00	_____
October	_____	_____	_____	$30.00	_____
November	_____	_____	_____	_____	$0.00

2. Scott charges a $480.00 refrigerator on his credit card. The finance rate is $1\frac{1}{2}\%$ per month. He plans to pay $80.00 per month. Make a chart to show how Scott will pay for the refrigerator.

Percents

Exercise M Solve these commission problems.

1. Marie receives a 6% rate of commission for selling a house. What is her commission for selling a $165,000.00 house?

2. Rashaan sells 9 electric drills at $29.95 each and 7 power saws at $39.95 each. How much is he paid if he receives a 6% rate of commission?

3. Miguel receives a different rate of commission for selling different items. Figure out his total commission for the sales in this chart.

Item	Machinery	Safety Supplies	Abrasives	Power Tools
Total Sales	$2,033.05	$254.15	$2,916.22	$3,011.88
Rate of Commission	18%	12%	14%	25%

4. Gwen receives a weekly salary of $95.00 plus 8% of all of her sales over $500.00. What are Gwen's weekly earnings if she sells $942.37 worth of merchandise?

5. Sam sells $7,896.00 worth of reference books. He is paid 2% for his first $4,000.00 of sales and 6% on all sales over $4,000.00. What is Sam's total commission?

6. Inga is paid $102.00 per week plus 1% of her sales. How much does she get paid for one week if she sells $2,908.00 worth of merchandise?

7. Li Chen is a salesperson for the Connally Machinery Company. She is paid a 2% rate of commission on the first $2,000.00 and 4% on all sales over $2,000.00. How much commission does she receive for $5,987.00 in sales?

8. A purchasing agent receives $4\frac{1}{2}$% for buying produce for her clients. What is her commission for buying 860 cartons of peaches for $16.85 per carton?

Exercise A Give the best name for each polygon.

1.

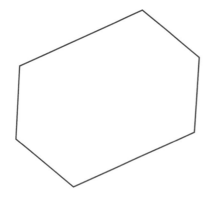

4.

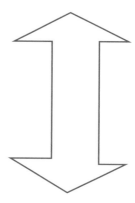

2.

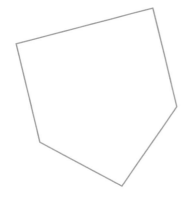

5.

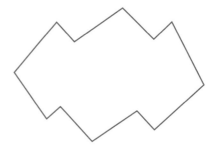

3.

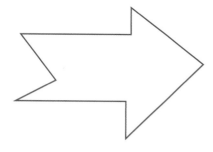

Exercise B Use the sides of the triangle to give the best name for each.

1.

3.

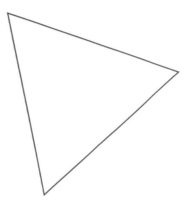

2.

4.

Exercise C Use the angles of the triangle to give the best name for each.

1.

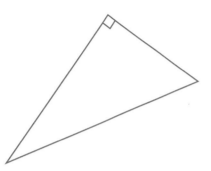

4.

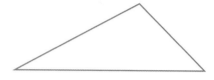

2.

5.

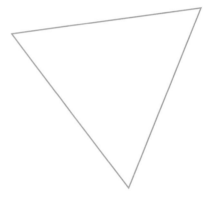

3.

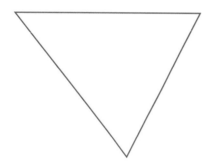

Exercise D Give the best name for each quadrilateral.

1.

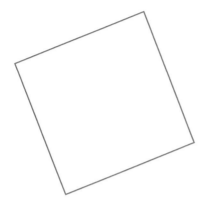

4.

2.

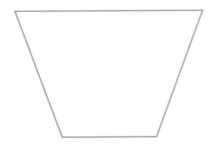

5.

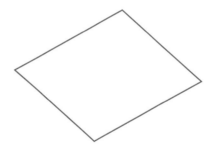

3.

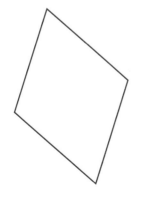

Exercise E Use the diagram to answer each question.

1. Which line is parallel to $\overleftrightarrow{GF}$?

2. Which line is perpendicular to $\overleftrightarrow{FC}$?

3. What kind of angle is $\angle GBA$?

4. What kind of triangle is $\triangle ADE$?

5. Where does $\overleftrightarrow{AB}$ intersect $\overleftrightarrow{FE}$?

6. What kind of quadrilateral is $ABFE$?

7. If $\angle BCE$ is 52°, what is the measure of $\angle GBD$?

8. What kind of triangle is $\triangle BCF$?

9. What kind of angle is $\angle DCF$?

10. What kind of triangle is $\triangle DBG$?

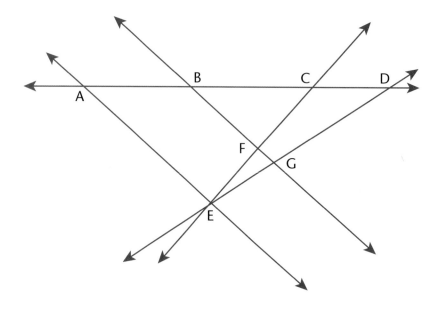

Photo Credits

Cover images: (background) © Andrew Brookes/Corbis/Stock Market, (inset) © Dynamic Graphics; p. xvi, © Marc Romanelli/Image Bank; p. 5, © Jon Riley/Stone; p. 14, © SuperStock International; p. 28, © Jeff Greenberg/Visuals Unlimited; p. 32, © Steve Callahan/Visuals Unlimited; p. 36, © Guido Alberto Rossi/Image Bank; p. 54, © Tony Freeman/PhotoEdit; p. 58, © Mark E. Gibson/Visuals Unlimited; p. 71, © David Young-Wolff/PhotoEdit; p. 81, © Arthur R. Hill/Visuals Unlimited; p. 85, © R. W. Jones/Corbis; p. 86, © Michael Newman/PhotoEdit; p. 90, © Visuals Unlimited; p. 101, © Robert E. Daemmrich/Stone; p. 117, © Bill Beatty/Visuals Unlimited; p. 118, © Michael Newman/PhotoEdit; p. 122, © Myrleen Ferguson Cate/PhotoEdit; p. 125, © Ken Biggs/Stone; p. 133, © Jon Riley/Stone; p. 134, © AFP/Corbis; p. 138, © Charles Gupton/Corbis/Stock Market; p. 141, © Elena Rooraid/PhotoEdit; p. 145, © David Young-Wolff/PhotoEdit; p. 157, © David Young-Wolff/PhotoEdit; p. 166, © Michael Newman/PhotoEdit; p. 170, © Susan Van Etten/PhotoEdit; p. 190, © Ted Horowitz/Corbis/Stock Market; p. 193, © Joel W. Rogers/Corbis; p. 200, © Christopher Bissell/Stone; p. 203, © Eric Anderson/Visuals Unlimited; p. 212, © Robert W. Ginn/PhotoEdit; p. 216, © SuperStock International; p. 221, © Don Smetzer/Stone; p. 231, © Michael Newman/PhotoEdit; p. 238, © Michael Newman/PhotoEdit; p. 242, © V. C. L./Paul Viant/FPG International; p. 249, © Matthias Kulka/Corbis/Stock Market; p. 260, © Kevin Smyth/Corbis/Stock Market; p. 265, © Kevin R. Morris/Corbis; p. 288, © David Young-Wolff/PhotoEdit; p. 297, © David Young-Wolff/PhotoEdit; p. 306, © Michael Newman/PhotoEdit; p. 329, © Bruce Ayres/Stone